Writing
RESEARCH PAPERS

Investigating Resources in

CYBERSPACE

P9-CJF-296

Jeannette A. Woodward
College of Santa Fe

NTC Publishing Group
Lincolnwood, Illinois USA

To Chris and Laura
With much love

Executive Editor: Marisa L. L'Heureux
Editor: Lisa A. De Mol
Cover and interior design: Ophelia M. Chambliss
Production Manager: Rosemary Dolinski

ISBN 0-8442-5929-2 (student edition)
ISBN 0-8442-5930-6 (instructor's edition)

Library of Congress Cataloging-in-Publication Data

Woodward, Jeannette A.
    Writing research papers : investigating resources in cyberspace /
Jeannette A. Woodward.
        p.   cm.
    Includes index.
    ISBN 0-8442-5929-2 (softbound)
    1. Report writing—Data processing. 2. Internet (Computer
network) in education. I. Title.
LB2369.W66 1997
808'.02—dc20   96-43725
                                                        CIP

Published by NTC Publishing Group
© 1997 NTC Publishing Group, 4255 West Touhy Avenue,
Lincolnwood (Chicago), Illinois 60646-1975 U.S.A.
All rights reserved. No part of this book may be reproduced, stored
in a retrieval system or transmitted in any form or by any means,
electronic, mechanical, photocopying, recording, or otherwise, without
the prior permission of NTC Publishing Group.
Manufactured in the United States of America.

6 7 8 9 VL 9 8 7 6 5 4 3 2 1

Contents

Preface xiii

Chapter 1
Understanding the Research Process 1

Chapter 2

Selecting a Topic   21

Chapter 3

Planning a Research Strategy   35

Chapter 4

Getting to Know the Library   51

Chapter 5

Investigating Library Resources 77

Chapter 6

Exploring the Internet   97

Chapter 7

Reading, Evaluating, and Note Taking 127

Chapter 8

Writing the Rough Draft 145

Chapter 9

Documenting Your Sources 171

Chapter 10

Revising Your Paper   233

Preface

The Computer Revolution in the Academic World

For hundreds of years, students and scholars have conducted their research primarily by investigating printed books and journals. They have devised techniques to cope with the world of ideas contained in the billions of printed pages available. Libraries have developed intricate methods for classifying and cataloging these published works, and researchers have evolved methods for searching, discovering, analyzing, writing, and documenting scholarly thought in their respective disciplines.

With the arrival of electronically digitized information, however, researchers find themselves suddenly having to reassess these techniques. The computer changes not only the technology for putting words on a page but completely revolutionizes the way one sets about a research project.

The transition from typewriter to word processor takes away much of the drudgery of formal writing but creates some unique problems as well. Similarly, the use of electronic reference sources enables the researcher to access vast collections of information that even ten years ago few could have anticipated. Yet those same electronic storehouses of knowledge may disappear overnight. Citations to documents found on the Internet often lead nowhere when those documents are moved to a different directory or removed entirely from their host computer.

Although there is speculation about the imminent death of the book, no one really knows what the fate of the printed word will be. Some researchers imagine that all written works will be scanned and available on-line in the near future. Others say that the prospect of reading thousands of pages on a computer screen is distinctly unpleasant. Although computer screens will undoubtedly improve, eye strain lessen, and computers become more portable, it is difficult to imagine a viewing device as efficient and attractive as a book. Amid the enthusiasm over computers, some forget that books do an excellent job of communicating large amounts of information. Ultimately, some greatly improved monitor will probably come along, but for the foreseeable future, most of us prefer to read a novel or history text on paper.

Writing Research Papers in the Digital Age

Writing Research Papers is a synthesis of the old and the new—of traditional methods of effectively combining research and writing coupled with new techniques for functioning comfortably and successfully in a digital world. It assumes that modern research methods require access to a computer and that students who develop good computer skills can produce superior papers. However, merely using a word-processing program and electronic information sources will not automatically improve the quality of your research paper. In fact, it might have just the opposite result. Writing with a computer encourages you to use shortcuts, some of which are beneficial. Others, like the ability to cut and paste from the works of others, can be potentially disastrous. Tools and techniques to organize information become absolutely vital when you can view only the text that is displayed on the screen at any one time.

Balance is called for in the area of technical sophistication. You and your classmates have a wide range of computer skill levels. Some of you have been playing video games for years, while others approach the computer with great trepidation. This book will attempt to walk the fine line between boring the experienced computer user and confusing the novice. Although a basic knowledge of computer commands is certainly useful, simply knowing which keys to press is only one small part of the writing process. More important are methods of working with information in a computer environment.

With this in mind, Writing Research Papers is designed to aid you in writing a well-thought-out research paper using electronic sources and equipment as well as more traditional methods. Chapter 1, "Understanding the Research Process," gives an overview of the research process. It clarifies the differences between formal and informal research, between primary and secondary sources, and between fact papers and thesis papers. This chapter also offers you helpful, practical advice on buying a computer, choosing software, and managing the large amounts of data you will generate in the process of writing your research paper.

Chapter 2, "Selecting a Topic," guides you through the all-important task of choosing a topic for your paper from doing preliminary research to refining your topic and writing the thesis statement. Chapter 3, "Planning a Research Strategy," can help you map out your approach to the research paper, from planning your time wisely through organizing your materials. The last section of this chapter is aimed at helping anyone who may not be accustomed to working with computers feel more comfortable with them. It includes hints on navigating in and around documents, adjusting to and reading documents on the computer screen, and composing with a keyboard instead of pen and paper.

Chapters 4 and 5 explore the resources available to you in a library. Chapter 4, "Getting to Know the Library," walks you through the library, explaining how to make use of the various indexes, electronic and card catalogs, and other search facilities to track down the information you need. Chapter 5, "Investigating Library Resources," explains the traditional research materials that are available for you to use. Beginning with encyclopedias and almanacs, the chapter also covers periodicals, government documents, accessing information at other libraries, and personal interviews.

Chapter 6, "Investigating the Internet," opens your field of research far beyond the library walls. A thorough explanation of the Internet, the chapter begins with the basics, such as on-line services and downloading files, for anyone who is not yet familiar with the Net. Such tools as the World Wide Web, Gopher, Telnet, WAIS, search engines, electronic mail, and discussion lists are explained. The chapter also includes helpful information on getting help on the Net, finding addresses, and accessing periodicals, books, and museums.

To help you gather information for your paper, Chapter 7, "Reading, Evaluating, and Note Taking" addresses reading critically, evaluating material, and effective note taking. In Chapter 8, "Writing the Rough Draft," guides you through the process of putting it all together, writing the rough draft of your paper. This chapter covers such essential skills as developing your tone and style, writing consistently and well, and using quotations correctly. It also shows how to use a computer or word processor most effectively when you are writing. It finishes by introducing the subject of acknowledging sources.

Chapter 9, "Documenting Your Sources," covers all you will need to know to correctly credit your sources, both print and electronic. It thoroughly explains the MLA, the APA, and the Chicago styles of documentation. Detailed explanations and examples for documenting various kinds of sources in each of these styles are included. Two student-written papers, one in the MLA style and one in the APA style, demonstrate these methods of documentation in use. A helpful section on how to use all of this information to write research papers in all of your classes is also included.

The final chapter, "Revising Your Paper," helps you revise and polish your drafts into your final paper. The appendix includes addresses and telephone numbers of various organizations to aid you in finding further material for research.

Working in Both Worlds

Electronic information sources are so new that the academic world is still reeling from their impact. This book is far from the last word on the subject. Standards for citing electronic sources, for instance, are still somewhat experimental, as are the new tools designed to access digitized information that appear almost daily. It is inevitable that electronic formats that today look so promising will be considered dinosaurs tomorrow. Books about the Internet are said to be out-of-date before they're published. This book, therefore, attempts to achieve a delicate balance, introducing you to new technology and new methods, while at the same time introducing the tools that are still necessary to access print information sources.

The introduction of the computer into the writing process is an exciting development. It can free you from the more tedious aspects of a formal writing project and allow you to expend your efforts on developing insightful ideas and expressing them in the most precise and compelling language. To that end, it is hoped that this book will enrich and enliven the process of writing your research paper; that it will not only help you with procedures and models but will aid you in acquiring the skills to adapt them to the technology of the rapidly emerging digital world of the future.

Chapter 1

Understanding the Research Process

Years ago, my seventh-grade classmates and I were introduced to the elaborate "tricks of the trade" employed by students and researchers to write research papers. High school and college honed our research skills, which stood us in good stead for years—until the arrival of the computer.

It is not that those skills have lost their value. Rather, the world of research has expanded. Information has doubled, tripled, even quadrupled, until we can easily become lost in a sea of data. The resources of our local libraries, though greatly increased, are often no longer sufficient, and our painstakingly handwritten cards are multiplying as rapidly as the endless books, journal articles, data files, conference proceedings, videotapes, CD-ROM disks, and multimedia presentations they document.

The computer has put resources around the world at our fingertips, but it is sometimes difficult to deal with such an embarrassment of riches. When we remember the agonies of unforgiving typewriters before the arrival of the word processor, it seems that the computer has made completing a research project easier. In fact, if we own even the least-expensive modem, we may not need to leave the comfort of home to complete a modest research project.

Now that it is possible to access all these resources, we are expected to do so. We can no longer use the old plea, "I couldn't find anything on the subject." Often, we are expected to identify a multitude of sources and to know how they relate to our subject. Trying to do this with old-fashioned research skills can be a traumatic experience. It's probably not even possible.

Remembering Research in the Good Old Days

Let's board a hypothetical time machine and look in on students writing a research paper just twenty years ago. For such students, research began and ended with a trip to an academic library. Such a trip might have involved checking the card catalog, looking up the subject in various printed periodical indexes, diligently perusing footnotes and bibliographies at the end of scholarly volumes, and finally staggering home with a stack of heavy tomes.

Printed sources were generally the only ones available, and the number of books and periodicals was limited. It was not possible to search every research library, and even if students with a great deal of time on their hands and money to burn could travel the world, they would not find much new material.

Doing Research in the Computer Age

It is difficult to say where today's students might begin, but, for the sake of simplicity, let's go back to the academic library. My, how it has changed! Books are still visible in abundance, but the card catalog is probably gone. Instead, there is a computer program that searches a file full of bibliographic information for keywords strung together with something called *Boolean connectors*.

The old printed periodical indexes are now rarely needed. Instead, you must learn to use half a dozen periodical indexing and abstracting programs, each of which works a little differently and has a different list of instructions. In addition, many libraries now have full-text programs like *Pro-Quest* and *InfoTrak* that allow students to pop in a CD-ROM disk and print out entire articles.

These programs will identify vastly more sources than were found by students of yesteryear, but you really can't stop here. There are still many places to look. To misquote the poet, you have miles to go before you sleep.

Using On-Line Services

Commercial database services like *Dialog* and *FirstSearch* can be accessed from most libraries, and each service may provide several hundred databases. Databases are large collections of information that can be rapidly searched and retrieved by a computer; each may contain several million records. Some examples are *Chemical Abstracts*, *Psychological Abstracts*, *ERIC*, newspapers from around the world, census data, government documents, patent claims, *Nuclear Science Abstracts*, and the MLA *Bibliography*.

Although a few of these databases provide complete texts, most require you to locate the cited articles elsewhere. The ability to decide which materials will actually be useful and which will simply take up precious time, divert attention, and add to the general confusion becomes a vital skill.

Investigating the Internet

Now that most colleges and universities provide access to the Internet, you have thousands of additional options. You may check the holdings of libraries in places as distant as New Zealand, Pakistan, or Finland. Text files and software housed at Princeton, Harvard, or the University of Michigan can be downloaded to your own computer disk through the magic of file transfer protocol, or FTP. Even the Library of Congress has its own World Wide Web site, which offers an assortment of research materials to the searcher.

Once, major reference works could be found only at large research libraries. Today, the Internet can bring them to even the smallest college library. Everyone from college students to world-class scholars can use the same materials.

Coping with Chaos

After only a few hours of effort, you can end up with far more information than you know what to do with. My seventh-grade teacher would surely be amazed.

Only research techniques that can deal efficiently with print, multimedia, data files, photocopies, printouts, screen dumps, on-line conference proceedings, and a welter of other formats stand a chance of surviving the onslaught.

Writing skills are just as important as ever, but today you need considerably better organizational skills than did your parents' generation. This book is intended to help you acquire those skills. We will discuss a variety of ways to tame the research monster, strategies for living and working comfortably in the computer age.

This chapter and those that follow will include a good measure of traditional term-paper wisdom—those axioms that have worked for researchers over the years—coupled with some practical advice on coping with the complexities of technology. In other words, we will be talking about ways to make the computer work for you—not against you.

Writing the Modern Research Paper

Though the research process has changed in the last twenty years, the end product is still much the same. Put simply, a research paper is a scholarly investigation or inquiry of a particular topic in the form of a written composition. It is a report you present to others about the conclusions you reach after extensive investigation of an issue. More specifically, you seek out and consider published and other sources of information on a topic. After testing a thesis, you then present your findings in a way that contributes to a better understanding of the topic.

In some types of research, you will simply report what others have said without adding personal comments. More commonly, however, you will not only present the ideas of others but will also evaluate or make judgments about them, even expand upon them. Though the point of view remains objective, you may add personal opinions and support one position over another.

During the course of your school years, you have probably written essays based on your own experience and opinions. For example, you may have written descriptive essays that presented information received through your senses, narrative essays that gave an account of something that happened, or argumentative essays that tried to persuade the reader to support your position.

A research paper, however, is a type of expository essay that explains a topic. In a short essay, you may already know enough about the topic to write your paper without consulting reference sources. Eventually, however, as the essay grows longer and more scholarly, you will need to go beyond what you already know. An important part of education is to seek answers by consulting experts.

The research paper is the result of your inquiry, your findings after extensive research. Many people see research as a kind of detective puzzle. Like a detective, you will want to obtain the most accurate information possible, and you will want to investigate a number of sources rather than taking the word of one person or one writer.

Understanding Subjective versus Objective Point of View

Your attitude toward your topic is called your *point of view*. Your point of view can affect the way you write and the conclusions you reach. It will affect your choice of words, your tone, the structure of your sentences, even your punctuation.

You may have written at least some of your essays from a *subjective* point of view: you presented information as seen through your own experience. You included feelings and impressions as well as facts, and your goal may have been to provoke anger, outrage, pleasure, enthusiasm, or some other reaction from your reader.

A research paper, on the other hand, must be presented from an *objective* point of view. The emphasis is not on you and your experiences but on the subject matter. The language of a research paper is neutral rather than emotional. You don't have to leave out your own ideas, but you must present them without emotion or personal prejudice.

Doing Informal versus Formal Research

Though you may not have thought about it, you have been doing research most of your life. For example, you consult the local newspaper to find out what movies are playing and at what time they are scheduled to begin. You turn on the radio to get the weather forecast. You consult the yellow pages to learn the address of a business. All are examples of informal research.

Formal research is similar, but there are a number of important differences. The most obvious is scope. Your goal when you carry out informal research is usually to find one piece of information. In contrast, your goal when writing a research paper is to gain a thorough understanding of your topic. To achieve this goal, you read, comprehend, analyze, evaluate, and take extensive notes on a number of different sources. This process takes much time and effort as well as the skills required to organize and carry out a large project.

Another way formal research differs from informal is in approach. With informal research, you need only find the answer to your question, whereas formal research involves a systematic, organized search for information. In addition, formal research requires you to understand and practice the techniques of careful analysis and critical evaluation.

Informal research may be carried out anywhere. Sources of information such as television, telephone directories, and newspapers are available everywhere. Formal research, however, is usually carried out in a library (or in your home, if you have a computer that gives you access to on-line information via a modem). You will find yourself making extensive use of library resources, so learning to use them effectively is an important skill.

Last but not least, formal research requires that you cite the source of the information or evidence you use. Called *documentation,* it lies at the heart of the research process.

Using Primary versus Secondary Research

In some cases, research is done through firsthand observation and investigation. When doing *primary research*, the researcher goes straight to the source. For example, an archaeologist digs in the ground to find physical evidence of the way people lived in the past. Another researcher might conduct a survey, carry out a laboratory experiment, or compile statistical information. Primary research also involves *primary sources*, such as historical documents like the Constitution, literary works like plays and poems, or the laboratory notes of a famous scientist.

Undergraduate researchers are usually concerned with the work done by experts in a given field. Such *secondary sources* are housed in the library. You might think of these sources as other people's research papers. With such sources, a student can construct a scholarly argument by taking a new look at existing information.

In a sense, the word *research* tells it all. When you write a research paper, you "search again." Examples of secondary sources include books written about literary works rather than the works themselves, and books or articles about historical events rather than the original historical documents related to those events.

Even papers that involve primary research, such as those based on psychological experiments, are firmly based on the work of others, who reported their findings in earlier publications. As you pursue your research, you will first want to identify what's already been written and then locate and absorb it. Then you will be in a position to develop informed ideas of your own.

Writing Fact / Report Papers versus Thesis Papers

In the business and scientific disciplines, papers that simply report the facts are more common than in the humanities. If you take a course in technical writing, you will encounter this type of writing. A thesis-driven research paper, however, is different. Unless you are writing a technical paper, merely summarizing the research you have read leads to a second-therate encyclopedia article. It is your thesis that makes the difference.

Your thesis is an opinion or judgment you have made about a specific topic. Your paper follows and supports this argument, weaving relevant information into a unified work that convinces your audience of the validity of your thesis. Though you are not on a voyage of discovery in an uncharted sea, you are nevertheless expected to see something that your predecessors did not see. Remember, the purpose of your research is to build on work that has been done before and to provide new information in the form of your own understanding and synthesis.

Occasionally, you will be asked simply to summarize the work of others, but with academic papers, your research should go beyond this narrow role. You are not simply a sponge, absorbing countless pieces of information, and you do not want your paper to be a tedious compilation of what is already known. Instead, it is your own work, your own perceptions and conclusions, resting solidly on the investigations of others. This independence and the opportunity for self-expression are really what make research enjoyable.

Thinking Critically

When you think critically, you first observe, and then question, investigate, analyze, and synthesize. These skills are important in all aspects of life, but they are especially important when writing a research paper.

The process begins when you ask questions about something you have learned or observed. In your everyday life, you may wonder why a cake fell, why a plant shriveled and died, or why the mercury in a thermometer rose as the temperature grew warmer. In considering more academic issues, you might wonder why an author chose to end a short story as he or she did, why General Eisenhower chose to land D-day troops at Normandy, whether states that have enacted strong gun-control laws are more or less violent than other states, or how Alzheimer's disease damages the brains of those afflicted.

To answer those questions, you would collect as much information on the subject as possible. As you read the information, you would make judgments based on your own knowledge and experience. Some of the information you found would probably contradict other information. You cannot simply accept other people's findings as true; rather, you must examine the evidence yourself, carefully and systematically.

Finding Evidence

As a researcher, you are looking for evidence that supports your thesis, much as a detective looks for evidence to solve a crime. The evidence you uncover as you pursue your investigation can be divided into three categories:

- **Facts.** Facts are pieces of information that are not in doubt. They are objective in the sense that they can be observed and measured. Examples include the chemical composition of the food we eat, test scores, and historical dates.
- **Inferences.** Inferences are statements about the unknown based on the known. For example, it is not feasible to poll all children or alcoholics or working women, so researchers make inferences or generalizations about them based on sampling typical members of the group. Conclusions based on such limited information may or may not be valid. Literary critics sometimes try to explain an author's intent when he or she wrote a particular passage, but there is no way to know what was in the mind of a long-dead author. The critic or researcher can only make an inference based on what is known about the author and his or her work.
- **Judgments.** A judgment is an expression of a writer's approval or disapproval of the actions or persons or occurrences he or she is describing. A

judgment states the writer's personal feelings. As you can imagine, judgments are often more interesting than facts, but in a research paper, they must be solidly grounded in fact.

Each of the three types of evidence has a place in a research paper. You gather facts in order to test your inferences or hypotheses about a given topic. You also collect the inferences and judgments of others, testing them against the facts. Finally, you make judgments of your own based on your findings.

In a sense, what you are doing is putting evidence together to create meaning. You must therefore put aside personal prejudices and biases. Evidence should be examined in a systematic, disciplined manner.

Acquiring Skills for a Lifetime

Is learning to do research of little use in the real world? Definitely not! Few skills will be more useful than learning to find answers to problems and being able to communicate your knowledge in clear, articulate prose. The investigations you conduct will not only increase your knowledge but also enhance your ability to think clearly and objectively. Moreover, both informal and formal research can result in evidence that will lend authority to your opinions or help you modify them when necessary.

Reports and proposals are common in the business world and in government. In fact, communicating effectively in written form will be important in whatever career you choose. In this day and age, however, being a competent writer may not be enough. Good writers and researchers should also be proficient in the use of computers and computer-based resources. These are skills you will want to hone and update throughout your life.

Joining the Computer Revolution

For some college students, the computer is as necessary and comfortable as an arm or leg. For others, it is a frightening monster. Those students whose experiences with computers have been disastrous would probably prefer to stay as far from cyberspace as possible.

If you are a student who is already proficient with computers, this book will provide ideas for using those skills to become a better student. Applying your computer expertise to your academic work will allow you to save time and to write better papers.

If, on the other hand, you are a student who avoids computers, this book will be a life raft. You may never be a computer whiz, but technology can still work for you, just as much as for the techie sitting across the aisle.

You needn't understand any of the jargon that you're accustomed to hearing from your hacker friends. Word-processing programs are among the most user-friendly software programs, and graphical user interfaces like *Windows* eliminate much of the confusion.

Visiting Your Campus Computer Center

Let's start with the student who knows nothing about computers. You may be feeling that you don't know where to begin. You wonder how and where other students got their experience. One of the best places to begin is your campus computer center. Called by different names at different universities, there is nearly always a place where students can type research papers and do other assignments.

Tell the lab attendant that you would like to work through a word-processing tutorial. A tutorial is a software program that takes you slowly and patiently through a program. Nearly every program nowadays comes with a tutorial, and some even show you how to use the computer's operating system. As you answer each simple question and press the keys you are told to press, you will progress painlessly through the program. When you finish, you will have mastered the basics of word processing and will have a foundation on which to build future expertise. Some of my best friends are tutorials. They never become impatient or behave as if I'm not very bright. I can go over the same instructions as many times as necessary until I feel confident.

Ask for help only when you have a specific question. Then make sure the lab attendant tells you only what you need to know. Listening to a barrage of technical information just invites a bad case of technophobia.

Here's another useful tip. Don't arrive at the computer lab with a handwritten paper a day or two before it's due, hoping to learn to use the computer and type your paper at the same time. A high stress level might cause you to make mistakes. Terrible things may start to happen, and you may even lose your file entirely. Learning the program and typing the paper should be two separate activities.

Buying a Personal Computer

These days, many view life without a personal computer as a form of cruel and inhuman punishment. With a word-processing program, for example, you can be the world's worst speller or typist yet still produce perfect copy. You can edit and re-edit until you are completely satisfied, without wasting a sheet of paper or typing the same phrase twice. Since your work is bound to be compared with that of others who can produce a pristine masterpiece, you can scarcely afford to cling to your typewriter.

Whether you buy a new or used computer, it's all yours! No one can play games while you wait impatiently, and no one (except you, of course) can accidentally reformat the hard drive, erasing the word-processing program minutes before your paper is due. Sharing computers with hundreds of other students often means that no computer is available when you need one or that the only available machine is in such poor condition that your file may disappear into the ether at any moment.

When you use a public or community computer, you may end up with a glorified typewriter, writing out your rough draft with pencil and paper in the same painstaking way researchers have done for centuries. When you have your own computer, you write in an entirely different way. As you become more comfortable, you write directly into the computer. Gone is the yellow pad. Everything—notes, quotes, rough draft—goes into a word-processing file. The computer is an integral part of the writing process, not just the machine that produces the final copy.

Deciding What Computer to Buy. Relying on your university's computer lab for word processing because you can't afford your own computer may be totally unnecessary. A used computer can be purchased for about the same price as a television set or a VCR. Prices on new computers go down each year, while their power and flexibility increase.

Moreover, used computers are generally good buys because computer users tend to upgrade to faster, more powerful models long before their old ones are showing signs of wear. If you are interested only in word processing or other text-based applications, you don't need speed or power. Your computer won't be doing anything most of the time but waiting for you to compose another line. You don't need much RAM (random access memory, so-called because any random byte or specific piece of information can be retrieved at once) because text occupies only a fraction of the space required for fancy graphics.

The same goes for buying a new computer. You don't need the newest state-of-the-art machine. Prices on one model plummet when a new model is introduced. Buying the older one will save you money and ensure that bugs and glitches have been identified and eliminated.

Be sure that the new or used computer you buy is IBM-compatible (unless, of course, you would prefer to work in a Macintosh environment). Personal computers that are not manufactured by IBM but are able to run IBM-compatible software are called *clones*. Most of these clones are excellent buys, so, no matter how limited your budget, there's probably a good, serviceable computer that you can afford.

IBM-compatible computers running under *Microsoft Windows* can run several programs at one time (as can Macintoshes). This capacity for *multitasking* is a valuable tool when doing research papers. For example, let's say you are composing your first draft on-screen. At some point, you may need to refer to notes that you have stored in a separate file. In a multitasking environment, you can stay in your first draft and open several note files at the same time (or refer to your outline). If you plan to run *Windows 3.1*, you will need four or more megabytes of RAM, while the literature for *Windows '95* specifies at least eight megabytes. Macintosh computers always come equipped with a graphical interface so you need not worry about this, but they too have varying amounts of RAM. The more RAM you have, the more documents you can open at one time.

CD-ROM Drives. A CD-ROM (compact disk—read-only memory) is a compact disk containing data to be read by a computer. A short time ago, CD-ROM drives were considered luxuries, well beyond the budget of the struggling college student. More recently, however, they have been included with most new computer packages. Although it depends on the exact year and model, most older computers cannot easily accommodate CD-ROM drives. By the time you spend the money to increase RAM and upgrade other boards, you could almost have bought a new computer. In addition, you have little assurance that your computer will run a CD-ROM reliably.

Although most of us would be delighted if someone offered us a free CD-ROM drive, it's far from necessary to have one. Of the home-market CD-ROM programs, the most useful are probably the electronic encyclopedias. *Microsoft Bookshelf* is another useful reference since it contains the core of several basic reference books on one disk. Major reference works on CD-ROM, however, may cost several thousand dollars and are beyond a student's budget. They are best purchased by your library, where they can be used by a number of people. Many of the lower-priced CD-ROM disks are not as useful for research as they claim to be. Although their enormous capacity provides space for large graphic files, home-market CD-ROMs have not yet achieved their potential in the reference area.

If you plan to add a CD-ROM drive to an existing computer, check with a technician to be sure they will be compatible. Most computer manufacturers maintain a toll-free telephone number, and manufacturers will know more about the computers they produce than a salesperson at your local computer store.

Retrieving information from a CD-ROM disk is slower than from a floppy or hard disk. How fast the information is loaded depends on the speed of your computer's microprocessor as well as that of the CD-ROM disk drive. When you are comparing prices, you may find terms like "quad speed" and "eight-speed" a little confusing. However, most product literature will list the "access speed" of the drive.

Printers. Even students who have their own computers often choose to do their printing at campus computer centers, thus saving money on paper, printer ribbons, toner, and repairs. Using the lab may give them access to an expensive laser printer that would otherwise exceed their budgets.

You may, however, want to own at least a low-cost bubble-jet printer for convenience. If you plan to type the final drafts of your papers on your own machine, avoid nine-pin dot matrix printers. The American Psychological Association has declared them unacceptable for the submission of papers, and your instructor may feel the same way.

If you decide to use the printer in your computer center, your home computer will need to be compatible with those on campus. As a rule, newer computers can understand older ones, but it doesn't usually work the other way around. Therefore, if your home computer is the older piece of equipment and you're taking a disk from home to campus, you should be in good shape.

Single-Function Word Processors. Several typewriter manufacturers entered the computer age with machines that are half typewriter and half computer, often just called *word processors*. When I use that term, I do not mean these machines. I mean a computer software program that can be loaded on a full-featured, multi-purpose computer.

The single-function machines often seem less expensive than a real PC or Macintosh and frequently include screen, keyboard, and printer all in one unit. Most typewriter/word processors, however, are not compatible with one another or with full-function computers. Their word-processing programs are unique, so you usually can't move information from one machine to another. An article downloaded from a machine in your library would be unreadable on such a machine.

A single-function word processor is only a good buy if you never intend to do anything with it but type your papers. You will usually be unable to connect by modem to the research databases described in this book or to download data from the vast storehouses of information available on the Internet. Too often, students purchase these typewriter/word processors and quickly outgrow them. Although they may seem like an economical investment, the money is wasted if you later upgrade to a full-function computer.

It is sometimes difficult to identify these typewriter/word processors because they vary greatly in appearance. In general, they tend to look something like a typewriter with a screen attached. The claims in their literature, however, often make them sound very much like a fully operational computer. In fact, one that is currently on the market advertises that it is equipped with a modem and can connect you to an e-mail provider.

Choosing Word-Processing Software

Although you will need word-processing software, your computer may come already equipped with a perfectly satisfactory program. If you must purchase a program, however, what should you look for? Even though the most recent versions of such giants in the word-processing industry as *WordPerfect* and *Microsoft Word* can almost jump through hoops while whistling Dixie, all you really need are the basics. Here's a list of essentials:

- the ability to import to and export from other programs.; you should not only be able to convert your file to another word-processing program but also be able to work with ASCII files (see "Understanding ASCII," page 15) that you receive by modem (all fairly recent programs can do this without difficulty)
- the ability to number pages automatically and to position page numbers where you want them (headers and footers are helpful for including your name and/or the title of the paper with the page)

- the ability to load several files at the same time or a clipboard utility (by no means essential, but it's nice to cut and paste information from one file to another)
- the ability to accent vowels for foreign spellings
- the ability to check spelling for errors

That's it. Come to think of it, you may not need everything on this brief list. Most word-processing programs can do far more than you will ever really need.

Choosing a Popular Program.

When learning to use a word-processing program, you need friends. If you are struggling with a manual that sounds as if it were written in a foreign language, nothing is so wonderful as a roommate or computer-center staffer who knows the program. With a few well-chosen words, he or she can get you over a hurdle that has caused you hours of misery.

For this reason, you might choose a program that is popular on your campus even if it costs a little more. Don't forget that your college or university is entitled to a substantial educational discount, so you may be able to purchase a high-end program at a more reasonable price.

Discovering Shareware.

Although the prices of commercial word-processing programs may seem astronomical, many excellent shareware or noncommercial programs are available. Shareware is a wonderful idea that has developed with the widespread use of personal computers.

Computer programmers, usually amateurs, may discover a need for a particular type of program, which they then write. To pay themselves back for the time they have invested, they distribute evaluation copies of the program free of cost. If you download or otherwise acquire a copy of the program, find that it suits your needs, and would like to keep it, you are honor-bound to register your copy and pay the programmer a fee. Such fees are far lower than the cost of a commercial program.

Shareware programs can be as good as their commercial counterparts. However, they can also be full of programming errors or limited in what they can do. It never hurts to try out a program. Experienced computer users will tell you that some of their favorite programs are shareware. However, you do have to take precautions.

Whether you select a program from one of the many shareware catalogs or download a program from a local bulletin board, be sure you run your virus checker on it immediately (see "Guarding against Viruses," page 16). Then try out the program and experiment with its various functions. Don't, however, become dependent on it before you put it through its paces, and be sure you have backup copies of any data you input. The title screen of a program usually includes the telephone number of the programmer, so it is often possible to get help in a crisis.

If you ask around, you will undoubtedly discover computer bulletin boards in your area that allow you to download shareware programs. Shareware can also be downloaded from the Internet. Remember, though, that if you keep the program and continue to use it, it is only fair that you pay the programmer's fee. If you purchase a disk from a catalog, remember that the money you pay (usually about $5 per disk) goes to the shareware vendor, not the programmer. The program itself will provide information on registration and cost.

Choosing Writing Tools. Most commercial word-processing programs now come with a variety of tools that can make a writer's job much easier.

- **Spell Checkers.** For the poor speller, spell checkers are wonderful programs. Most word-processing programs come with their own spell checkers, but if yours doesn't, you can download or purchase a separate program that can interact with your word processor. The process is a little cumbersome, but it works.

    Spell checkers are a necessity, and not only for poor spellers. We all make occasional typos, and the number of typos tends to increase when we use a word processor. The computer allows us to type so rapidly that we can almost keep up with our thoughts. We type as we think, and we don't want to interrupt the flow of ideas. Having to pay attention to each word and letter we type would halt that flow. It is much easier to go back later to clean it up.

    A spell checker will not catch all your errors. It won't understand that you really meant to type *their*, not *there*. All it understands is that both *there* and *their* are words in its database. You will still need to proofread carefully to be sure you have not only typed the word correctly, but used the one that means what you intend it to mean.

- **On-line Thesauri.** Do you sometimes waste precious minutes searching for just the right word? The computer can't really tell you the word you're looking for, but a thesaurus program can be helpful. Just set your cursor on the word that doesn't sound right and invoke the thesaurus. On the screen will appear half a dozen words with similar meanings. You choose the most appropriate one, and the program types it in place of your original word. A thesaurus can be especially useful when you feel as if you're repeating the same word too often.

    Thesauri, however, whether printed or computerized, can be addictive. This is especially true when you are experiencing a touch of writer's block. Problems occur when you lack confidence in your writing and invoke the thesaurus for every third word. Eventually, your writing sounds like a confusing string of unrelated words, and every noun is modified by three adjectives.

    Bear in mind that two words rarely mean precisely the same thing. It is better to repeat yourself than to add an unintended shade of meaning that may confuse your reader.

- **Grammar Checkers.** Although most writers would never want to work without a spell checker and thesaurus program, grammar checkers are optional. They are not as reliable as these other programs and must be used with caution. Computers do an excellent job with spelling, for there are at most two correct ways to spell a word. Computers understand *yes* or *no*, *right* or *wrong*, but they don't like *maybe*. The English language, however, is complicated and full of *maybes*.

  Each of us writes differently, and the computer doesn't really understand what we have written. All it can do is check to see if we have followed certain rules that have been programmed into it. If you lack confidence and follow the admonitions of a grammar program slavishly, you will waste time, and your prose may actually suffer. If, on the other hand, you take the program's advice with a grain of salt, you may find it helpful. Grammar checkers are wonderful at noticing technical errors you might miss, such as a verb that doesn't agree with its subject. However, when they begin telling you what's wrong with your writing, seek out your instructor for a second opinion.

Understanding ASCII

Unfortunately, word-processing, database, and other programs do not communicate well with one another. Each program uses different codes for bold type, underlining, margins, and line spacing that are embedded in a file and cannot be understood by other programs. However, it's possible to strip all this information from a file and store it in what's called an ASCII file. Short for American Standard Code for Information Interchange, ASCII is a kind of Esperanto, a universal language intended for transferring information from one computer to another.

Newer word processors allow you to load an ASCII file with either hard or soft carriage returns. If you have this option available to you, it's generally best to choose soft. A hard return occurs when the author of a file hits the "Enter" key (usually at the end of a line). A soft return occurs when the computer is allowed to use its own judgment about how to break lines. Loading a file with hard returns often results in text being spread out on many more lines than needed because the hard return was determined by the old margin setting. Since most downloaded files have more characters per line than you will be using for a research paper format, the extra text will spill over onto a new line. Soft returns let the text fit into your own format.

You will probably use ASCII most often when you are loading a file copied from a library database or downloaded from the Internet. Since ASCII files lack special formatting like boldface and underlining, you will probably prefer to use translation modules within your word processor to change your document from a *WordPerfect* to a *Microsoft Word* document or vice-versa, for example.

Guarding against Viruses

When working on a paper, you may be importing data from a variety of places. You may also be importing viruses. A computer virus, like its biological counterpart, has a self-replicating code that can "infect" a computer program. Viruses are usually planted illegally by hackers to damage or shut down a system or network or to make an individual program misbehave.

Most new computers come equipped with a virus detection and cure program. If you have a registered copy of the software, you are usually entitled to free updates for a specified period of time. If your computer does not have an antivirus program or if it is out of date, you might purchase a copy of the popular *Norton Anti-Virus* program or a good shareware equivalent. If you choose shareware, be sure to check when it was last updated since new viruses are being created all the time. New viruses called *macro viruses* that have appeared in the last few years are especially dangerous. They are transmitted in word-processing files and are let loose to cause havoc on your hard disk when you invoke a word-processing macro. Recently, *Microsoft Word* has been the target of many of these viruses, but Microsoft maintains software at its World Wide Web site that can eliminate the intruders.

A good "fix-it" or recovery program like *Norton Utilities*, *PC Tools*, or their shareware counterparts is also helpful to deal with unexpected crises. Whether you are using someone else's equipment for printing or downloading files from the Internet, you need to guard against the ubiquitous virus.

If you're in a hurry, you may forget to run your virus checker every time you load a new file. Most virus checkers, however, can be loaded as memory-resident programs. Called *TSRs*, memory-resident programs load when you first start up your computer, but they stay in the background, automatically checking new files. An alarm sounds if they discover a hostile invader. You then have the opportunity to clean the file or disk on which the virus is encamped.

Managing Data

Though not absolutely essential, it's helpful to have a database program of some sort to keep track of bibliographic and other information. It can be the mail-merge module in your word processor, an integrated database program that may come packaged with your word processor, or a separate program like *FoxPro*, *D-Base*, or *Inmagic*. For example, *Microsoft Windows* comes with a handy little card-file program. The cards resemble the ones you use for notes, but the program has the advantage of being able to search for any word or phrase.

Most newer computers come equipped with an integrated software package that includes some sort of database module like *Microsoft Access*. Even if you are not especially fond of the program provided, it would be wise to become accustomed to using it. Commands will be similar to those in the word-processing program, so there is less to learn. In addition, it is possible to move reports from the database into word-processing files with a minimum of effort.

Some colleges and universities offer powerful reference managers to handle bibliographic information. These programs, which include *ProCite, Endnote,* and *Nota Bene,* can alphabetize citations and format bibliographies in whatever style you're using. They're worth their weight in gold, but, unfortunately, that's about what they cost. Except for the lower-end programs, you will probably be able to use them only on campus. Many schools offer workshops covering the basic skills needed to use the programs. A few of these programs not only do a good job of handling bibliographic information but are in the $100 price range.

As with word processors, shareware is a good alternative to expensive commercial database programs. If cost is an issue, shareware programs like *Wampum* and *Winfile* often do the job as well as—or better than—more expensive commercial programs.

If you are using a separate program (not one that comes with your word processor) to store your bibliographic citations, be sure you can later import them into your word-processed document. Then you can easily alphabetize your citations, create a report, and append the report/bibliography to your document (usually in an ASCII format).

Communicating by Modem

Modems are like telephones. Using your phone line, you can connect to other computers all over the world. A modem links you to the outside world, allowing you to receive (download) as well as send (upload) information. By connecting to the Internet or an on-line service provider, for example, you can hold conversations with experts all over the country simply by typing on your keyboard.

Despite the fact that a serviceable new modem costs as little as $100, many computer owners do not have one. Modems are one of the few bells or whistles that, until recently, were not included with a new computer, yet they increase its usefulness many times over.

With a modem, you can check the holdings of libraries all over the world. You can download files from large university computers and discuss your research problems with faculty and students in an Internet discussion group. In addition, you can access large commercial data services like *Dialog* and *FirstSearch* or use the on-line research services provided by the Library of Congress, the Colorado Library Alliance (CARL), and California's MELVYL.

Understanding Baud Rates.
The term *baud,* which is a count of data bits per second (bps), refers to the speed at which a modem can send or receive messages. In the past, computer users thought 300 bps was lightning-fast, but newer modems send data at 14,400 and 28,800 bits per second. When you subscribe to on-line services, check to see if they charge a flat rate for the time you're on-line or if they have a higher charge for faster baud rates.

Choosing Communications Software.
Your modem is controlled or directed by a software program. Communications software allows you to use your modem

to send and receive data over telephone lines. Most of the newer programs make it easy for you to connect to other computers, storing the numbers you dial most frequently and letting you speed-dial as you would with a telephone.

Some of the best communications programs on the market are shareware. *Q-Modem*, *Telex*, *Procomm*, and *Crosstalk* are all high-quality, widely available programs. However, most of the on-line services like *Prodigy*, *America Online*, and *CompuServe* provide their own communications programs. They store some of the data on your own hard drive so that it need not be repeatedly sent over the phone line. These programs, however, are intended only for accessing a specific service. Your university may also require that you use custom software to access its on-line resources or may provide you with a copy of a World Wide Web browser like *Mosaic* or *Netscape*. If you wish to communicate with other computers, you will also need an all-purpose program.

Saving Information. Any information you see on your screen when you are on-line can usually be saved to a file, and whole book-length files can be downloaded to your PC in a matter of minutes, depending on the speed of your modem. Whichever communications program you choose, be sure you know how to save the information you discover. You can choose to save whole files (logging), or you can save one screen at a time (screen capture).

If you set your program to save everything automatically to a file, you can later load that file into your word processor. It will be in an ASCII format. In other words, it will be in a "stripped-down" format that is compatible with most computers. Some of the electronic documents available on the World Wide Web and in on-line databases are enormous. Be sure to delete all the unnecessary information and don't turn off your computer until you have pared the file down to a manageable size, because at least half of the text will be composed of log-in routines, help screens, menus, and other unneeded information. Having to wade through all this extraneous data every time you bring up the file takes precious time away from more important tasks and uses scarce storage space.

Finding these files can also be difficult. I spent days trying to find the file I had saved after my first experience with the screen-capture command. Some programs allow you to name the file, but others give it a preassigned name and put it wherever they like. Here's how to find a file:

1. Be sure that your computer is set to the correct date and time before you go on-line.
2. After you have logged off from an on-line session, close your communications program and open your word-processing program.
3. Type the command to open a document.
4. Choose the directory in which you have stored your communications program.
5. Look at the list of files in that directory. Only one file should have been created on the date and at the time when you were last on-line.

(Always check this immediately after you go off-line so that you won't forget.)

6. Choose the file with the correct date and time. Your word processor will probably ask if you want to load it as an ASCII file with hard returns. Choose ASCII with soft returns instead.

7. Check to be sure you have the right file. It may look different from what you expected because it's a collection of screens exactly as they appeared, including menu options.

8. Delete all unwanted information and save it to your word-processing directory. Give it a new name that makes sense, for you don't want to lose it again. Your communications program may continue saving downloaded information to the old file name, overwriting the file you just edited. Once you have saved it to your word processor, it's safe.

Services like *America Online* allow you to download articles from magazines, journals, and reference works. They use their own communications software and intend that you view your downloaded file while you're off-line but still in their software program. Use the *copy command* in the program to copy the file to your word processor. Once again, give it a name that will allow you to find it easily.

You can accumulate a lot of these downloaded files, so create a directory just for them. If you were collecting photocopied articles, you would probably keep them together in a folder or notebook. A separate directory serves the same purpose.

Most World Wide Web browsers allow you to save documents to whatever file you choose. Sometimes, however, your university network is not equipped to send the file directly to your remote computer, so saving a file becomes a two-step process. The file is saved to the university's computer. You then load the appropriate software and download the file to your home computer.

Preparing for Last-Minute Crises

Novice computer users are often discouraged by the horror stories they hear from friends. Who has not known the tearful student who stayed up all night typing a paper only to have it go up in a puff of smoke before he or she was able to print it? These things happen, but they are usually not the computer's fault. Face it. When we are anxious and tense, we do dumb things.

When you save a file to a floppy disk, you are depending on magnetic impulses that grow faint with time. Magnetic storage is never permanent. And spilling Coca Cola on a floppy disk or leaving it in the back window of a car on a sunny day will not make it more readable. Although they are more solid and substantial, computer hard drives have their problems as well. Hard drives can be accidentally reformatted, file fragments can get lost, or the drive may crash for any one of a number of reasons.

If your paper is stored in only one place, whether it be hard drive or floppy disk, don't assume it is safe. Having two separate copies of a file is absolutely necessary, and three would not be excessive if the paper is an important one. For example, you may want to keep important files on the hard drive (assuming you have your own computer) and on two separate floppies.

However, most computer users go for years without a serious problem. As long as they back up their files on a regular basis, they usually encounter few difficulties. It's important, though, to have a crisis plan just in case. Novice users, especially, need all the comfort and reassurance they can get. Such a plan gives them (and even experts, for that matter) a needed sense of security.

Imagine that your computer dies suddenly. What would you do? Suppose your computer is chugging along merrily, but your printer starts typing Chinese characters. Think ahead. What are your options? Where can you find another computer equipped with your word-processing program? Does your campus computer lab use your word-processing program? Do you have your program stored on backup disks so that you could temporarily transfer it to a friend's computer? Work out a complete disaster plan.

Be sure that, in an emergency, you will have access to backup file copies as well as backup hardware and software. It often seems that just having the plan assures that you will never have to use it.

Now that you have identified or acquired your hardware and learned to use a word-processing program, you're ready to think about your paper. Just what will you write about?

Chapter **2**

Selecting a Topic

Like many students, you may experience something like sheer panic when an instructor assigns a paper. Whatever will you write about? There are literally thousands of possibilities, but at that moment you can't think of a single one.

Choosing Topics Rather Than Subjects

In your panic, you might snatch at a subject, any subject. Perhaps you decide to write about the Civil War. You dash to the library and print out or photocopy everything you can find on the Civil War. You then piece together these articles and find you have something that looks more like a crazy quilt than a research paper.

Let us assume that your instructor has assigned a ten-page paper. The number of pages published on the subject of the Civil War must be in the millions. You obviously can't distill those millions of pages into ten pages. For this reason, papers should never be written about general subjects. Instead, you will do better to focus your efforts on a *topic*—one specific aspect of that subject.

Compared to a general subject, which can usually be expressed in one or two words, a well-defined topic requires a more detailed description. The Civil War, violent crime, and Flannery O'Connor, for instance, are all general subjects. A topic tells us what aspect of a subject a research paper will discuss. For example, a student might write about one of the following specific topics: the role of women in the Civil War, strategies for reducing violent crime among teenagers, or the theme of parent-child conflict in Flannery O'Connor's "Everything That Rises Must Converge."

Choosing the Right Topic

Nothing can ruin your paper as quickly and as thoroughly as choosing the wrong topic. But how do you know which is the right one? Here are some basic guidelines:

- Choose a topic that you really care about. Your interest in your topic will help you to focus and you will have original ideas to contribute. Your paper will develop naturally as you answer the questions that occur to you.
- Choose a topic that matters, one that deals with important issues, such as efforts to deal with toxic waste. There's no point in wasting your time researching a topic that really doesn't matter, such as the food preferences of a current rock singer.
- Don't begin with a strong bias or personal prejudice unless your instructor assigns an argumentative paper. Keep an open mind.

- Think about your audience and capture their attention. You are not the only one who should be interested in the topic. Even though your readers may know more about the topic than you do, you want them to find your paper fresh and interesting, not a boring rehash of well-known material.
- Like Goldilocks, choose a topic that's not too large or too small but just right. Until you have done some preliminary research in the library, however, you may not be able to judge the just-rightness of a topic. Be prepared to narrow or expand your topic as needed.
- Choose a topic that's appropriate to the course and one that will increase your knowledge of the subject matter. In that way, your work in class provides ideas for your paper and, conversely, your classwork is enriched by the research you are doing on your paper.
- Choose a topic you understand. If it is excessively technical, you might be making your task more difficult than it need be, and you are unlikely to do a good job.

Focusing on Your Instructor's Input

Listen carefully and take notes when your instructor discusses your assignment in class. Be sure you understand his or her expectations:

- **Subject Matter:** Has your instructor assigned a topic? It's more likely that he or she has specified the general subject matter of the paper. Your instructor may even have given you a free hand to write about whatever you wish.
- **Length:** How long should the paper be? A topic that you can only do justice to in twenty-five pages may not be suitable for a shorter paper. If your instructor assigns a ten-page paper, does he or she mean at least ten pages or would a longer paper be acceptable? Some instructors encourage students to write longer papers if the topic warrants it. Others may want students to learn how to express their ideas concisely in a given amount of space.
- **Style:** Which bibliographic style should you use? Research papers have a formal structure that varies greatly from one discipline to another.
- **Tone:** How formal does your instructor expect your paper to be? The more formal the paper, the more formal the topic. Must you write entirely in the third person or would an occasional *you* or *I* be acceptable?
- **Sources:** How many sources should you consult?

No matter how carefully you have followed instructions, get your instructor's approval before going ahead with a topic. If you have chosen poorly or misunderstood some point, now is the time to find out—not after the paper is written.

Avoiding Certain Topics

Years ago, my English instructor assigned two research papers. The first one I completed was about Elizabeth Barrett Browning. I worked hard, followed instructions, and received an "A."

The second paper was a labor of love. I was going through my "flying saucer" phase and decided to write on that subject. I probably logged at least twice as many hours on this paper as I had investigating Elizabeth Barrett Browning, and I was convinced I had created a masterpiece. Unfortunately, I had failed to discuss the topic with my instructor. When at last the papers were returned, I found not the "A++" I expected but a "C." Looking back, that seems a little harsh after all my work, but my instructor's response was not that unpredictable. I had managed to break most of the rules governing the selection of topics. Consider the following suggestions about topics to avoid.

Controversial Topics. There is a time and a place for controversy. If you're asked to write an argumentative essay, you will need to take a controversial position and defend it. Most formal research papers, however, should weigh more heavily on the side of fact than of opinion.

In my own example, I defended the existence of flying saucers with all my heart but with little involvement from my head. Most of my points were merely opinions. I would have been unlikely to understand scientific works relating to the subject, so instead I chose popular and sensational sources that presented few facts to support my ideas.

Overused Topics. How many papers, I wonder, had my instructor received on flying saucers? How many papers has the average college instructor read on the subject of abortion or gun control? Can a student really expect his or her audience, in this case the instructor, to be interested in a paper that contains nothing new or engaging? You would find it tedious to read the same thing over and over again. So does your instructor.

Trivial or Sensational Topics. As a rule of thumb, a subject that appears routinely in the tabloids is not a suitable topic for a research paper. These might include sensational yet questionable medical treatments, fad diets, or the philosophical observations of film stars. It is almost impossible to apply sound, scholarly research methods to such topics, so you are forced to rely on publications that lack authority or credibility. Such publications deal with trivial subjects, and the information they contain does not stand the test of importance or academic respectability.

Recycled Papers. Don't try to recycle a paper you did for another class. The subject matter is probably inappropriate, and every instructor has different expectations for what they want done. However, a paper that you wrote last semester might lead to unanswered questions and ideas for further research. You may want to use the old paper as a starting point for the new one, but talk to your instructor first.

Excessively Neutral Topics. You don't want your paper to sound like an encyclopedia. Though excessive controversy is undesirable, blandness can be even worse. Your paper should explore areas that are uncertain or in dispute, rather than simply state the facts.

Topics for Which There Is Insufficient Available Information. Your library probably has more information on your proposed topic than you might think, but some topics are too specialized for most academic libraries. Regional or local topics can also create problems. You are unlikely to find much information about water pollution in your home state of Massachusetts if you are attending college in Illinois.

Brainstorming

Are you one of those students who has a panic attack when asked to choose a topic? Do you become convinced you have nothing whatever to write about? Everything you have learned in this and other courses suddenly evaporates. You don't know anything about any issue that anyone else would want to read about. In reality, of course, you have lots of ideas, innumerable observations, bottled up inside you. Your previous courses have given you insights into a number of subjects. You probably read the newspaper and wonder why things happen as they do. You have stored up more than enough ideas to get you started on a research paper. But how do you set them free and allow them to flow onto paper?

Don't we all share that fear of the blank screen or the blank sheet of paper? That was why the great American writer Ernest Hemingway made it a rule to end each sheet of paper in the middle of a sentence. That way he began the next page with something. He never had to look at a perfectly blank sheet of paper.

Like Hemingway, most successful writers have their own ways of dealing with writer's block. The following techniques have helped many students and writers alike.

Freewriting. Often you can release the flow of ideas by simply making yourself write for ten minutes or so without stopping. You will need a starting point, some rough idea of your potential topic, but from then on, let yourself go. Write quickly about whatever comes to mind. Don't worry about spelling or grammar, which can distract you. Write everything you can think of that has to do with the topic. Write about what you know. Write about what seems interesting. Follow any random thoughts that cross your mind. Don't stop or you may interrupt the flow. Write long enough to become tired. This will enable you to get past whatever is at the surface of your thoughts or at the top of your mind. If you find yourself eventually pausing, the flow has slowed and you are probably ready to stop.

Sometimes, you may find you can't concentrate on your assignment because you are worrying about something else. Freewriting can be a way of releasing these feelings by putting them into words. Your mind may feel clear after a few minutes and you will be able to move on to ideas about your topic.

Listing and Clustering. Put aside the pages you have filled. Take a break so that you can come back to your topic with a fresh and objective viewpoint. Then reread what you have written.

Think it over and see if you can find a center or focal point for the ideas you expressed. Sometimes this is called a center around which your other ideas cluster. Maybe there is not one focal point but many. Make a list of the main ideas you discover as you read through the wandering prose you have produced.

Are all of these ideas separate and distinct from one another or do some of them connect with others? Look for connections and separate out any groups of ideas that seem to go together. Do these groups suggest ideas for developing your topic?

What do your feelings tell you? A good topic is one you enjoy thinking about. Whether you know a lot about it or very little, it appeals to you in some way.

Where has all this writing, listing, and clustering taken you? If all has gone well, you are moving toward a clearer idea of what you want to write about. It may be helpful now to repeat the process. Give yourself some time, maybe even a day or two, and then try the freewriting exercise again. You will be amazed at how your thoughts have come together.

Using CD-ROM Encyclopedias to Jog Your Memory. This is a very new technique that has been made possible by recent software innovations, especially the ability of a search program to find every incidence of a word or phrase in an encyclopedia. Although encyclopedias are generally used to find information, they can also serve as a way of jogging your memory, of bringing thoughts to the surface in much the way freewriting does. All you really need to begin is a word or two.

Load the CD-ROM encyclopedia and invoke the command for searching the entire text. Type a word or phrase related to something that interests you. Be careful that the word you choose is not too common or widely used because you could end up with a thousand hits, rather than the dozen or so you're hoping for. Look at what you have found. Some of the hits will be unexpected. Ask yourself how one article relates to another. Read a little of the text surrounding the word you typed, but remember that your goal is not to read the articles but to nudge your brain in the direction of creative thinking. Let the headings you discover stimulate your own thinking. What do you already know about the subjects that come up on your screen? Which aspects are more interesting to you? Which relate more closely to your assignment? Do the headings suggest ideas for narrowing or widening your topic?

Writing about Popular Culture

Before we leave this subject, let us spend a moment discussing popular subjects like rock music. Your instructor may have his or her own guidelines concerning such subjects, but if you are in doubt, the following rules of thumb will be helpful.

Contemporary music, to continue this example, is a perfectly respectable field of study, but choosing a topic presents special difficulties. Your topic should not be trivial or sensational. You will need to approach it in an academic and professional manner.

While many serious works have been written on, let's say, the influence of the Beatles, a paper on a performer who currently has a best-selling CD may not work. You will need access to a body of literature written about this performer in respected publications by people with established credentials in the field. In addition, you must have reason to believe that the topic of your paper is important and that six months or a year from now the performer will not be totally forgotten.

Lightweight, fan-directed music magazines are not adequate sources, so find out what is available before you commit yourself to such a topic. The longer this performer has been in the public eye, the greater the likelihood that a reliable body of sources can be amassed. Ask your librarian about reference books listing the credentials of people in the music world.

Similarly, it is difficult to write a paper about a Hollywood star without it sounding like an article in a fan magazine. However, a paper on a director and his or her contribution to a particular film, making use of the professional literature such as film journals, might be successful.

As you write the paper, keep your audience in mind. You must convince your instructor that your subject matter is worthy of a serious paper. Be sure to state the credentials of the authorities you cite to counter any skepticism, and connect your subject to major developments and issues in the field.

Refining Your Preliminary Topic at the Library

When you have progressed far enough with your brainstorming to have a sense of direction, it's time to make your first exploratory trip to the library. You will need more information before you finally commit to a topic.

Be sure to bring your notes with you. In fact, you might want to add a few sentences describing the kind of information you want to find. What questions do you hope to answer?

Even though you have not yet settled on a final topic, don't go to the library empty-handed. Students sometimes think that if they wander around the library, something will catch their eye and an idea for a topic will occur to them. Maybe a book will seem to jump out at them, or they will come across an interesting title in the book catalog.

This may have been possible years ago when academic libraries were smaller. However, a modern university library of ten or more stack levels and hundreds of stack ranges is more likely to intimidate than inspire you. Your academic library may have half-a-million books, as well as thousands of journals, dissertations, conference proceedings, government documents, and enough miscellaneous publications to totally confound an inexperienced college student.

To use the library's catalog effectively, you will need to look up specific words. The computer screen will prompt you for a subject or keyword. If you key in a vague term like *music* or *literature* or *history*, you may sit for several minutes while the program selects thousands of records containing that word in the subject, title, contents, abstract, or keywords. When the first dozen or so items appear on the screen, most will mean nothing to you. Librarians are available to help you, but there is little they can do unless you have specific questions. In such a large and complicated place, you can easily find yourself overwhelmed and develop a bad case of library-phobia.

If you come prepared to investigate one or more preliminary topics, such as the causes of the American Revolution, you will have a starting point, and your notes will yield keywords that can be used to search for books and articles.

Chapters 4 and 5 will tell you more about using specific library resources, but for now just locate the reference section on a library map or ask a librarian for help.

Finding Out about Campus Libraries

If you are attending a large university, you may have a choice of several libraries. The easiest way to select one is to follow your instructor's recommendation. If none has been specified, find out whether a special undergraduate library is available. Some universities have established smaller libraries especially for undergraduate research. Librarians in these smaller libraries will be more experienced in dealing with undergraduate research projects. If no undergraduate library is available, you will probably want to begin your research at the large general library.

Visiting the Reference Collection

Reference books are those heavy volumes like encyclopedias that are used to look up specific information. Both general and specialized dictionaries and encyclopedias would be helpful at this point. For example, if you're writing a paper on Napoleon, a general encyclopedia like *Encyclopedia Americana* will provide a brief biographical article while the *Dictionary of World Biography* will give you more specific information. If you're researching DNA, you might try the *McGraw-Hill Encyclopedia of Science and Technology*. Reference works, however, are not limited to dictionaries and encyclopedias. You will find a wealth of handbooks, almanacs, yearbooks, and bibliographies.

Exploring Computerized Encyclopedias

Many of these same reference works are available in CD-ROM or on-line. Computerized reference works are not always better than their print counterparts, but computerized encyclopedias are an exciting innovation.

When you use a printed encyclopedia you have two choices. You can look up your topic alphabetically in the volume devoted to that letter, or you can use the index. When you use the keyword-searching option of a computerized encyclopedia, the program will find every mention of your topic in the entire encyclopedia. You will usually end up with a list of "hits" showing how many times your keyword is mentioned in each article.

Some, of course, will be of little use. In the case of DNA, the first hit, an article entitled "DNA," will probably contain ample information to get you started. However, some of the other "hits" will both surprise and interest you. They can give you an idea of how DNA relates to other topics, and you may discover some specific aspect of the topic you would like to write about. Most important, the list of hits will start you thinking about your paper. You will begin making decisions about what should be included or left out. The hit list will also give you an idea how much information is available.

CD-ROM Encyclopedias.
If your own computer is of recent vintage, it may have come with a CD-ROM drive and several disks, including an encyclopedia. If so, you might begin your research on your home turf. These home-market CD-ROM programs are entertaining and may provide some preliminary information on your topic. However, many, like Microsoft's *Encarta,* are aimed primarily at children or high school students. You can learn quite a bit from them, but they're not the equivalent of the *Encyclopaedia Britannica* or other adult encyclopedias.

On-Line Encyclopedias.
Some of the on-line services like Prodigy, America Online, and CompuServe also have on-line encyclopedias and other reference works available. Prodigy provides access to a collection of reference works called Homework Helper. America Online has a similar service called Academic Advisor. Although these services are also aimed at younger students, they will provide quite a bit of useful information to get you started.

Reading an Encyclopedia Article Like a Road Map

Whichever encyclopedia format you use, take a good look at the articles on your topic. Each paragraph of an article tells you about some aspect of the topic. It gives you a sense of the scope or extent of your territory. The article can serve as a kind of road map, pointing the way to different areas of interest. In fact, the headingsused in the article almost serve as an outline of available information. Since the headings indicate aspects of the subject that have been studied by others, they can be used to narrow your topic.

General encyclopedia articles are helpful in formulating your topic, assessing the extent of available information, and structuring an outline; however, they are usually not useful for actual research. Once you begin gathering information for your paper, you will find encyclopedia articles too superficial to be helpful.

Using Periodical Indexes

Another good source for introductory information is a general periodical index. At this point, you don't really want scholarly information. You're just hitting the high spots, finding out how broad or how narrow your chosen subject really is and getting a rough idea of what has been written about it. General indexes are ideal for this purpose.

The Reader's Guide to Periodical Literature is usually the first general index we think of. It's now available in a printed version, on CD-ROM (WilsonDisc), and in an on-line version (Wilsonline). ProQuest's General Periodicals Collection is another good place to find introductory magazine articles.

Reading Journal Abstracts

Until recently, magazine and journal abstracts were treasures little known to undergraduates. These one- or two-paragraph summaries of the information contained in an article only appeared in the more serious scholarly services, such as Psychological Abstracts or Chemical Abstracts.

When computerized indexes became common, it was obvious that the title of an article did not provide enough information. Students who might locate citations for fifty or a hundred articles could not possibly go to the shelves and look up each and every article. They needed more information. If abstracts were available, students could decide which articles were pertinent to their research and which could be safely eliminated.

Abstracts are precisely what you need at this stage of your research since you are not ready to plunge into the articles themselves. Abstracts can provide an overview of the subject matter, a bird's-eye view of the information available on your topic.

Computerized journal indexes can also help you narrow your topic. The ProQuest service actually has an index arranged by subject. If you look up a broad subject, you will find narrower headings listed underneath. EBSCO's Magazine Summaries has a similar index. These divide the subject just the way the headings in the encyclopedia article did. One of these subheadings might be the basis of just the topic you're looking for.

The library has many other resources available to you, but it's probably time to collect your thoughts and see where you are with your topic.

Narrowing the Topic

Now that you have a bird's-eye view of the information available, you will want to narrow your topic to one issue or problem you can cover in the space and time you have available. When you begin a project, you wonder how you will ever fill ten or twenty or thirty pages. You know so little about the topic that you doubt that you could fill up a postage stamp. As you go deeper, however, you find more and more information, and you begin to realize how much more there is to know. Unfortunately, it is necessary to narrow your topic while you are still at the "postage stamp" stage.

After your preliminary reconnaissance at the library, you are ready to make some educated guesses about the information available on your topic and what size chunk can be covered in the required number of pages. Both the subheadings of encyclopedia articles and the journal indexes gave you an idea of how your subject is usually divided. The more you pare down now, the less material you will need to identify, locate, read, file—and ultimately discard.

Working through the following questions can help you narrow your topic:

- What broad subject are you considering, or what is the general subject matter of the course (for example, American history, sociology, or art history)?
- After consulting some of the library's reference works, what five broad areas can you divide the subject into? In an American history course, for example, five possible areas might be colonization, the Revolution, the Civil War, the Great Depression, and World War II.
- Which of these five areas is most interesting to you?
- When you have made a choice, break it down once again. What five aspects of this area can you think of to research? Suppose you chose the American Revolution for your history paper. You might research the causes, the economic impact, the British point of view, a particular battle, or treaty provisions.
- Which of these aspects interests you most? Let's say you chose the British point of view.
- Do you think this aspect of the subject will interest your readers?
- What in particular would you like to know about the British point of view? For example, you might be curious about how supportive the British people were of their government's actions against the American colonies.
- What specific questions might you ask about British attitudes?

Almost every subject can be divided and subdivided and even sub-subdivided into smaller and smaller parts. Experiment with this technique, beginning with different subjects. You will find yourself with more good topics than you know what to do with.

Avoiding Too-Narrow Topics

Although it doesn't happen often, there is such a thing as a too-narrow topic, one so specific that not more than a few brief articles have ever been written about it. Such a topic might be called a dead end. Either no one has gotten around to writing about it or there just isn't anything to say.

However, the problem may not be the topic itself but the limitations of your library. Finding enough information on a highly specialized topic may require the resources of a large research library. Interlibrary loan expands your library's collection considerably, but you can't depend on it for the majority of your sources.

Writing a Thesis Statement

Now that you have made your preliminary investigation and narrowed your topic to a manageable size, it is time to write out a trial thesis statement that will hold your paper together. You might think of it as an idea you are going to test or a statement you will spend your paper developing.

In the scientific disciplines a thesis may be called a *hypothesis*. You might define the thesis statement as your answer to the central question or problem that you raise. It incorporates not only your topic but also your point of view.

Keeping your thesis statement clearly in mind will help you stay on track and see your destination ahead. You will know how far you have come and what else you need to say before you finish. It can also keep your paper from becoming a paraphrase of other people's thoughts.

The thesis statement provides the framework around which you will shape the information you discover, eventually molding it into a unified whole. That does not mean, however, that your thesis is a permanent unyielding wall. Your research may alter your original thesis. You may feel, at this early stage, that you don't know enough about your topic to make such an important commitment. Don't worry. You can revise it as often as necessary. You should never think of the thesis statement as a burden that you are stuck with and must drag around, allowing it to distort or handicap your paper.

Finding a Starting Point

So where do you begin when you write a thesis statement? It is helpful to start with your purpose and audience. What purpose are you setting out to achieve? Do you want to describe something? Explain something? Are you arguing for a certain viewpoint, or do you want to persuade your reader to act or think in a particular way? Who are your readers? Can you assume that your readers will already be interested in the subject, or must you awaken their interest? The choice of audience will give your paper a slant or point of view.

Next write down what you have learned in your preliminary research. Do not try to write polished prose. Just jot down the thoughts and questions that occur to you. Eventually, a focus will begin to develop. Describe what you might write about and what information seems particularly interesting. Since your investigation was brief, it probably raised more questions than it answered. Write down those questions.

Understanding Why Scholars Write

If you are having difficulty formulating a thesis, you might stop to consider why people write books and articles. What purpose is served by their work? Here are the most common reasons authors choose to put pen to paper or fingers to keyboard:

- To propose a new point of view
- To agree with, support, or defend someone else's point of view
- To combine the two previous reasons, agreeing in part with the research in question but expressing some disagreement or an alternative interpretation as well
- To make an existing point of view clearer or better in some way
- To criticize or dismiss a point of view because of its inadequacy or irrelevance
- To reconcile two positions that appear to be in opposition to one another

Wording and Placing Your Thesis

At this point, you are formulating a trial thesis statement, but you should remember the form that your final statement will ultimately take. For example, even though your thesis should embody the main idea and the basic subdivisions of your paper, it is usually only one sentence long.

Although you will be seeking answers to your questions, the thesis statement should be an assertion, not a question. It should express an opinion, not state a fact.

Let's say that you have chosen to write about the attitudes of the British people toward the American Revolution. Your thesis statement should not simply indicate that you are going to investigate the nature of these attitudes. Instead, you must go out on a limb. In what direction is your preliminary research pointing? You could, of course, say something bland and boring to the effect that some Britons were supportive and some were not. However, you will lose your reader before you begin. Instead, look for the unexpected. What did you find in your preliminary research that surprised you? Although you still have insufficient data, be somewhat daring (as long as you have good reason to believe you are on the right track).

Write your thesis statement as a complete sentence that you can later use in your introduction. The thesis statement is usually, though not always, the last sentence of your paper's opening paragraph. It tells your readers what to expect and focuses their attention. We all find it easier to read a book, a journal article, or a research paper when we know what to look for.

Revising Your Thesis Statement

Your thesis statement is not written in stone. In fact, you may change it several times as you discover what sort of information is available and which aspects interest you most. As you continue your research, go back and look at your thesis. Are you still satisfied with it? Are you finding material to support it?

Feel free to change it if necessary, but don't forget that your thesis statement should impose some discipline on your research. Don't keep squeezing and stretching it just to accommodate new information you discover.

In this chapter, you have accomplished some of the more difficult tasks in writing a research paper. Choosing a good topic can make the difference between success and failure. Your preliminary investigations at the library have given you a sense of direction and sufficient information to write a provocative thesis statement. With this solid foundation, you are ready to plan your paper.

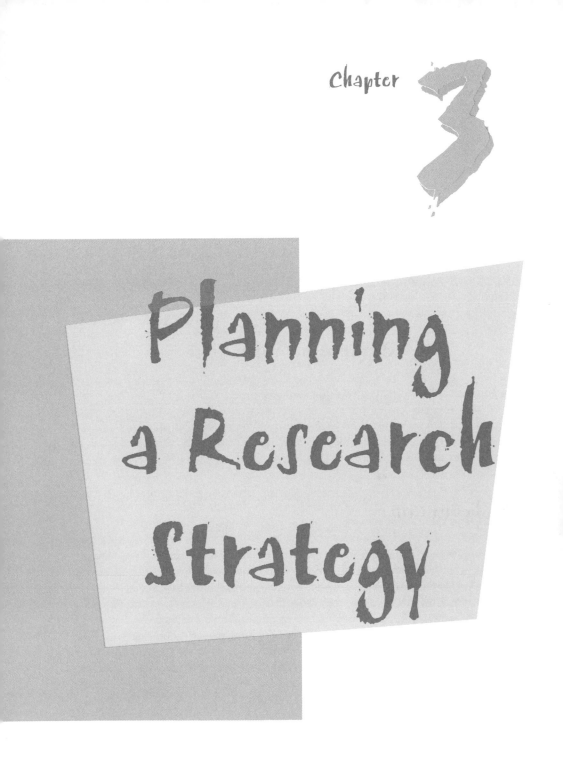

Chapter 3

Planning a Research Strategy

Now that you have a topic and a trial thesis statement, you are ready to begin your research in earnest. If you are feeling overwhelmed and unsure of yourself, maybe you need a pep talk. Approaching your paper with confidence and enthusiasm will make all the difference. You are in charge of this paper, and you will shape it into its final form. Don't be passive, accepting whatever information happens to come along. Don't borrow the words of others when your own will add clarity and cohesiveness. You can mold your paper into exactly what you want it to be.

At this point, you need a plan of attack. Only you can make the many decisions that lie ahead. You should plan not just your time but the way you will approach what may look like an overwhelming job at first. There is a world of information out there that you must explore and through which you must find your way. At every turn, you will find something to divert your attention. You certainly don't want to get sidetracked and spend precious time on information you don't need.

Organizing Your Time

You have a big job ahead, and you undoubtedly have other important activities and projects that you must juggle at the same time. You probably have several courses demanding your attention. You also have a life away from the classroom—friends, work, hobbies, and family obligations. The most difficult part of college is doing justice to each aspect of your life. Successful students usually find that the only way to keep important things from falling through the cracks is organization.

Predicting Crises

On the first day of class, instructors usually distribute class syllabi listing major assignments and their due dates. Armed with syllabi from all your courses, you can begin to create a schedule, listing all the dates when assignments are due. A wall calendar with big blank squares allows you to see everything at a glance.

You are bound to discover that assignments are not spread evenly over the semester, and it's not uncommon for two or more major projects to be due on the same day. When this happens, you will need to plan time for each project, and one project will have to be completed ahead of schedule to allow time for the other. Next, add your work schedule and sports and social events to the calendar, as well as the birthdays of family and friends. Rough out the time you will spend on each project—and allow plenty of room for the unexpected.

Failing to organize your time can lead to last-minute crises, such as the painful realization that you don't have the information you need just minutes after the library closes. What if your printer ribbon self-destructs as you are printing the final draft fifteen minutes before class? What if your research does not support your thesis? Many students have faced these disasters, and you must be prepared to cope with similar problems.

Trying to get things together even a few days before the due date can be fraught with peril. Let's say that your paper is due in two days, and your library does not have all the books and articles you need (or they're checked out). Since it's now too late for interlibrary loan, you may have to make do with sources that don't really support your thesis. In fact, your thesis may get lost entirely as you struggle to piece together the materials you managed to find on those few rush trips to the library.

There is no way to predict in advance exactly what direction your research will take. Some paths lead to dead ends. You may even have to change direction midway and scrap much of your work if you conclude that your thesis is invalid.

Doing Your Best Work

Under stress, one's writing style tends to suffer, and a paper can easily become a rambling hodgepodge of hurried, ungrammatical prose that doesn't hold together. A formal paper just does not lend itself to the casual, off-the-cuff style that characterizes midnight efforts. Detailed documentation takes time to do right, and the night before the paper is due, time is what you haven't got. Proper documentation also requires an alertness that half a dozen cups of coffee can't produce.

Allowing Time for Your Ideas to Develop

While you are planning your paper, remember that there is more to writing a research paper than simply reading and writing. You also need time to think, to let the material sink in and become the focal point around which your own ideas develop. Unless you take the time to let your thoughts gel, you will have only your own unformed ideas or a paraphrase of someone else's.

Enjoying Your Research

Maybe the most important reason to avoid last-minute all-nighters is that it takes all the fun out of writing a paper. "Fun?" you say. *Fun* may be the last word you would ever use to describe a research paper. However, research is fun for precisely the same reason that detective stories are enjoyable. Just like detectives, writers search for evidence. There really is a sense of elation when you track down that evidence and find the answers to your questions. It's almost as good as knowing "Who Done It."

It is also a delightful feeling to be right, to be convinced you have made a discovery that others have missed. Don't underestimate the importance of your own work. The germ of many great discoveries and literary insights can be traced back to undergraduate papers.

Constructing a Timetable

The day your paper is assigned, make yourself a timetable. When is the paper due? Start with that date and work backward. Has your instructor assigned any interim deadlines? Is your topic, outline, rough draft, or bibliography due on a certain date? Put those dates into your timetable. Don't, however, depend on your instructor for all your deadlines. Set your own.

Here are some goals that should be included in your timetable:

- Selecting a preliminary topic
- Selecting a final topic
- Drafting the trial thesis statement
- Finalizing the thesis statement
- Creating an outline
- Visiting the library
- Placing interlibrary loan requests
- Conducting Internet searches
- Completing a rough draft
- Revising
- Proofreading

When you use a word processor, the different tasks involved in writing a research paper tend to run together. For example, you can polish one part of your paper while you are still writing the rough draft of another section. A third section may be awaiting the arrival of a volume on interlibrary loan. That means your timetable can be flexible, but don't race ahead until your topic, thesis, and outline are all nailed down. Also, make sure that the resulting sections go together; in the final paper, they should be fully integrated and should develop your thesis in a logical and orderly manner.

If your paper is due December 1, ask yourself how much time you will need for proofreading and final editing. Let's say you will need at least two weeks, thus bringing the completion of the rough draft to November 16. The Thanksgiving holiday comes between these two dates. Will you be traveling during the holiday? Will you have more or less time to work on your paper during the holiday? Will you have access to your computer? Will you be able to get to a library? Your local public library is unlikely to have many of the books and articles held by an academic library, but if you plan ahead, you may be able to take some of your references with you. Adjust your schedule to reflect reality. You might allow another two weeks to write your rough draft, but during this period you may also have to prepare for a test in another course. Should you allow yourself more time? Keep working your way back to the selection of your topic, doing your best to predict any major interruptions.

Anticipating Problems

Research papers rarely progress as you expect them to. Something inevitably goes wrong. You might think of it as exploring unknown territory. You don't know a great deal about your subject, so you can't predict what lies ahead. Maybe you will discover that your thesis is incorrect. You have to change it, which may mean a whole new outline and plan of attack. Maybe what first seemd to be a narrow topic turns out to have all sorts of ramifications you can't possibly cover in a fifteen-page paper. Once again, you're going to have to alter your plans.

Suppose you make these discoveries the night before the paper is due, when it's too late to do anything about them. You don't have time to find new sources or write a revised outline, so you're likely to continue with the old plan even though you know your argument is invalid. If your topic is too large, you will have to live with gaps in your research and a lopsided, confusing paper.

Making Several Trips to the Library

Research isn't done all in one sitting. You may have gathered up a dozen books and articles, but you haven't finished your research. As you read, ideas take shape. You may need to go back to the library to follow up on a point mentioned in one of your sources. The book that answers one question raises another, and so it goes. The more you read, the more ideas come to you, and, each time, you may want to return to the library for further information. Papers consist of connected ideas, not bits of information strung together like beads in a necklace.

Using Interlibrary Loan

If your library does not have a book you need, you can borrow it from another library via interlibrary loan. Ask your librarian how long it usually takes to get a book or article with interlibrary loan. Take that delay into account in constructing your schedule.

Now that it is possible to search the catalogs of other libraries on the Internet, you nearly always discover sources that would improve your paper. Nevertheless, books are sent out "snail mail" and are sometimes incredibly slow in arriving. Allow time for your library to send out the request and receive the material, as well as time for you to incorporate the new material into your paper.

Keeping a Pocket Notebook

A notebook that is small enough to carry in your pocket is a wonderful way to keep yourself organized. A notebook helps you keep track of all the small tasks that go into a research paper. You may find yourself with a few minutes between classes that might be put to good use, but all of your notes are back home or in your dorm room. A small notebook may be the answer.

What should you put into your pocket notebook? Every researcher goes about the task somewhat differently, but here are some suggestions: Write down ideas as they occur to you. As you become involved in your research, you find yourself turning over possibilities. The paper begins to take shape in your mind, and you discover interesting directions to pursue. Jot these down. You can follow them up in the library or flesh out a thought later in a few paragraphs.

You might just get a cup of coffee at the snack bar and take a good look at your thesis statement. What questions does it suggest? Where might you find the answers to those questions?

Here are some other possibilities for a pocket notebook:

- Make a note of any keywords you might use to search journal indexes for relevant articles.
- Keep track of information you still need.
- Include a copy of your timetable, your thesis statement, and possibly even your outline.

Making To-Do Lists. Research always generates bits of unfinished business, so your pocket notebook can be a good place to remind yourself of the little things you have yet to do. For example, you may discover that you don't have the bibliographic form for a pamphlet or that you forgot to jot down a publisher's name before you returned a book to the library. If you have your notebook, you can take care of these small tasks between classes.

Try making a page for each type of activity. For instance, one page might be headed "Internet Addresses," another "Request on Interlibrary Loan," and still another "Ask Instructor About."

Keeping Track of Sources. Your notebook can work in tandem with your bibliography cards or printouts. While you are in the library, you will probably browse through many books and journals that you will later reject and put aside. Before you forget them entirely, jot down enough bibliographic information to locate them in the stacks. You might even make a brief note to yourself about their contents in case you change your mind. Nothing is more frustrating than having a vague memory of a perfect quotation you discovered the last time you visited the library but having no idea where you found it.

Keeping a Writer's Journal

You may find the pocket notebook useful but not quite large enough. Many successful writers keep a journal. They jot down the thoughts that come to them after a day's research and comment on what they have read. A journal allows you to include your own personal thoughts, those elusive ideas that reading seems to trigger. A journal is informal and private, a place where you can write freely and let your thoughts flow without worrying about readers or grammatical rules. Feel free to write not just about the paper but about any of the thoughts it generates, whatever is interesting or worrying you at the time.

Creating a Preliminary Outline

Soon after you have done some preliminary research and written a trial thesis statement, you are ready to make a rudimentary outline. An outline provides both an overview and a structure for your paper. It can help you to see how each section relates to the others. You can also follow the logical progression of your argument, noticing at once when you lose the thread of the discussion or become sidetracked. At this point, your outline will be very general because you know so little about your subject. Later, as you become more knowledgeable, you can add and rearrange sections.

Some instructors require an outline, but whether they do or not, an outline is really meant to help you. Although some very brief papers may not really need outlines, they can transform your research project, saving you time and greatly improving your finished product. The outline of your paper is developed from the thesis statement. Your thesis and outline work together, guiding you systematically through the maze of print and computerized resources.

An outline is also important in setting up a workable system for collecting material. Because you have so many sources of information available to you, both in print and on the computer, you may find yourself becoming overwhelmed. As you progress deeper into your research, you may find more books, articles, electronic documents, and other materials than you ever imagined. Where do they fit in or do they really fit anywhere? Having so much information at your fingertips can be disconcerting, and, without a framework to follow, you can get lost wading through all of it. Your paper then turns into a chaotic mass of facts, dates, and other randomly arranged information.

As you collect books and articles, notes and bibliographies, store them with other related materials in the appropriate section of your outline. You can literally keep computer data within your outline if you have it stored as a computer file. Printed material can be stored in a notebook organized according to the headings of your outline. If you can't decide which section something belongs in, perhaps it doesn't belong at all.

Your outline also breaks your work up into manageable chunks and allows you to work on one chunk at a time. Your paper will gradually evolve as each heading is developed, the rough draft fleshing out your outline.

Understanding Types of Outlines

Over the years, many different kinds of outlines have been developed. Your instructor may prefer a particular format, or you may be free to choose the one that works best for your subject matter. The most common form is the topic outline.

Each heading consists of just a few words identifying the topic covered in that section. Other outlines may consist of full sentences or complete paragraphs, although paragraph outlines are not generally used for student papers. Whichever style you choose, be consistent.

At some point, you probably learned a formal outline structure that alternated Arabic and Roman numerals with capital and lowercase letters. The point of all this was to distinguish between main headings, subheadings, and sub-subheadings. In other words, information should be presented in a logical order, and specific facts and observations should follow more general ones.

■ Example of Formal Outline Structure

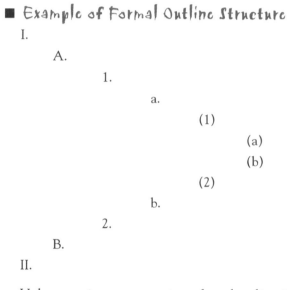

I.

  A.

    1.

      a.

        (1)

          (a)

          (b)

        (2)

      b.

    2.

  B.

II.

Unless your instructor requires a formal outline, it is not particularly important to remember when to use Roman and when to use Arabic numerals. However, nest your ideas in a logical way so that one thought is fully developed before you move on to the next one.

Building a Framework

Each heading in your outline should correspond to an idea you will develop in your paper. And, no matter how you choose to organize your outline, information should flow rationally and coherently.

Some alternative ways of organizing your outline are shown below. Although each can result in an effective paper, some will be more appropriate for your subject matter than others.

- **The Chronological Approach.** With this approach, you describe events or discoveries as they occurred. This technique can add a quality of immediacy, making the reader feel that he or she is witnessing the event.

For example, you might describe a battle as it actually occurred or the progress of a scientific discovery, including dead ends and false starts.

- **Divide and Conquer.** With this approach, you go back to your thesis statement and divide it into its basic parts and the questions you plan to answer about each. For instance, if your paper is about an environmental issue, you might discuss several points of view as well as any technical issues that must be explained.

- **Cause and Effect.** With this approach, which is especially useful in the social sciences, you consider an issue or problem and discuss its causes. For example, you might discuss the causes of the Great Depression, or you might describe various economic policies and their impact.

- **Compare and Contrast.** As its name suggests, with this approach, you compare two or more things to show how they are the same or how they differ. For instance, you might compare the health-care systems of France and the United States

- **Process.** With this approach, you describe how something works or how something is done. For example, you might describe the steps of a scientific experiment or how meditation techniques work.

A paper may move from the general to the particular (deductive) or it may use specific incidents or examples as building blocks upon which to rest more general conclusions (inductive). You may also define the problem, classify the different aspects or components of the problem, or analyze its ramifications. Supporting your arguments with examples and descriptive details also adds interest.

Outlining with a Computer

Working with computer files rather than printed sources is almost impossible without an outline. The easiest way to work with computer files is to summarize the information and then to move your summary to the relevant section of your outline.

If you don't have an outline, you can summarize the information on note cards, but moving information from computer file to card file to computer file is inconvenient. A better solution is to move your summary to computer note cards. Many note card and database programs are available, but most are separate programs, not part of your word-processing program. You will thus have to move your summary first to the computer clipboard, then to the note card program. Moving data to your outline file within the word processor can be done more easily, and the exercise of constantly deciding where in your outline a chunk of information belongs will keep you focused on your thesis.

When you write your paper, you will want to have your notes in front of you. *Windows* and Macintosh permit you to alternate between two programs, and it is sometimes possible to use two programs simultaneously. However, an outline in your own word-processing program is, once again, a lot easier.

Excellent computer outlining programs are available, but they are really not needed. In fact, if they are part of a separate program, it is difficult to incorporate them into your work. The word processor I use has a very sophisticated tool for outlining a document but I rarely use it. It normally doesn't really matter to me whether I use Arabic or Roman numerals or how many spaces I indent. You, on the other hand, may want a more formal structure.

Revising Your Outline

Although you will always have the freedom to change your mind and hence change your paper right up to the day before it's due, it becomes increasingly difficult to do so. Therefore, it's a good idea to set a point about midway in your research when you make what you might call a "Go–No Go" decision. Take a good look at your thesis statement and outline. Are you completely satisfied with them? How do you know if you should be satisfied with your outline? Ask yourself the following questions before proceeding further:

- Does your outline really support your thesis statement? Does it do what you promised to do? Prove what you promised to prove?
- Is your outline organized in a logical way? Does each section pick up on and expand the one preceding it, and then evolve naturally into the one following?
- Is the method of organization that you used appropriate for your subject matter?
- Are there loose ends in the outline—points that don't seem to go anywhere? They should be removed entirely or placed in a section where they are appropriate and can help develop your argument.
- Does the information you have gathered so far support the outline? What are you going to do with the information that does not seem to belong? Does your outline need expanding? Are your notes relevant?
- Does your outline support your argument? Do any of your points weaken it? You want to be truthful without allowing your argument to be watered down.
- Will you be able to find information you need to support each point in the outline?
- Have you found any information that would lead you to believe your assumptions are incorrect?
- Have you discovered disagreements among the authorities that you should include in the outline?
- Based on your outline, will the resulting paper be the assigned length?
- Reading over the points in your outline, do you see new connections between ideas? Should the outline be expanded to include them?

Organizing Source Materials

What are you going to do with the mountain of "stuff" you find? Soon you will be collecting books, articles, and data files galore. If you're not organized, you may have photocopies littering the floor and spend hours looking for that article you downloaded to disk. Get ready now for the onslaught—it does not have to be chaos.

Getting Organized

The right supplies can help you keep track of your material. Here are some basic items to start with:

- A large, three-ring, loose-leaf binder. Punch and file papers immediately to prevent crucial pages from floating away.
- A three-hole punch. Many libraries make them available to patrons, but it's wise to carry your own.
- A copy of your outline—printed out and punched—at the front of your loose-leaf notebook
- Notebook dividers labeled with major outline headings
- A plastic disk pocket or sleeve (also three-hole punched for use with your notebook)
- Two floppy disks: one for information downloaded from someone else's computer and one for your own files (those you are using for this paper), stored in a plastic sleeve
- Loose-leaf notebook paper
- A few pages copied from the style manual you will be using (MLA, Turabian, APA, etc.); select examples of the most common bibliography and note formats so you won't have to keep looking them up

The point of having all these items is to allow paper and computerized information to coexist peacefully together. You will need a separate notebook for each research project.

Organizing Computer Files

Just as your notebook is organized according to the headings in your outline, your basic computer files should also start with the outline. Type your outline right into your research paper file. That allows you to keep it in your document file and in all the other files you will be working with. Unless your instructor requires you to turn in your outline in a specific format, you might want to type it all in capital letters. The capital letters are easy to spot when you need to delete the outline in the final draft.

Some writers type their outline first into a file of its own, then copy it into a file that will eventually become the rough draft, then into a file for notes and another for quotations. Finally they copy it into a bibliography file. Each file is then renamed.

Naming Files. Incorporating your outline into each of your files will help keep them organized, but you also need to keep track of the files themselves. Always name your files consistently. A file name that makes perfect sense to you today may look like gibberish tomorrow, and nothing is more frustrating than searching through several dozen files trying to find the one you need.

Since some computer systems allow you to use only eight characters plus an extension of three characters to name a file, these designations can quickly become meaningless (Macintosh is more flexible in this regard and can accommodate more descriptive file names). Begin a new paper with a new directory. A directory might be compared to a file drawer that contains a number of files. The name you give the directory should tell you immediately that it contains files related to this research paper. If you get into the habit of putting related files in the same directory, you will find it much easier to locate them later.

Keep your directories small enough so you can back up the complete directory on a floppy disk. The storage space required for all the files you will be using for this paper will probably not exceed the capacity of a high-density disk. However, electronic documents downloaded from the Internet or a library CD-ROM program can take up a great deal of space, so remember to delete unneeded information. Although it is not difficult to back up files individually, it requires a little more effort. You will want the "back up habit" to become automatic, something you do without thinking just before you shut down your computer.

One way to name your files is to choose a term related to your paper. This is not difficult with the Macintosh or *Windows '95*, but it can be quite challenging if you're using DOS or DOS-based Windows. If you are writing about crime, for example, begin every file name with that word. That will take up the first five letters. The other characters could be numbers, for example, "crime1," "crime2," and so on. Even better, you might name your outline "crimeout," your text "crimetex," your notes "crimenot," and your quotations file "crimequo." Notice that I have deleted end letters rather than internal letters because otherwise I might abbreviate differently the next time I name a file.

Before you begin gathering information, create all your basic files. Store one copy of each on your hard disk and a backup copy on the disk in your notebook.

Sometimes you may not be sure what is useful and what is not. The thought of throwing needed information away may worry you. Then, too, an article that's not useful for this paper may be vital to the next one you write. But don't clutter your hard disk with these "maybe someday" files. Store data files on floppies you have designated as "archives." Then you need not handle them again while you're working on this paper. If you find yourself collecting a lot of these files, shareware programs are available for cataloging your disks.

Backing Up and Locating Information. When you use a computer for a research paper, you make hundreds, even thousands, of additions and changes. You should thus save files frequently or risk losing vital information. However, when you add information to one copy of a file but forget to update the other copy, it is easy to end up with several versions of the same file. You might, for instance, update your hard drive but not your backup floppy.

When you save a file you have been editing, the screen normally asks if you want to replace the old file. The answer should almost always be yes. Depending on the word-processing program you're using, the default setting may leave your old file as it was before you began editing, then create a whole new file. You then waste time trying to figure out which file has the most recent information.

If your computer does not have a working clock, be sure you always set the time and date each time you turn it on. Then you can at least see when a file was last saved. Some people type the time and date at the top of the file (or use a date stamp if their program has that capability) just before they save their file or leave the word processor.

Avoiding Toxic Disks. In the list of supplies, I included two floppy disks, one of which is your backup floppy. Always use the second disk for the information you download from other computers. Though you will probably need a lot of space to store all the information you are accumulating, there's another reason for keeping the information on these disks separate.

You may end up using five or six different computers in the course of a research project in addition to your personal computer. For example, you may use several library computers on which are loaded catalogs as well as indexes and reference programs. If your access to the Internet is from your university's computer center rather than from home, that is another, and if you use a printer that's not your own, that's still another. You may even work on your project at the office during your lunch hour.

In a nutshell, this is how viruses spread, and a virus is the last thing you want to bring home to your own system. Think of that second disk you carry in your notebook as toxic. Before you load any file stored on it into your own computer, run it through your virus checker. In the last year, it has become necessary to check for both the usual type of virus and something called a "macro" virus. Macro viruses are transmitted in word-processed documents and hide inside the word processor. The most common macro viruses now attack files created with *Microsoft Word,* although it will not be long before other word-processing programs have similar problems.

Of course, the disk containing your own files should be checked regularly, but if you load and save those files only on your own computer, the danger of infecting them is rather low. However, many seasoned computer users say that the chance of eventually contracting a virus when using a public computer is 100 percent. Remember, no word-processed document is ever safe on a virus-infected computer.

Eliminating Unnecessary Information

The student writing a paper twenty years ago had to struggle to gather a limited number of sources. Photocopiers were not so common, and their quality left much to be desired. Today, the same amount of effort can produce ten, even fifty times that number of sources. Neither an excellent outline nor a gross of notebooks will allow you to deal with all this information unless you can rid yourself of as much extraneous "stuff" as possible.

There are many reasons why we pile up information we cannot use. Often it is wishful thinking. You hope that an article or file will contain just what you need, but instead it contains no more than a sentence or so of useful information. You don't want to take the time to make such decisions now so you simply keep the entire document. You may possibly have room to store all this verbiage on your hard disk or in your notebook, but such mountains of material can only sidetrack and waylay you when you're trying to focus on your topic.

Suppose you are in the library, and you have been able to download an article to the disk you keep in your notebook. Do you really need the whole article? Much of it may be irrelevant for your present needs. As soon as you can get to a word processor, load the file containing the article, read it, and delete the sections you know you won't use. If possible, summarize the remaining information so that you are saving only your own words. Don't carry the entire article around with you. Keep only what relates directly to your thesis. Just be careful you don't delete the bibliographic citation.

Printing Articles

If at all possible, limit your printouts and save anything you can to your own floppy disk. It may be, however, that the library program you're using does not have the ability to save a file to disk. The *ProQuest* system, for instance, stores the text of articles in a graphic format. Although you can download *ProQuest's* bibliographies to disk, you can't download the articles themselves. Then again, your library may not permit downloading since many libraries fear viruses.

If you encounter either of these situations, you have no choice but to print out an article or data file on paper. Though this may be an unnecessary waste of a tree, you often have some control over what you print. Many programs allow you to highlight sections of text or print out only the pages you need. Try to be as sparing as possible when you're selecting material to print.

Many students print out everything they find in the library because they don't want to take the time to read it. Their plan is to gather the material now and digest it later. However, this plan can result in heaps of useless information.

Skim the article before copying it to find out whether it is useful. Also, keep your outline in mind to avoid gathering too much material for one section while totally neglecting another. You don't want an unbalanced final paper—or hysterical midnight marathons at the library when you discover the omission.

Reading and Writing with a Computer

Some students who are accustomed to reading an article that's been printed on paper feel uncomfortable reading the same text on a computer screen. They feel they can understand the print better and can scribble notes and underline the important points. Therefore, students often print out reams of text. Once you become accustomed to a computer, however, you will find it just as easy to read text on a monitor, if not easier. Instead of highlighting important sections, you can delete unimportant ones. If you're too cowardly to do that, most programs allow you to underline or italicize blocks of text. All that extra paper just wears out your printer ribbon, destroys the environment, and leaves you floating in a sea of "stuff."

Similarly, students accustomed to using pen and paper may at first have difficulty composing text directly into the computer. The most efficient way to compose a rough draft is to type it right into your outline. Although this may seem rather startling, it is the best way to have a sense of the whole paper, not just the text that appears on your screen.

The computers allows you to type almost as fast as you can think. Typos can be cleaned up later, so you needn't interrupt your train of thought. Likewise, looking up a word in the dictionary will break the flow of your thoughts, so you will want to wait until later to run a spelling check. If you are missing a key piece of information, work out a system that allows you to come back and insert the missing data. If you let yourself write without interruption, your sentences will be more cohesive and your thoughts will be expressed in a more natural and logical way.

Navigating within Your Document. When you write or type on paper, you can not only see the whole page but can also leaf through other pages to see what you've already covered. The computer screen doesn't allow you to do this easily. You can see only a fraction of a page at a time. When you scroll up or down, you can no longer see the part you've just been working on. Without the structure of the outline, you tend to get lost.

Although most word processors show the page and line number at the bottom of the screen, you may still feel disoriented. It is difficult to see how the lines you are writing relate to the lines you can't see. This makes it easy to repeat yourself or leave out important information.

An outline embedded within your rough draft also gives you the ability to work on different sections as inspiration strikes. When you write with a computer, you don't have to start at the beginning and progress in a linear way to the end. You are able to skip around, so while you're working on one section, you may have a sudden thought about a point that should be included five or six pages ahead.

If you were writing with pen and paper, you might tear off a sheet of paper and head it "Notes for Historical Section" or some other heading in your outline. When you are typing into a computer, you need some place to store these thoughts. Fragments are easily lost. Yet the computer has an enormous advantage over handwritten notes. It allows you to incorporate information exactly where you need it. There is no possibility of loss and the information will be immediately available when you are ready to write your rough draft. Those handwritten notes, if they didn't disappear altogether, would be edited and copied into the text of the rough draft, recopied as part of interim drafts, and finally copied once again into the final draft. When you are satisfied with a piece of text typed into the computer, it need never be retyped.

Growing Accustomed to Your Computer Monitor. New computer users often think they must print out a copy of their paper every time they attempt to revise or proofread. Most experienced users, on the other hand, limit themselves to printing only the final draft. Others print the very last version of the rough draft, just to be sure they have caught each and every error. They are able to do without interim printed copies because they develop a mental image of their papers and a sense of where different sections are located in relation to the text they are currently editing. They also train themselves to notice errors in the text. Once you get used to it, a computer file is no more difficult to work with than paper and pencil. Often, it's a lot easier.

The more of your paper you can see, the less confusing it is to edit and proofread, so it is usually wise to set your word processor to single space. Although it's never possible to see more than part of a page on your screen, you want to see as much as you can. Since instructors usually require that research papers be double-spaced, many computer users set this as their default without thinking how simple it is to change the spacing when they finish. Once again, they are still working as though they were using a typewriter. One or two keystrokes is all that you need to transform a single-spaced paper into a double-spaced one when you are ready to print.

Taking Information with You

One of the few times you can't avoid printing is when you must carry information with you. It would be wonderful to have a laptop computer ready with all the information you need for your research, but if you can't afford such a luxury, you still don't need to lug reams of paper around. Just take along the information you know you will need, including bibliographic citations, sections of a few vital articles, and names of persons and events you plan to look up. You might copy and paste the needed information into a temporary file, then print it out. Just be sure to delete the temporary file to avoid confusion later.

Since your outline is already in your notebook, your printout should require no more than a couple of sheets of paper. Not only does this save trees, but it saves time since you won't be leafing through pages and pages of material looking for a particular name or fact. Don't forget to punch each page you print and insert it in the appropriate section of your notebook.

Chapter 4

Getting to Know the Library

Now that you have developed a strategy for tackling the task that lies ahead, you're ready to begin looking for more detailed information about your topic. The best place to begin is still your local academic library. While it's true that many computer resources are only a telephone call away, the better databases are often costly for individual subscribers. Libraries generally provide them free or at low cost to their users.

However, cost is not the only reason to use an academic library whenever possible. The most important one is rarely appreciated or taken full advantage of by student researchers: librarians. Librarians are paid to help you find your way through the maze of print and computer resources, yet most of us fail to use their professional expertise. If you're not finding the kind of information you want, a librarian can often point you in the right direction.

Taking a Quick Library Tour

Every library is different, but most have certain things in common. Becoming familiar with the layout and services of your library will make your research tasks much easier. Libraries often make students feel uncomfortable because they're very large, quiet places. You may, therefore, assume that they're unfriendly as well. Libraries can certainly be confusing with their millions of books, journals, and other materials. However, it is not difficult to learn your way around, and a librarian is always there to help you.

You may find a library especially intimidating when you first pull open one of those massive doors and stand on the threshold. The first thing you need is a map. If there's a wall map within range, it should be your first stop. If you don't see one, however, ask a library staff member where you can find a printed map or library guide.

Visiting the Information Desk

A good place to begin your search is the information desk. Most larger libraries have one, often located just inside the front door. Here you can usually find a wide variety of literature, including a library map and handbook. Libraries produce and distribute materials that can save you hours of fruitless searching. The staff member at the information desk can also point out a few important locations, like the computer catalog, elevators, and restrooms.

Information desks provide general information about the library. Since they are not usually staffed by librarians, one of the first questions you should ask is the location of the reference desk. The reference librarian can help you decide which library resources will be most useful and give you any help you need to use them effectively.

Making a Library Action Plan

Once you have collected some information about the library, sit down and look it over. You will probably want to begin your research by investigating reference works to get an overview of your topic. Then you will start collecting lists of books and journal articles. On your map, identify the location of the OPAC or library book catalog. Next, find out where reference works, periodical indexes, and journals are kept. Check to see if printed periodical indexes are located near their electronic counterparts or in a different area. Circle these locations on your map. Your map will also provide information about other useful library services and policies. Once you have looked over all this literature, it's time to take a brief tour.

Investigating the Reference Room

Encyclopedias and dictionaries, as well as other fact-filled volumes like directories, handbooks, and almanacs, are called *reference works*. They are often located in a separate room or stack area. Reference books are usually (though not always) arranged in call-number order. They can't be checked out of the library because of heavy demand. Reference collections are usually small enough to browse through. For instance, if your paper is on politics, it's easy to discover where political science reference books are located. A brief outline of the classification scheme can usually be found on a wall sign or in the library handbook. In the Library of Congress system, political science sources would be under the letter "J." In the Dewey Decimal System, political science is found in the 300s.

Discovering the Library OPAC

Most academic libraries list the books in their collections in a computerized On-line Public Access Catalog (OPAC). It is usually possible to search for information under the author's name, the title of the book, the subject of the book, or any important words (keywords) used in the title, subject, contents, or notes field of the library's record. OPAC terminals are often located throughout the library to make them more convenient, and there are usually a number of them in the reference room. It is probably best to begin your search with these terminals since the reference librarian is close at hand if you need assistance.

Before computers became common, libraries listed their books on cards and filed them in large card catalog cabinets. Many libraries have not completed the process of transferring all their records to the OPAC, so the old card cabinets often remain. Be sure you use the OPAC first. Card files are no longer kept up to date, but they can be useful for locating older and less frequently used books.

Each library OPAC contains somewhat different information. Most include records of all the books held at all the libraries located at a particular college or university (except the older books mentioned above). Many also include records of audiovisual materials, journal titles, and microform holdings. Some provide information about books owned by other libraries in the area. Remember, however, that OPACs do not include information on journal articles. To learn what articles have been written on your topic, you need to use either printed or computerized periodical indexes.

Newer OPACs let you know if a book is checked out and the date when it is due to be returned. With this information, you can go straight to the circulation desk and request that the book be held for you when it is returned.

Exploring Book Stacks

Academic book collections are usually large, so most of the library will be taken up with book stacks, probably filling several floors. You may discover that Library of Congress letters "A–D" are on one level and "E–F" on another. Newer books are often classified by the Library of Congress system (spine labels begin with letters like "BL" and "PR"), while older ones still use Dewey Decimal (spine labels begin with numbers like 243.02 and 821). Don't waste time wandering through the stacks without knowing the specific call numbers to look for. Once you have some call numbers, you will be headed toward the right stacks for your topic; at that point, browsing among those stacks can be useful as you might find resources that your computer or card catalog search didn't reveal.

■ Library of Congress Classification System

A	General Works
B–BJ	Philosophy, Psychology
BL–BX	Religion
C	Auxiliary Science of History
D	History: General and Old World (Eastern Hemisphere)
E-F	History: America (Western Hemisphere)
G	Geography, Maps, Anthropology, Recreation
H–HJ	Social Sciences: Economics
HM–HX	Social Sciences: Sociology
J	Political Science
K	Law
L	Education
M	Music
N	Fine Arts

P	Language and Literature
Q	Science
R	Medicine
S	Agriculture
T	Technology
U–V	Military and Naval Science
Z	Bibliography, Library Science

■ Dewey Decimal Classification System

000	General Works
100	Philosophy and Psychology
200	Religion
300	Social Sciences
400	Language
500	Natural Sciences and Mathematics
600	Technology and Applied Sciences
700	Fine Arts
800	Literature
900	Geography and History

Checking Out the Reserve Room

Instructors sometimes place books and journal articles on reserve. This allows you to share materials with other students, thus reducing the number of texts you are required to purchase. Materials are either on closed reserve, which means they cannot be removed from the library, or they can be checked out for a limited period, usually a day or two. The OPAC will sometimes tell you when an item has been placed on reserve. However, if you don't find a book in the regular stack area, check the reserve room.

Finding the Photocopy Area

What modern student could possibly survive without a photocopy machine? Check to see if your library sells copy cards, which are inserted into the photocopier instead of coins. They allow you to make copies more easily and at a lower cost. In most cases, you purchase a card from a machine and reinsert it every time you need to increase your credit. The machine electronically records the amount of money you deposit. Remember to be gentle with the books you copy—spines can be easily damaged with too much pressure.

Obeying the Copyright Law. When you use a photocopier, you are subject to the provisions of copyright law. It is usually perfectly legal for you to copy an article from one of the library's journals. However, it is not legal to photocopy large sections of a textbook to avoid having to purchase it. Although the law is rather complicated, you can answer many questions by simply asking yourself whether the publisher is losing a sale because of your actions. As a student, you are obviously not expected to subscribe to every journal needed for your paper. However, you are responsible for purchasing your own textbooks.

Visiting the Circulation and Reference Desks

Most libraries have two main public-service desks. The circulation desk is the large one where you apply for a library card and check out books. It is not usually staffed by librarians, so it's not the best place to ask questions. The reference desk, on the other hand, is staffed with librarians who are specially trained to help you find answers to your research questions and will even accompany you to the stacks if necessary.

Exploring the Documents Depository

If your academic library houses a government documents collection, it is probably located in a separate area. The collection consists of the publications of the United States government and often of your state government. Federal documents are shelved not by Library of Congress number but by something called a SuDoc, or Superintendent of Documents, number. State documents are probably organized with another system of their own.

The U.S. government recently began publishing many documents on CD-ROM disks. Some others are only available by accessing one of the government's Internet sites. Since this makes the document area a little more confusing than other sections of the library, be sure to read any literature provided. And get to know your documents librarian, especially if you will be making extensive use of the collection.

Investigating the Microform Room

Libraries often purchase magazines, journals, and newspapers in a microfilm or microfiche format. These are rolls or small sheets of photographic film that look something like the negatives of photographs. They enable the library to store a large collection of materials in a relatively small space. Microform readers or view-ers are usually located near the microform storage cabinets, and some of these machines can print out full-size paper copies just like photocopy machines. Since some microform readers are tricky to load, ask the librarian for help if you have trouble.

Compiling a Working Bibliography

In Chapter 2, you did some preliminary research in the library before you settled on a definite topic. Now you are ready to compile a bibliography to work from. You might want to reread your notes to see what you have already dis-covered. What do you now know about the topic? What do you want to learn?

Write out a few sentences about what you have learned so far and the questions that have arisen as a result of your preliminary research. This is an exercise you will want to repeat again and again as your research progresses. Since you will be exposed to such a large number of different sources, many of them irrelevant to your topic, you may get off track. It is helpful to periodically take stock of where you are and where you want to be.

Identifying Keywords

From the sentences you have written, pick out the terms that best describe your topic. These terms will be a good starting place for continued research. Most of the library's computer programs search for information using "key" words that you pro-vide. You can zero in on the specific information you want by combining these keywords in a variety of ways. For example, if you're writing about DNA, some key terms might be *genetics, heredity, deoxyribonucleic acid, nucleic acid,* and *nucleotides,* as well as your original term *DNA*. If you didn't already know them, all these key-words or phrases could easily be found in a brief encyclopedia article.

Only a few of these terms may be useful, however. You don't want to be deluged with everything the library has on DNA, which may range from several hundred to several thousand books and journal articles, as well as many megabytes of infor-mation gleaned from computer databases. If you were to investigate the holdings of other libraries, you might well find citations numbering in the millions.

Be sure that your keywords are specific enough to focus on what you want and to eliminate the material you can't use. To make this a little clearer, think about the information you discovered in your preliminary search. What aspects of the topic have little or nothing to do with your thesis? With your thesis in mind, divide your keywords into two columns, the first for words or phrases that relate to the information you want and the second for information you don't want. These lists will be useful later on when we discuss Boolean connectors. Most library com-puters allow you to specify that you want one thing and not another. You might request *DNA* not *RNA*. You might want Shakespeare's *sonnets,* not his *plays*.

Focusing Your Research

While making your preliminary investigation, you may have looked at a computerized encyclopedia or peeked into the OPAC. If there was a bibliography at the end of the encyclopedia article you used for your preliminary research, print out or photocopy it. This list of books and journal articles can be a starting point for your research.

If you locate one of the sources listed in this bibliography, it may, in turn, lead you to other sources and bibliographies. The research process leads you from one source to another to another. You might say that your path twists and turns as you discover new aspects of your topic. Many reference books, such as *Contemporary Authors*, *Who's Who*, and specialized encyclopedias, contain bibliographies. As you find them, make copies.

Your OPAC can also produce a printed bibliography listing books on the topic you request. Such printouts usually include the library call number of each book. Take advantage of this service—it will save you time. Make printouts from computerized journal indexes as well. Don't, however, allow your working bibliography to become too large before you have done a little reading in some of your sources. This will allow you to keep refocusing your search and avoid collecting large numbers of useless citations.

■ Sample OPAC Bibliography (Melvyl)

Search request: FIND SUBJECT WATER RESOURCES
Partial result: 200 records at all libraries

Display: DISPLAY

1. A 20 year legislative policy and program for the development of the water resources of the state of California. [Sacramento, Calif.] : Weber Foundation, 1959.
    Series title: Weber Foundation Studies.
    UCB   WRCA   G407 H9-3

2. 1985-1986 report of the Interagency Ecological Studies Program for the Sacramento-San Joaquin Estuary : including technical report 10—Suisun Marsh
    vegetation survey, technical report 11—Striped bass egg and larvae...
    Sacramento : Dept. of Water Resources, 1987.

Series title: Technical report / Interagency Ecological Study Program
for the Sacramento-San Joaquin Estuary ; nos. 10-12.
3.   Abbas, B. M. (Borhanuddin Mohammed)
The Ganges waters dispute / B. M. Abbas. Dacca, Bangladesh : University
Press, c1982.
UCB Main   HD1698.I4 A2227 1982

The advantage of having a large working bibliography is that you can use your
time more efficiently. When you go to the stacks, you have several books to look
for, and you can do the same with journal citations. Check which journals your
library owns and mark them on your list so you won't be chasing missing journals.

■ *Sample Bibliographic Citation From ProQuest*

Access No: 02622554 ProQuest Periodical Abstracts
Title: Water
Authors: McDowell, Judith
Journal: Amicus Journal [IAMC] ISSN: 0276-7201
     Jrnl Group: Socio/Environmental
     Vol: 17 Iss: 4 Date: Winter 1996 p: 46-47
     Type: Feature Length: Medium Illus: Illustration
Companies: Natural Resources Defense Council
Subjects: Water pollution; Environmental protection; Ecosystems

Abstract: The Natural Resources Defense Council (NRDC) understands
the science and respects it, balancing scientific understanding with
its fundamental goal of protecting the environment. The NRDC's
participation in protecting the waters and their ecosystems in the US
is detailed.

■ *Sample FirstSearch Bibliographic Citation*

Ownership: FirstSearch indicates your library owns this item or magazine
AUTHOR: Marxsen, Craig S.
TITLE: Ecology: Can America Afford Clean Water?

JOURNAL NAME: USA Today.

VOL, ISSUE: Volume 125, Number 2614

PAGES: pp. 60

PUB DATE: July 01

YEAR: 1996

TYPE: Article

ABSTRACT: The bill for complying with Environmental Protection Agency
pollution control regulations runs almost $4,000 a year per
household. However, the consequences of impure water must be
balanced against these costs.

ISSN: 0161-7389

J ALT NAME: Intellect

■ Sample New York Times Citation

Access No: 9300099224 ProQuest - The New York Times ® Ondisc

Title: PERSONAL COMPUTERS; CRUISING THE WEB WITH A
    BROWSER

Authors: PETER H. LEWIS

Source: The New York Times, Late Edition - Final

Date: Tuesday Feb 7, 1995   Sec: C Science Desk p: 8

Length: Long (910 words)   Illus: Drawing

Subjects: ELECTRONIC INFORMATION SYSTEMS; SOFTWARE
    PRODUCTS; INTERNET (COMPUTER NETWORK)

Copyright 1995 The New York Times Company. Data supplied by
NEXIS ® Service.

Article text:

AS with all truly great communications tools, including the printing press,
the television, the telephone and the personal computer, the Internet's World
Wide Web is both a dynamic information source and a prodigious producti-
vity waster.

As an information engine, the Web has the potential to transform business,
education and other aspects of daily life. As an entertainment source, it
also has the potential to be a time-sucking black hole. It is a speed trap on
the data superhighway, a Bermuda Triangle in the information ocean, the
junk food aisle in cyberspace's digital supermarket.

Storing Bibliographic Information

After you have looked up call numbers and searched the stacks, you will want to make notes about what you find. One book will have little useful information, while another will be just what you were looking for. Make notes about what you discover next to the citation in your bibliography so you don't have to cover the same territory again.

As you progress through the library, you will accumulate a dozen or more bibliography printouts. Some books and articles will appear only once; others will be repeated on several lists. All your discoveries will not be on computer terminals, however. Jot down citations for books and articles you find in the course of your reading or browsing. If your library still uses a card catalog to access older works, take notes on these books as well.

To avoid confusion, you need some way of organizing and storing this information. Four good methods are listed below:

'Real' Bibliography Cards.

Enter the bibliographic information on 3" x 5" note cards. Use one card for each book or article. Write the author's name (last name first) on the top line so you can alphabetize cards by author.

If you're citing a book, also include the following:

Title

Other authors and editors

Edition (if one is given)

Publisher

Place of publication

Date of publication

If it's a journal article, you will also need:

Article title

Journal title

Volume number

Issue number

Page number

Write the call number in the upper-left corner and use the rest of the card for notes to jog your memory. Have you looked at this material? Did you find it useful? Note any information about content if you plan to return to it later.

The advantage of real cards over virtual ones is their portability. You can carry them with you wherever you go. The disadvantage is that card files tend to become large and hard to manage. They are also prone to getting lost. And since they easily get out of order, frequent alphabetizing and filing may occupy quite a lot of time.

Sample Bibliography Card (Book)

NX	
65	Bronowski, Jacob.
.B696	The Visionary Eye. Cambridge: MIT Press, 1978.
	Essays about the arts. Bronowski is a philosopher, scientist and television personality ("Ascent of Man").

Virtual Bibliography Cards. Both *Windows*-equipped personal computers and Macintosh computers come with note card programs. Note card programs are also among the simplest and most common shareware programs, so if yours is an older computer, you should be able to find a similar program.

Enter exactly the same information as you did on the index cards. The advantage of computer cards over their cardboard cousins is the ability to search any word on the card. This option is helpful when you have a large number of sources and can't remember who wrote the one about *semiotics* or *sassafras*. At the bottom of each card, type a few subject headings or words that describe the book to make it easier to find later. Virtual cards are also self-alphabetizing, so you cannot inadvertently lose a couple of your most important sources.

Unless you have a portable notebook computer, virtual cards can't go to the library with you. Some also have limited printing options. Since it's helpful to keep printouts of sources in your three-ring binder, you might choose a program that can print either one long bibliography or individual cards.

Card file programs can be downloaded from local bulletin boards and on-line services. Shareware catalogs almost always include a few of these useful programs.

Personal Library Programs. Personal library programs have a lot of different names, such as *Book Librarian*, *Personal Librarian*, and *Bookworm*. They are most often shareware programs, intended to help you organize your own personal book collection. However, they work fine for organizing bibliographic references copied from your printouts. They can be more useful than a note card program because they're intended for storing only bibliographic references. Each screen has a blank

Sample Bibliography Card (Journal Article)
Microfiche
(downstairs)

Martin, William F.
"Immune Cells Gain Wider Recognition."
Science News 147
(May 13, 1995): 292.

T-Cell Research

for author, title, and so on. Most of these programs can search by any word in the record, and some even print out in standard bibliographic formats. Most shareware collections on CD-ROM or shareware catalogs include a few of these programs in Macintosh, *Windows,* and DOS formats

You can also create a library record-keeping program of your own using a general-purpose database. Macintosh computers come equipped with a database, and *Microsoft Works* and *Microsoft Office,* which may come with *Windows*-equipped computers, include a database module. *D-Base* and *Alpha 4* are two popular stand-alone programs, and *Wampum* is a serviceable shareware look-alike.

The advantage of the do-it-yourself database is that you can design it to meet your particular needs. For example, you can allow lots of room for notes. Unfortunately, because databases are more powerful, they take more time to learn. However, their use is not limited to bibliographic citations, so the extra time invested may be worthwhile.

Some word processors allow you to create bibliographic records right in the word processor. Although you lose some of the advantages of a database, you are able to alphabetize your citations and manipulate them to some extent.

Professional Reference Managers. Although it is unlikely that you will want to invest in the more expensive of these commercial programs, many campus computer centers have one or more available for student research papers. They may even conduct brief workshops to help you get the most out of them.

Like personal library programs, they are intended for storing bibliographic citations. However, reference managers can store more citations, print out perfect bibliographies in any one of a dozen bibliographic styles, and allow you to select different sources from the database for different papers.

Some programs let you download bibliographies from your OPAC or on-line
journal indexes like *ProQuest, Dialog,* and EBSCO's *Academic Index* and import
them directly into the database. The program can tell which piece of data is the
author, title, or subject and store it in the appropriate field. This means that, theoretically, you could produce a perfect bibliography with no typing at all. In reality, however, you must keep an eagle eye on the output of such programs. They follow the rules with which they have been programmed, and they are lost when a
piece of information is not where they expect to find it.

Some of the most popular programs are the following:

- **EndNote Plus:** Available for *Windows*, MS-DOS, and Macintosh and
  compatible with most word processors. A plug-in module is available for
  Microsoft Word that adds *EndNote* functions to *Word* menus. Imports data
  from several on-line services and CD-ROMs. Citations can be output in
  more than two hundred bibliographic styles.

- **Library Master:** Has twenty-eight predefined templates for different
  types of materials. Can import MARC records and records from on-line
  databases and CD-ROMs. Available for MS-DOS, Macintosh, and
  Windows.

- **Papyrus:** Available in MS-DOS, *Windows*, and Macintosh versions. Less
  expensive than most of the others. Under $100 retail and much less on
  campus with an educational discount. Has many satisfied customers. For
  further information on *Papyrus*, ftp teleport.com in the directory/ven-
  dors/rsd (see Chapter 6 for information on ftp).

- **ProCite:** Available for MS-DOS, *Windows*, and Macintosh. A compan-
  ion package called *Bibliolink* imports downloaded citations from on-line
  databases and CD-ROMs. Can also import from many OPACs. Twenty
  predefined work forms for various types of materials (books, journals, and
  so on). Supports twenty-eight different bibliographic styles. For more
  information, e-mail sales@pbsinc.com.

- **Reference Manager:** Available for MS-DOS, Macintosh, and *Windows*.
  For more information, check World Wide Web site at
  http://www.risinc.com.

- **RMS-III: Reference Management System:** Available only for MS-DOS.
  Shareware. Registered users pay about $45. For more information, e-mail
  74267.2713@compuserv.com.

Using the On-Line Public Access Catalog (OPAC)

At this point, you must make a choice. Will you look first for books or for journal articles? The answer depends on how recent your information needs to be. Books take a long time to write, edit, and publish, and a book "hot off the press" may contain information that is already out of date. Books about Shakespeare written fifty years ago are still useful, but an important DNA discovery may have been announced last month.

Journal articles are shorter than books and require less time to write. Since journals are published several times a year, new articles are available much sooner than new books. However, a discovery announced last month is unlikely to be available in a printed, scholarly journal, though it may be discussed in a newspaper article or weekly news magazine. A thorough discussion, however, may only be available in an electronic journal. Chapter 6 discusses these and other resources available on the Internet.

Let's assume that our information need not be current and start with the book catalog, or on-line public access catalog. Each library has a slightly different system and most share basic characteristics. Computerized book catalogs generally allow you to search by title, author, subject, or keyword. If you don't have any particular book in mind, you will have to choose either subject or keyword.

Using Keywords

When keyword searching is available, it's probably your best choice. In computerized book catalogs, *subject* refers to the specific subject heading used by the Library of Congress, which may or may not be useful to you. Once you have found a book that's exactly what you are looking for, you can check the subject headings at the bottom of the screen. Armed with an exact heading, you can look for other books on the same subject.

Even though modern libraries have many state-of-the-art computer services and it is possible for students to find information on the most obscure topics, research shows that the information they actually find is no better than before the computers were installed. This isn't the fault of the computer programs. It has to do with the way students use them. We are tempted to key in simple search terms, often just a single word. Then we take the first citations we find, no matter how old or how distantly related to the topic. By failing to narrow down our topic and paying no attention to publication dates, we probably end up doing a poorer research paper than we might have done using traditional library tools.

It was possible to search for title, author, or subject in the old card catalog. Keyword searching, however, is unique to the computer because it can search every word in its database in less time than it used to take to pull out a catalog drawer and find a card with the correct heading.

If your library has both an OPAC and a card cabinet, you might find some excellent books on Shakespeare that have not yet been entered into the computer catalog, but the card catalog is not the place to look for the latest on genetic engineering. In other words, check out the card catalog if your topic doesn't require very recent sources, but don't rely on it if you are writing on a "hot" topic.

Using Other OPAC Options

Although OPACs differ greatly, most offer these same basic search options:

- *TIL:* Searches the title: book title, journal title, or series title.
- *AUT:* Searches the author, illustrator, editor, or organization.
- *A-T:* Searches a combination of author and title.
- *SUB:* Searches the subject heading assigned by the library.
- *KEY:* Searches keywords taken from a title, author, or subject.
- *BOL:* Uses Boolean connectors to search title, author, subject, or keywords.
- *RES:* Searches items on reserve

Your OPAC may call these options by slightly different names. For example, some use just a single letter to indicate the type of search.

Discovering Gateways

As you look at the main menu on one of your library's public access terminals, you will probably see headings describing resources both at your university and at other locations. These are called *gateways*. When you choose one of the gateway options, your computer terminal will connect you to your library's book catalog, other universities' catalogs, and networked information resources on your own campus or others at remote locations. Sometimes this is done through your internal campus network or a direct telephone link to a remote computer. More and more often, you are actually connecting to the Internet. As a library user, you are normally unaware of the mechanics.

A gateway may allow you to use a centralized or union catalog of library materials belonging to several academic libraries. Libraries in the same city or state often get together and store records of their holdings in one central computer. You are then able to look at the holdings of your own college or those of all the libraries in your region. If you're planning to visit one of these other libraries, the gateway makes it possible to do much of the work before you go. Just be sure to keep track of where different titles are located. You won't want to waste time searching the stacks of your local academic library when the books you want are housed elsewhere.

Understanding Boolean Logic

If your computerized catalog allows you to search by keyword, it probably can do Boolean searching as well. This capacity can be vital to your research strategy.

George Boole was a nineteenth-century mathematician who developed a system we call *Boolean algebra*. However, you don't need to be a math whiz to use Boolean search strategies. Just three words—*and, or,* and *not*—will make it possible for you to zero in on exactly the computerized information you need.

Let's start with a simple topic like *dogs* and assume you're using the library's computerized book catalog. If you type in the word *dogs*, you will get a lot of hits (or matches). The word *dogs* may have come up in the title, subject headings, contents, or notes field of many book records.

The and Connector. To focus your search, you probably want to narrow the subject down by using *and*.

> *dogs* **and** *training*

Both the words *dogs* and *training* will then appear in each record that is selected. The list will be much shorter. Most of the books on the list of hits will have something to do with dog training.

Some OPACs require that you type the word *and*. Others assume that if you simply type a list of words like *dogs training obedience*, you mean to connect them with *and*. This may not be what you really mean. Other programs assume that if you type the words *dog training* together, you want only records in which the two words occur beside one another. In such a system, you would probably get no hits at all if you typed *dogs training obedience*. For these and other reasons, students often fail to find the information that is available. Take some time to read your OPAC's "Help" screens.

The or Connector. If you want a longer list, think of all the synonyms or words that mean roughly the same thing as *dog*. These can be strung together with the connector *or* to produce a more comprehensive list. For example, you might type the following:

> *dog* **or** *canine* **or** *spaniel* **or** *poodle*

If you combined the hits from this list with *training*, your search might look something like this:

> (*dog* **or** *canine* **or** *spaniel* **or** *poodle*) **and** *training*

Some programs ask that you use parentheses to tell the program what to do first. In this case, it will produce a large hit list of all those doggy words and check each to see if *training* appears in them. Your final list will include only those records or titles that contain at least one of the *dog* words plus *training*. Once again, take care to read the instructions. Computer programs never assume you mean *or*, so it is sometimes more difficult to communicate this information to the computer.

The not Connector. Finally, there's the connector *not*, which tends to be used less often than the other two. *Not* is helpful when you are finding a lot of information you can't use.

Let's say that you are looking for information about all types of dogs except poodles. You might indicate this by typing:

dogs **not** *poodles*

Depending on the program you are using, you might also type:

(*dogs* **or** *spaniels* **or** *retrievers* **or** *beagles*) **not** *poodles*

The program might also ask that you type the *dog* group on one line and *poodle* on the next line. Again, follow instructions carefully.

Admittedly, the likelihood that you are writing about cocker spaniels is very remote. To use an example that might actually come up in a research paper, let's say you are writing about Napoleon's military campaigns and type the following:

Napoleon **and** *military*

or

Napoleon **and** *campaign*

These entries will bring up a number of book records. At this point, you may want to narrow the topic further by adding another *and:*

Napoleon **and** *military* **and** *Italy*

On the other hand, you may just want to nibble away at your subject by eliminating specific campaigns that don't fit into your paper. In this case you might type the following:

(*Napoleon* **and** *military*) **not** *Russia*

Some OPACs cannot to this, or they may require that you do it in two steps. Ask the reference librarian if your system's capabilities are not clear. *Not* is usually used only after you have been working on your search for quite a while. Until you have made several attempts, you don't know what is likely to come up in the literature.

Using Truncation. Getting back to our first example, you will get one group of hits if you type *dog* and another if you type *dogs*. Since you would probably be interested in either group, you could type *dog* **or** *dogs*. However, an easier way is to truncate or cut off the last letters of a word and use some symbol to let the computer know you don't care what letters follow. Truncation is handled differently in different Boolean search programs. In some programs, typing *dog?* or *dog** will allow you to search for *dog, dogs,* or any other word that begins with those three letters. Although you might get some strange hits, like dogmatic or dogwood, you will have identified every useful record.

Using Different Programs. Though the principle is the same, each program has a different procedure for Boolean searching. Some provide a series of small boxes. You type one word in each box and then choose the appropriate connector. Others expect you to type your complete search strategy, connectors and all, onto a long blank line.

Although we have been assuming that you're searching the computerized book catalog, nearly all computerized library reference programs use some form of Boolean searching. It would save time if they all did it the same way, but, unfortunately, you will need to follow different instructions for each program.

Getting Help

If your search didn't result in as much useful information as you expected, press the "Help" key and follow the directions exactly. If you have chosen a reasonable topic, it is likely that plenty of information is available, so perhaps your search strategy isn't working.

Finding Books in the Stacks

If you have followed your computerized catalog's directions, you should have a list of book titles useful for your research. Your list should include call numbers leading you to a book's shelf location.

Most OPAC programs are able to sort your "hit list" by call number, then print it out. This saves time when you take your list to the stack area because the list is in the same order as the books on the shelf. If your OPAC can be accessed from home, you can print the list before going to the library.

Understanding Library Classification Systems

Libraries shelve books according to either the Dewey Decimal or the Library of Congress System. Larger libraries most often use the Library of Congress system. You can tell the difference easily because Dewey call numbers begin with a number, while the first line of a Library of Congress call number starts with a letter of the alphabet. If you are using a card catalog or your OPAC screen looks like a catalog card, the call number will appear in the upper-left corner of the screen. If you are enrolled at a large university, the catalog may include entries for a dozen or so libraries located all over campus. The call number in such large systems often includes an abbreviation for the library and may be confusing. Ask the reference librarian if you are unsure.

Consult a library map to find the location of the first book on your list. Let us say it has the following classification:

DA

428.5

E43

F55

1995

Look on the map for the "D" section. Each book in a library has an exact location, and the call number is typed on a label placed on the book spine. If the book has been shelved properly, it should be easy to find. You simply find the books with the same top line of the call number, then the second line, and so on. If you cannot find a particular book, ask the staff at the circulation desk to check its status. If the book is checked out for several weeks, you may need to get another copy of the book through interlibrary loan.

The book you're looking for may have just recently been returned to the library but not yet have been reshelved. Most libraries have a number of "waiting" areas for returned books located throughout the library. If you see a staff member shelving books in the stack area where you are searching, ask him or her where to look for your book.

Browsing

Once you have found the first book on your list, look around. Even though computers have revolutionized libraries, browsing is still a good way to find useful information. The books to the right and left of your target book are probably about the same subject, and you may find some useful sources that the computerized catalog missed.

Finding Information in Periodicals

As mentioned previously, current information can only be found in journals, magazines, and newspapers. Such periodicals cover the same subjects as books but often offer a wider variety of perspectives. The term *periodical* just means that something's published periodically. This term includes both journals and magazines as well as newspapers. Different disciplines make more or less use of periodicals than others. For instance, the physical sciences place a high value on the newest information available, while a scholar in philosophy or history would be more content with older materials.

Journals usually contain scholarly or academically oriented information for particular audiences, such as sociologists or linguists, whereas popular magazines such as *Newsweek* or *Popular Mechanics* are written for more general audiences. Most instructors will ask that you use journal articles for your research since they are written by experts in their fields. For example, an article about child psychology in the *Journal of Psychology* is going to be far more authoritative than one in the popular magazine *American Baby*. You may enjoy reading the latter article, but it probably has no place in a research paper.

Researchers have traditionally located periodical articles through printed indexes. For example, you may have used the large, green *Readers' Guide to Periodical Literature* volumes. These are published monthly, quarterly, and/or annually. Each volume must be searched separately. Printed indexes also use subject headings similar to those used to catalog books, but each index tends to have its own set of headings. Looking up a subject in a printed index is thus a time-consuming process.

In many disciplines, computer programs have largely replaced printed indexes. If you are looking for recent material, and there is an appropriate index in your subject area, you will find computer programs have many advantages over their print cousins. Unfortunately, they have a few disadvantages, too, which we will discuss later.

Using Computerized Indexes and Abstracts

Library book catalogs and periodical indexes are both available on computer, but students often fail to understand the difference between the two. Compared to OPACs, which contain records of the books and other materials actually owned by the library, as well as holdings of other libraries in your area, a periodical index is usually produced by a commercial publisher that sells the program to many libraries. You will need to find out which journals your library actually subscribes to and which can only be found elsewhere. Some commercial programs allow the library to indicate their holdings in the program, but more often this information is kept in a printed periodicals list; periodical holdings may also be listed in the computerized book catalog.

Getting Help

Since periodical indexes are probably the resources you will be using most often, look around the area where the library's computerized indexes are kept for instruction sheets, which are probably stored in literature racks. If you are not familiar with computers, these printed directions will get you started.

If you are used to computers, you might try to omit this step and begin experimentally pressing keys. You might pull up some useful information but also miss many of the better resources. One problem with computerized indexes is that each program tends to work differently. You will miss much of what is available unless you take advantage of the more advanced techniques of a specific program. If your library does not have instruction sheets, spend some time with the "Help" screens and experiment with different strategies before you begin your search in earnest.

Comparing CD-ROM-Based Indexes and On-Line Indexes

Computerized periodical indexes can be divided into two basic categories: those available on disk in your library and those accessed through on-line services that allow you to call up centrally located databases. Most libraries offer a combination of CD-ROM programs and on-line services. If all your library's computer resources are available on a network, you may not be aware of the difference.

Accessing CD-ROM Disks. CD-ROM disks are accessed on microcomputers equipped with a CD-ROM disk drive or player. One compact disk can store the equivalent of 275,000 double-spaced typed pages, so they are a convenient way for libraries to store the index citations as well as the full texts of magazine and journal articles.

Some libraries network their CD-ROMs so you never touch the disk. You simply select the right program from a menu on a library computer screen. Other libraries request that you check a disk out at a service desk and load it yourself. Even for those unfamiliar with how a CD-ROM drive works, they are not difficult to use. You may, however, want to ask a librarian to help you the first time. Though some services like *ProQuest* use hundreds of CD-ROM disks, they are simple to use because the disks always remain in plastic cases and slip in and out of the drive easily.

Some libraries also list their own periodical holdings in CD-ROM-based indexing and abstracting programs. Since CD-ROM disks are read-only, the library's holding information is actually stored in a program on a hard disk that interacts with the CD-ROM. Most libraries, however, also have printed lists of their periodical holdings in binders, usually kept near their computer terminals.

Using On-Line Services. On-line databases are accessed either by calling direct via modem or via the Internet to a distant computer. On-line services allow libraries to share a central computer on which many databases are loaded. Since each library pays only for the time it actually uses, even small libraries can offer many of the same resources available at large research libraries. However, the number of indexing services is now in the hundreds, and most libraries can only subscribe to a few of the more heavily used ones.

CD-ROM programs tend to be faster and easier to use than on-line services, have attractive graphical interfaces, and offer more "Help" screens and search options. On-line programs, however, have much larger databases. They are also more current. Some are updated quarterly or monthly, and others boast that new information is loaded daily.

Some databases supplied by on-line services are not available in printed form. They are so current that information would be obsolete by the time paper copies were printed and distributed. At the present time, on-line databases tend to have longer backfiles than their CD-ROM counterparts. Another advantage is not having to change disks when searching for past years.

Since the subscriber pays only for actual use, many businesspeople and scientists subscribe to on-line services directly and bypass the library. Services like CompuServe also act as gateways to hundreds of resources. On-line services available at your library, however, are less expensive, and librarians are available to help you. Your library may offer free CD-ROM searching or charge for at least some on-line databases. Check with the reference librarian to find out which databases are available free-of-cost to students and which ones charge a fee.

One group of on-line databases, however, is usually free to student users. These databases are provided by FirstSearch service. Produced by OCLC, Inc., a nonprofit library organization, FirstSearch provides a wide variety of databases, including WorldCat, the world's largest bibliographic database for books. Not only does this database include bibliographic citations but also library holdings information. FirstSearch also provides access to ERIC (Education Resources Information Center), the Government Printing Office Monthly Catalog, Consumers Index, PsycINFO, BIOSIS, and many other databases.

As you might imagine, FirstSearch is a wonderful way to identify books and articles not owned by your local academic library. Armed with information about libraries that have the sources you need, you can request materials via interlibrary loan or visit the libraries where they are available.

Home-User Services. Occasionally, students may find that their college or university library simply isn't large enough to meet their needs. Students involved in long-distance education programs also have this problem since their home campus may be hundreds of miles away. One option is to purchase a library card at a university library in your area. Universities may, however, limit database access to students enrolled in their programs. If you are unable to find another way of obtaining the resources you need, you may want to consider subscribing to one of the commercial database services.

Several on-line services have a lower-priced home-user version. One of these is DIALOG Information Retrieval Service, which offers approximately six hundred databases on a variety of subjects. This service is available at most academic libraries and includes databases in science, business, social sciences, economics, chemistry, law, medicine, and engineering. If your local library does not provide DIALOG, or if the cost is high, you might want to subscribe to *Knowledge Index*. This is a lower-cost, nonprime-time version of the service.

Address: DIALOG Information Retrieval Service
                3460 Hillview Avenue
                Palo Alto, CA 94304

Telephone: (415) 858-3785
Toll-free: (800) 3-DIALOG

Understanding the Limitations of Computerized Indexes

Since computerized indexing services are relatively new, their staffs have not had time to enter citations for older articles. Manycomputerized indexes go back only to the 1980s, so if you are looking for older material, you will have to use printed indexes.

Printed indexes have always been selective. In other words, they attempted to include only the best of the magazines or journals in a particular category. Index publishers often sent out questionnaires to determine which magazine and journal articles should be included since the limited space available required that they be quite selective. As we shall see below, this is not the case with computerized indexes.

Applying Critical Judgment to Your Search

In the past, most of the books and journals you might have found in an academic library were selected because of their high quality and the excellent credentials of their authors. With the arrival of computerized information resources, this is no longer the case. Many of the journal articles that are now available to you on services like *ProQuest* and *Academic Index* were not selected for research purposes. They simply came in the "package" sold by a database vendor. Most of these vendors attempt to include as many magazines and journals as possible, but they do not select titles based on any sort of quality standards. They include whatever is available.

Novice researchers are sometimes shocked to discover that all books and articles are not necessarily accurate or authoritative. In the course of your investigations, you are bound to encounter a number of sources that are misleading, inaccurate, and inappropriate for use in a research paper. How can you know what to avoid?

Most reputable journals list the academic qualifications of the authors. Many are also published by universities. A distinction is made in academic circles between refereed and non-refereed journals. Articles in refereed journals are selected by a group of experts. They are not told the name of the author and the author does not know who is doing the refereeing. This ensures the integrity of the process. Articles in non-refereed journals are usually selected by the editor or an editorial board. Consult *Ulrich's Guide to Periodicals* for a list of refereed journals. Although there are many good non-refereed journals, you are assured of high quality when you use a refereed journal. Others may require that you do some further investigation.

One of the problems with electronic publishing is the difficulty in establishing authority. Many electronic journals, however, are refereed, exactly as printed journals are refereed, and you can establish the credentials of the authors just as you would for a printed article.

Checking Up on the Author. Sometimes, the author's credentials are not listed in the magazine or journal. One way of establishing the authority of a work is to look up the author's career and publication record elsewhere. Nearly every discipline has some sort of biographical directory of authorities or well-known individual. Examples are *American Men and Women of Science* and *American Scholars*. More general sources like *Who's Who in America* can also be useful. If you cannot identify authors in these standard sources, you should at least be able to find them in the *American Faculty Directory* if they have any claim to academic standing.

It is often more difficult to check on the author of an article than to check on the author of a book. However, you might check *Books in Print* to learn if the author of your article has published books as well. Since books are easier to evaluate than articles, you might check reviews for any books you find listed under the author's name. Although this will not provide specific information about your article, you will discover whether an author is considered competent in his or her area of specialization.

Book Reviews. Book reviews usually provide information not only about books themselves but about the author's background and knowledge of the subject. Printed and computerized versions of *Book Review Digest*, *Magill Book Reviews*, and *Book Review Index* are the most commonly used sources of reviews. The on-line version of *Books in Print* contains reviews as does EBSCO's *Academic Abstracts*.

In order to find a book review, you need to know when the book was first published. This information can usually be found in *Books in Print* or on the back of the book's title page. You're looking for the copyright date (the letter C enclosed in a circle), not the printing date. Books are usually reviewed only when they are first published, but later editions are sometimes reviewed as well.

Checking the Publisher. If you are unable to locate reviews or if the author does not appear in standard biographical sources, you may start to wonder about the credibility of the work. Your next step might be to investigate the publisher. Publishers vary greatly in the types of periodicals and books they publish and the level of scholarship they require.

It is not unusual for a magazine or journal to be published by an organization attempting to make its point of view more widely known. Their aim is to influence public opinion. Although these publications may be interesting, keep in mind that they will not be objective, a quality that is important in a research paper.

University-press books and journals are nearly all written and edited by scholars. They can be relied upon for accurate information, though possibly not for readable prose. At the other end of the continuum are what are called *subsidy* or *vanity* publishers that require payment from an author to publish a book. Authors are usually unwilling to pay to have their books published unless they have been turned down by commercial or academic presses. These books are frequently sent free to libraries and are sometimes added to collections. Most directories of publishers like *Publishers Trade List Annual* exclude subsidy publishers or place them in a separate section.

If the publisher is neither a university press nor a subsidy publisher, check some other titles. You can do this using your library OPAC or *Books in Print*. Do these titles seem solid and reliable, or do they include anything that sounds a bit bizarre or extreme? Once again, if it seems important, you can always find book reviews.

Currency of Information. Even if a journal article or book is well written, the information it contains may be out of date. When you discuss your research project with your instructor, ask how recent your sources should be. Every discipline is a little different. The more frequently discovery and change occur within a discipline, the more recent your material must be.

This chapter has provided a brief introduction to the library and its organization. It has also equipped you with some basic tools for using library databases and reference works effectively. In the next chapter, you will have the opportunity to apply these newly acquired talents to specific library research sources.

Chapter

5

Investigating Library Resources

In the last chapter, you found your way around the library, discovering search techniques to help you locate and use library resources. You discovered the power of Boolean searching, visited the reference collection in search of general information, used both print and computerized encyclopedias, and investigated general periodical indexes. In this chapter, you will be investigating specific sources available to researchers. We will focus on two students—Javier and Yvonne—and their particular needs. Since reading about dozens of reference works and indexes can be confusing, following our two imaginary students will allow us to progress logically through the research process in a more realistic way.

Javier has decided to write his paper on the subject of affirmative action in higher education, and Yvonne is interested in the conservation of water resources. These subject areas will give us an opportunity to explore reference works dealing with current events, education, sociology, biology, chemistry, ecology, and other related disciplines. However, we will also show how the same techniques can be used in other fields of study.

Both students have written their thesis statements so they can focus on the specific information they need to write their papers. That will save them a lot of time. They can zero in on their topics and avoid extra work.

Exploring Reference Works

You will notice that the term used here is not *reference books* but *reference works*. That is because a modern library stores reference information in a variety of ways, ranging from books through microfilm and microfiche to CD-ROM and on-line formats. Most of the newer reference works are available in more than one format, and it's up to your library to decide which one to purchase.

Many reference works are available in CD-ROM since that medium is especially easy to use. Javier and Yvonne will not have to consult a dozen or more annual volumes of printed indexes if a CD-ROM program is available. Multiple years can be searched together by subject, title, or author, or they can choose other access points, like journal title, language, or keywords. (See Chapter 4 for a discussion of keyword searches.) They can also use the many on-line databases discussed in Chapter 4.

In many libraries, there is a charge for some of the more sophisticated on-line databases. If this is the case, do as much of your research as possible in the databases that are available free of cost. If, in the end, you are missing some specific information that an on-line search might provide, it could be worth paying for a computer search. Discuss your options with a reference librarian and exhaust the free ones first.

Old-fashioned bound volumes have some advantages over the computer. If your library still subscribes to both formats, you may find that it's best to use both. Browsing is easier with a book. Leafing through the pages of a printed index can give you a sense of how the information is organized and what sort of headings are used to describe your topic. Computer searching is best when you know exactly what you are looking for and can combine terms to locate specific information.

Discovering What's Available

One way to discover what reference works the library owns on your topic is to check for the general call number used to catalog books in that discipline. There's usually a wall chart or a library handout that lists the general categories. Then you can walk through the reference stacks looking specifically for those spine labels. For instance, the Library of Congress uses the letter "L" for books related to education. Since Javier is writing about a topic in this field, he could browse through the "L" section in the reference stacks. In the Dewey Decimal System, education is classed in the 300s.

Javier is using a large university library, so the reference collection may be too large to browse. Typing keywords like *education and encyclopedia* into the OPAC might give him more specific information. However, it would be even more useful to look for particular titles of reference works. To find these titles, Javier can check a work that identifies and describes reference works. *Guide to Reference Books*, edited by Eugene Sheehy, is one of the best available, providing information about handbooks, encyclopedias, indexes, and a wide variety of other reference tools. Since it is arranged by subject, Javier will need to look in only one place. Another useful work is *The Master Index to Subject Encyclopedias*, which includes a comprehensive list of topics, together with citations for specialized encyclopedias, where these topics can be found. These guides also describe the contents of each reference work so that Javier can choose the best ones for his purpose. Once he has identified some reference titles, he can look them up in his library's OPAC.

Encyclopedias and Dictionaries.
Although you are probably familiar with general encyclopedias like the *Britannica* and the *Americana*, you may not be aware of the wide assortment of specialized titles. Both Javier and Yvonne have used a general encyclopedia to get overviews of their topics, but now they need more specific information. Either by going directly to the reference stacks or by using one of the guides described above, Javier found *The Encyclopedia of Education*. This contains over one thousand signed articles with bibliographies, so he should be able to find quite a bit of useful information.

He also discovered the *Dictionary of Education* and the *International Encyclopedia of Education*, both of which are published in England. However, he decided that since his topic is concerned with affirmative action, he had better stick to reference works published in the United States. If the place of publication and, therefore, the national emphasis is important to your topic, be sure to check the bottom of the title page or the copyright page to see where a book was published.

Yvonne, who is writing about the conservation of water resources, discovered *The Encyclopedia of the Environment*, *The Dictionary of Ecology and Environmental Science*, and the *Environmental Encyclopedia*, each containing useful information on her topic. *Environment and the Law: A Dictionary* is a title she would probably not have found if she had simply browsed through the reference stacks since it is shelved with the law books. *The Handbook of Water Law* is another of her discoveries in the law section.

Unlike Javier, Yvonne really doesn't care whether a reference work is published in the United States or in another country, since water conservation is an international problem. What is important to her, however, is the audience for which the work is written. Yvonne is a college freshman, and, though she is interested in her topic, she has not had the advanced chemistry and biology courses needed to understand highly technical information. The guides to reference works and encyclopedias listed above would have told her whether a title was written for laypersons or specialists. The introductions of most reference works will do the same. If you are writing about a subject that is new to you, begin with more general discussions aimed at a lay audience. Later, when you know more about the subject, you may want to consult more technical ones.

A brief list of specialized dictionaries and encyclopedias in other disciplines follows. You might call it the tip of the iceberg:

- *Encyclopedia of World Art.* This work covers genres, artists, periods, and movements in the world of art. Excellent bibliographies are included with most articles.
- *Benet's Reader's Encyclopedia.* A one-volume encyclopedia containing brief articles on famous people in the arts, literature, and music.
- *Encyclopedia of Philosophy.* Covers the field of philosophy, including signed articles by experts and bibliographies.
- *Encyclopedia of Psychology.* Definitive encyclopedia on the subject.
- *Grzimek's Animal Life Encyclopedia.* All aspects of animal life, including their appearance, behavior, and habitat
- *New Grove Dictionary of Music and Musicians.* Standard music encyclopedia in English. Covers musicians, composers, musical terms, instruments, and periods.
- *McGraw-Hill Encyclopedia of Science and Technology.* Articles on all fields of science and technology. Excellent bibliographies follow the articles.
- *Dictionary of American History.* Detailed historical information.

Biographical Sources. Many of the reference works in a library provide information about people. Students use these titles frequently. For example, Javier might look for the biography of an important figure in American education, or Yvonne might find information on a major environmentalist. Titles that they might find useful include:

- *McGraw-Hill Encyclopedia of World Biography.* Biographies of persons in all fields. One useful feature is the annotated list of further readings on the subject.

- *Biography Index.* Index to biographical information in magazines and books.
- *Current Biography Yearbook.* Biographies of people who have recently made news. Published monthly and compiled into an annual edition.
- *American Men and Women of Science.* Biographies of living American scientists.
- *Biography and Genealogy Master Index.* Lists publications containing biographical information on an individual and identifies the relevant edition. Serves as an index to subject encyclopedias, biographical dictionaries, *Who's Who,* and other reference works.
- *Dictionary of Literary Biography.* Multivolume set listing hundreds of authors.
- *Who's Who in America: A Biographical Dictionary of Notable Living Men and Women.* Contemporary American Biography.
- *Author Biographies Master Index.* Indexes entries about authors in biographical dictionaries.
- *Personal Name Index to the New York Times.* Covers all individuals mentioned in the *New York Times* for a given time period.
- *Dictionary of American Biography.* Biographies of famous men and women of all periods who lived in the United States (includes only persons who died prior to publication).
- *Dictionary of National Biography.* Similar to the above but British.

Almanacs. Almanacs are books of facts. They may be general in scope and include facts on every subject imaginable, or they may deal with a specific subject area. They tend to be most useful early in your search or when brief factual information is needed.

In Javier's case, almanacs might provide important dates in the history of American education or statistics on school enrollment or educational expenditures. *The Negro Almanac: A Reference Work on the African American* is a specialized almanac that might include sections on affirmative action, as well.

Since environmental issues are often in the news, the current events sections would be of interest to Yvonne. The following three general almanacs can be used for a variety of topics:

- *World Almanac and Book of Facts.* Information on every subject.
- *Whittaker's Almanac.* Similar to the above but with a British slant.
- *Information Please Almanac.* Facts and figures on almost any subject you can think of.

Directories. Directories are reference works that tell you where to find something or someone. Your home telephone book is an example. Since a number of organizations are concerned with affirmative action, Javier would do well to spend some time looking over these sources. One useful directory is the *Encyclopedia of*

Associations. Javier will find hundreds of organizations concerned with issues relating to women and minorities, as well as many dealing with education.

Hardly any issue has given rise to as many organizations as the environment. Yvonne should also be able to find a number of organizations concerned with water-conservation issues in the *Encyclopedia of Associations*. In fact, if Javier and Yvonne have enough time, they could write to several organizations to request their literature. Remember, however, that both affirmative action and water conservation are politically controversial issues. The literature they receive will probably represent one particular point of view. Controversial or biased information can be interesting, but since it may not be objective, it should be treated with care.

The *Encyclopedia of Associations* is not, however, the only useful directory. Your library has dozens, possibly hundreds, of others. Some of the more widely used directories include:

- *The Career Guide: Dun's Employment Opportunities Directory*
- *Awards, Honors and Prizes: An International Directory of Awards*
- *World of Winners: A Current and Historical Perspective on Awards and their Winners*
- *Directory of Financial Aid for Minorities*
- *Barron's Guide to Medical and Dental Schools*
- *Peterson's Guide to Graduate and Professional Programs*
- *Summer Theatre Directory*

Bibliographies. The more research papers you write, the more you will come to love bibliographies. That's because they do much of the work of locating sources for you. There are whole volumes that contain nothing but bibliographic citations. Usually arranged by subject, they can be gold mines. Here are a few samples:

- *A Bibliography of American Naval History*. Arranged chronologically beginning prior to American Revolution.
- *A Bibliography of Theatre Technology*. Topical arrangement.
- *Modern Language Association Bibliography*. Index to material about English and American literature. Other volumes cover European, Asian, African, and Latin American literature.
- *Women in American History: A Bibliography*. Lists abstracts of articles from approximately 550 periodicals, arranged by subject.
- *Bibliographic Index*. An index to bibliographies published separately or as parts of books, pamphlets, or periodicals.

Indexes to Information in Books. Although we usually think of indexes in connection with periodical literature, several include books or sections of books. *The MLA Bibliography* and *The Bibliographic Index* listed above are two of these. Other titles in this category include:

- *Dissertation Abstracts International.* Index to dissertations submitted at both American and international universities.
- *NTIS.* National Technical Information Service of the U.S. Department of Commerce index to U.S. government-sponsored research.
- *Essay and General Literature Index.* Indexes collections of essays in all subject areas.

Tracking Down a Book

Javier's instructor has recommended a great book on his subject but can't remember who wrote it. Yvonne read an article last month about water pollution but cannot cite it without complete bibliographic information. These are the sorts of problems that always seem to come up at least once with every research paper. Maybe you see a reference to a book that would be helpful, but you have no more than an author's name or title. How can you get more information? The following reference works should be helpful:

- *Books in Print.* Listing of English-language books currently in publication.
- *Subject Guide to Books in Print.* The same information arranged by subject for most nonfiction books.
- *Forthcoming Books.* Lists soon-to-be-published books.

Exploring Periodical Indexes

Whether your library provides CD-ROM disks, on-line databases, or printed volumes, periodical indexes are probably the resources you will be using most often. Before you begin your search, however, look around the area where the library's indexes are kept. There should be some instruction sheets available, probably stored in literature racks. If you are not familiar with computers, you will be much more comfortable if you can follow a set of written directions.

Each of the periodical indexing programs tends to work differently. There is little standardization among them. Computerized indexes are still in their infancies, and this lack of standardization is one of their most frustrating problems. It is usually fairly easy to do a simple search, but you will miss much of what is available unless you take advantage of more advanced techniques available for a specific program. In fact, a search using a printed index may result in better hits than a bad computer search. If your library has no instruction sheets, spend some time with the "Help" screens and experiment with different strategies before you begin your search in earnest.

Javier and Yvonne began with some general CD-ROM indexes, including *Readers' Guide, ProQuest,* and *Academic Index.* Both students found a lot of good articles in these indexes, but they tend to be aimed at a popular audience and give superficial information. Thus, time the two students moved on to more specialized and scholarly indexes.

Most periodical indexes are available in more than one format. The older titles are still published in a printed version, while the newer ones may be available in only a CD-ROM or on-line version. Javier found more useful articles in the *Education Index* and ERIC. Produced by the U.S. Department of Education, ERIC covers a wide range of subjects that affect education. One section is the *Current Index to Journals in Education (CIJE)*, which includes articles from all major education journals. The other section, *Resources in Education (RIE)*, consists of a variety of documents, including conference proceedings and research reports.

Another index that Javier would find useful both for education and for its coverage of minority issues is *PAIS International* (Public Affairs Information Service). It also includes publications on public policy, business, law, economics, government, and international relations.

Yvonne might choose a specialized environmental index or a more general one like *Biological and Agricultural Index* or the *General Science Index*. Even more specialized indexes are available devoted entirely to water resources. However, these tend to be highly technical and thus will not be really useful until Yvonne knows a lot more about her subject.

No matter what subject you are writing about, there are both general and specialized indexes that you will find useful. Some of the most widely available titles include:

- *ABI/INFORM*. Indexes periodicals in business, management, and industry.
- *AgeLine*. Covers health, economic, sociopsychological, and political aspects of aging.
- *Art Index*. Indexes U.S. and foreign fine arts periodicals.
- *Disclosure Database*. Full-text financial database.
- *ENERGYLINE*. Indexes energy information from journals, reports, monographs, conference proceedings, and other sources.
- *Family Resources Database*. Cites articles, books, and other materials dealing with marriage and the family.
- *Food Science and Technology Abstracts*. Articles in food science and technology.
- *GEOREF*. Indexes literature in the geosciences, including economic geology, geochemistry, geomorphology, and other related disciplines.
- *LABORDOC*. Literature in labor-related fields, including industrial relations and management.
- *Harvard Business Review/Online*. Text of articles from *Harvard Business Review*.
- *Humanities Index*. Indexes English language periodicals in the humanities.
- *NEXIS* and *LEXIS*. *NEXIS* provides databases in areas that include trade, technology, and business legislation. *LEXIS* offers legal research information, including state, federal, and foreign case law.

- *Psychological Abstracts or PsycINFO*. The most important source for articles, reports and dissertations on psychology and related disciplines. *Psychological Abstracts* is the printed version; *PsycInfo* the on-line version.
- *Reader's Guide to Periodical Literature*. The old standby, covering general-interest magazines.
- *Religion Index One*. Covers articles from both U.S. and foreign religious periodicals.
- *Reuters Textline*. Full text of news and comments from international publications.
- *Social Sciences Index*. Mainly American journals in the social sciences.
- *Sociological Abstracts*. Indexes publications in the field of sociology.
- *SPORT Database*. Abstracts of journal articles, books, and other publications, on sports-related topics.

Finding Information about a Magazine or Journal

Just as you occasionally want to cite a book but have incomplete information, you may also need more information about a journal. In the case of journals, there's the added problem of frequent name changes and similar or even identical titles. The following reference works provide bibliographic information about journals:

- *Ulrich's International Periodicals Directory*. Information on well over a hundred thousand serials, including both magazines and journals.
- *Gale Directory of Publications and Broadcast Media*. Covers newspapers and other periodicals as well as radio, television, and cable-TV stations.
- *Benn's Media Directory*. Emphasizes British media outlets.

Using Microforms

Microfilm or microfiche is usually just another format for storing newspapers, magazines, and journals. Most libraries purchase at least some periodicals on microfilm or microfiche to save storage space. Often these are less frequently used titles.

Some collections of research materials can be found only in microform. Either the individual items were published long ago and are no longer in print or there is so much information that it would be impractical to print it. A few examples are given below:

- *Television News Index and Abstracts*. Indexes network evening news programs.
- *Herstory*. A set of 821 newsletters, journals, and newspapers by and about women, most of which were published between 1968 and 1974.
- *College Catalogs on Microfiche*. Complete collection of college catalogs.
- *National Criminal Justice Reference Service*. Collection of materials relating to criminal justice.

Gradually, however, these collections are becoming available on the Internet, especially the older ones for which the copyright law does not restrict access.

Accessing Newspaper Indexes

A few years ago, students' access to newspapers was limited to their own hometown paper and the *New York Times*. Today, with the emergence of electronic sources, lengthy newspaper files can be stored on a single CD-ROM disk or maintained by an on-line service. Researchers are discovering that newspapers like the *Los Angeles Times*, *The Atlanta Constitution*, and *The Cleveland Plain Dealer* cover many stories of national importance and frequently run in-depth series on contemporary social problems. Electronic newspapers are self-indexed, but if your access is to microfilm or printed copies, you will need a separate index, usually available as a bound volume. Here are some samples:

- *Chicago Tribune Index*
- *Christian-Science Monitor Index*
- *Los Angeles Times Index*
- *New York Times Index*
- *Times (London) Index*
- *Wall Street Journal Index*
- *Washington Post Index*

Most CD-ROM disks cover just one newspaper. On-line services, however, may provide as many as a hundred different titles, searchable either together or individually. While some give only a citation and an abstract, others supply the full text of most articles. Even if the full text is not available, newspaper articles are so numerous that the abstracts alone are a gold mine of information. Here are a few of the on-line services available:

- *VU/TEXT*. On-line index to newspapers. Includes full text.
- *Knight Ridder's DIALOG Information Service*. Includes most major American and some international newspapers in a full-text format.
- *Newspaper Abstracts*. CD-Rom program. Provides abstracts of articles in many major newspapers.

Investigating Government Documents

Many people don't realize the enormous number of books, journals, and pamphlets published by the government. The United States government is the world's largest publisher, and you would be amazed at the breadth of subject matter. Among the topics covered are travel, technology, home repairs, nutrition, trade policy, and energy conservation. Both Javier's and Yvonne's topics lend themselves to documents because the government is deeply involved with both affirmative action and water resources. In fact these may be among the best sources our two students discover.

Understanding the Federal Depository Library Program

Although it's possible to obtain government publications directly through the United States Government Printing Office (G.P.O.), it's easier to use the collection in your local library's government documents depository. This program was established by Congress to make government publications available to all citizens. Approximately 1,400 libraries participate in the program. They make available large collections of government publications, but you won't find every publication at every depository library.

Most are partial or selective depositories, which means the library selects only what it thinks it can use. Fifty-three libraries, however, are designated as regional depository libraries and maintain complete collections of documents. Each state usually has one regional depository, although population plays a role in the location of selective depository libraries.

Most state university libraries are government-document-depository libraries. Ask your librarian whether yours is a depository. If it's not, the librarian should be able to tell you the location of the nearest one. If for some reason you are still not able to locate a collection, write to the following address:

Federal Depository Library Program
U.S. Government Printing Office
Superintendent of Documents
Stop: SM
Washington, DC 20402

The Superintendent of Documents Office is a unit of the United States Government Printing Office charged with the responsibility of selling copies of government publications, including pamphlets, periodicals, and books. Although this is a good starting place for obtaining documents, it is far from the only place. And since many government agencies publish their own information, tracking down a particular publication can be a time-consuming operation.

Locating Government Publications

The biggest problem with using government documents in the past was that they were difficult to locate and that you had to know what you wanted. The arrival of electronic indexes, however, has made it considerably easier to locate such documents.

Javier and Yvonne begin their search with a CD-ROM version of the *Monthly Catalog of United States Government Publications*, which lists most, though not all, government documents. Printed issues are organized in Superintendent of Documents classification number order. Author, title, and subject indexes make it easier to find publications, but MO CAT, as it is fondly known, is not the most user-friendly index. Luckily, libraries now have their choice of several excellent computer programs that allow you to search the documents database, including *Knight Ridder's DIALOG Information Services*. Files available include the *GPO Publications Reference File* and the *GPO Monthly Catalog* file. DIALOG subscribers can place an order through DIALORDER, although this is an expensive way to obtain a document if you have access to a depository library.

While computer programs have replaced many printed aids, you may still need to know about the following titles if you are doing a lot of work with government documents. Many can be found at your local depository library:

- *Publications Reference File*. A catalog of publications and subscription services for sale through the Superintendent of Documents, available both on microfiche and on machine-readable tape. Search by subject, title, or keyword.
- *The Out-of-Print G.P.O. Sales Publications Reference File*. Records for publications that were once available through the G.P.O. as far back as 1972.
- *American Statistics Index*. Guide to U.S. government statistical information.
- *Guide to U.S. Government Publications*. Annotated compilation of the important series and periodicals published by U.S. government agencies.
- *Public Affairs Information Service*. Previously mentioned periodical index that also includes citations for government documents. The service produces a variety of printed indexes as well as *PAIS International Online*.
- *Subject Bibliography Index*. Lists all the available subject bibliographies.
- *U.S. Government Books*. An annotated catalog of almost one thousand new and popular books. Available from:

  U.S. Government Printing Office
  Superintendent of Documents
  Stop: SSOP
  Washington, DC 20402-9328

- *The Consumer Information Catalog*. Lists free and low-cost consumer publications. For a free copy write to:

  Consumer Information Center
  Pueblo, Colorado 81009

- *Government Periodicals and Subscription Services* (Price List 36). Available free from the GPO address above.

- *New Books*. An annotated list of all new titles made available during the preceding two months, also available from GPO.

The Government Printing Office publishes indexes and catalogs that are free of charge to individuals. Also available are more than 230 subject bibliographies.

Using Government Reference Works

Many of the library's basic reference works are published by the government. Both Javier and Yvonne need the *United States Government Organization Manual*. This official handbook of the federal government describes the purpose and programs of government agencies and lists addresses and telephone numbers. Several of the programs listed relate to our students' topics. The *Federal Regulatory Directory* describes the work of large regulatory agencies. This resource will be especially useful to Yvonne because many government regulations concern water quality.

Both students may also wish to consult state publications. Every state has its own agencies devoted to education and the environment. To learn more about them, Javier and Yvonne might consult *The National Directory of State Agencies*, a guide to state agencies and their staffs.

Exploring Other Sources of Government Publications

Nearly every large government department or agency, including the State Department, the Departments of Agriculture and Education, the Bureau of the Census, and the federal Archives, publishes some of its own materials. Quite often, these publications are not listed in GPO catalogs. How then do you find them? If your library research has failed to turn up sufficient material, you might consider contacting the agency directly to obtain publications providing more detailed information.

Investigating ERIC

In addition to being a periodical index, ERIC is a government document. ERIC is an acronym that stands for Educational Resources Information Center, which provides access to a vast body of education-related literature. Established in 1966 by the U.S. Department of Education Office of Education Research and Improvement, the service is probably the world's largest source of education information. Over 700,000 documents, including monographs, conference proceedings, and journal articles have been indexed and abstracted.

ERIC indexes are available in libraries throughout the country as print volumes, on microfiche, on CD-ROM, as well as through on-line services. Information is collected from sixteen subject-specific clearinghouses that provide research summaries, bibliographies, and reference and referral services.

ERIC is actually divided into two main sections. The first, *Current Index to Journals in Education,* indexes articles from journals. The second, *Resources in Education,* provides access to what are called ERIC documents—a term that includes most of the other literature in the field. Most college and university libraries provide some type of ERIC access. If, however, you would like to know the location of your nearest ERIC collection, write to the following address:

> Educational Resources Information Center
> U.S. Department of Education
> Office of Educational Research and Improvement
> 555 New Jersey Avenue NW
> Washington, DC 20208-5270
> Toll-free Number: 800-USE-ERIC

Obviously, Javier will find ERIC useful for articles and documents concerning affirmative action in higher education. However, it is surprising what a wide range of information it covers. If Yvonne is interested in environmental education, she too will find helpful information in ERIC. It also covers the disciplines of psychology and library science, although in less depth.

Using Resources in Other Libraries

What can you do if your library does not have the materials you are seeking? You need not limit your research to your own academic library. If your computer has a modem and you can connect to the Internet, you can visit libraries around the world.

Library Catalogs

Most academic libraries as well as the larger public libraries make their book catalogs available on the Internet. Although each uses a different OPAC program, they are all somewhat similar. If you have any difficulty using a program, there is always a "Help" screen to deal with problems.

Check the holdings of libraries in your own geographical area. If you find a library that has a good selection of materials relating to your topic, ask your librarian if students at your university have borrowing privileges there. Groups of libraries often get together and agree to extend borrowing privileges to one another's users.

Union Catalogs

Although almost any of the on-line catalogs will be helpful, the most useful are the union catalogs. These list the holdings of not one library but of many libraries located within a particular geographical area or belonging to the same library association. Just be careful to note which libraries have the titles you're seeking. California's Melvyl system is not a single library's catalog but a union catalog of University of California libraries.

E-Mail Bibliographies

Many libraries, including Melvyl, will send you a bibliography of the titles retrieved from their OPACs. Since it arrives by e-mail, it saves on-line time and gives you complete bibliographic information for requesting books through interlibrary loan or visiting the library in person.

Screen Capture

If you've surfed to a library that does not provide e-mail bibliographies, don't forget to save the screens displaying the bibliographic citations for the books you're seeking. Screen capture allows your communications program to save everything that appears on your computer screen.

The Library of Congress

The largest book collection in the United States is, of course, at the Library of Congress. LC's Gopher, which it calls *Marvel*, provides access not only to the book catalog but to an extensive collection of government-related databases. While you're there, you might like to take a look at some of the fascinating collections of documents and stunning graphics, like the American Memory Project. Although the Library of Congress does not usually lend its collection, you may want to make a visit if you're in the Washington area. It really is a fascinating experience.

Visiting Other Libraries

There is no substitute for visiting a library in person. Although OPACs allow you to search for specific titles and keywords, you can't browse through the stacks, opening first one book and then another, checking indexes and tables of contents. Although it may be inconvenient to journey to a distant town just to use a library, you might squeeze in a library visit when you travel. Take advantage of home visits and vacations to check out libraries. Before you leave campus, look in the *American Library Directory* to find out what libraries are located in the city you plan to visit.

Prepare Before You Go. If you must travel to another city to use an unfamiliar research facility, you will not be able to return whenever you need an article or bibliography. Since your time is limited, use it efficiently. This does not mean, however, that quality must suffer. Much of the work can now be done before you leave home.

Search the OPAC of the library you will be visiting on-line so you can go fully equipped with a list of needed books and call numbers. You can also take complete bibliographic citations for the journal articles you're seeking, having first searched the appropriate indexing and abstracting services and checked the library's periodical holdings in their catalog.

You will find that it's much easier to do your thinking at your home computer or in your home library. Unfamiliar surroundings and a strange collection will be confusing. Being prepared with a list of what you want will keep you focused. And since you're not spending your time looking up call numbers or searching indexes, you will have more time to evaluate information and bring back only what you really need.

Cooperative Agreements. If your library has a reciprocal borrowing agreement with the library you are visiting, you may need to bring a form signed by a librarian on your home campus. Some libraries call these *passports*. Other libraries simply allow you to check out materials with your own university library card or student ID. Find out before you go. You would not want to drive all the way to another library only to find when you got there that you didn't bring the necessary paperwork.

Interlibrary Loan. If, however, the books you need are not at a library where you have borrowing privileges, you can request them from your library's interlibrary loan department. Your library probably belongs to the OCLC national library network. Once you have made your request, a staff member checks the computer to learn which libraries own copies of the books you are requesting. A message is left for those libraries, and, if all goes well, they will soon ship the books to your library.

Although the computer makes it quick and easy to find a lending library, the Post Office makes it slow and inefficient to send materials. They usually travel fourth-class mail and may take over a week in transit. It is usually necessary to allow at least two weeks for the arrival of interlibrary loan materials. You will want to identify these books and articles soon after your paper is assigned to allow sufficient time.

Finding Information Outside the Library

Although Javier and Yvonne will probably find most of their information in their local academic library or at a larger one nearby, there are other possibilities they might want to investigate. Interviews, questionnaires, surveys, and the observation of some type of behavior, whether human or animal, are all important non-library sources of information.

If you think your proposed topic might lend itself to a questionnaire or opinion survey, discuss your plans with your instructor. Ask him or her to suggest books on constructing a survey instrument and interpreting the results obtained. If you are writing a research paper for a course in the social sciences, this information may be covered in class. Although creating a questionnaire may seem a very easy task, your data may be useless if you are unaware of the factors that could bias or alter the responses you receive. Collecting data must be done in a professional manner to ensure accuracy, and you may need to bone up on some elementary statistical techniques if you plan to make inferences from the responses.

Discussing Your Topic with an Expert

Occasionally, what you need is not a book or journal article but an expert. You may have specific questions and would like to talk to someone who knows the answers. Such an expert may be as near as your own university faculty, or you may need to go farther to find your answers. In the Appendix of this book, you will find a list of organizations, one of which may have your expert on its staff or membership rolls. Someone in the organization's administrative offices may be able to tell you where you can find the information you're seeking.

Experts can also be found in your hometown. If you are writing about drug abuse, for instance, you might contact your local substance-abuse treatment center. Call the number listed in the telephone book and tell the person answering the phone that you would like to speak to someone knowledgeable on the topic. Be as specific as possible because staff members have different specialties. When a name is mentioned, ask about this person's job and academic and professional credentials. Anyone you interview for a research paper should have some claim to expert knowledge. You will probably be transferred to one of the professional staff or told that someone will get back to you. Explain the nature of your paper and ask if you might arrange an interview.

Both Javier and Yvonne might use a discussion with an expert to break up the flow of factual information and make their papers more interesting. Javier could locate an attorney who has been involved in a significant affirmative action court case. Yvonne might identify a chemist, biologist, or hydrologist on her own college faculty who has interesting information to contribute. Both students, however, must be careful to distinguish the expert from people who simply have an opinion on the subject. This is not to say that some comments from the general public would not make a good addition to their papers. Javier, for instance, might include quotations from his fellow students representing a variety of views on affirmative action. He must take care, however, to make it clear that these are simply a few random comments, not a scientific sample or the views of especially knowledgeable people.

Yvonne might wish to contact the author of one of the articles she has read. Most scholarly and many popular articles provide biographical information, such as the university at which the author is employed. Nearly all universities and many other organizations are on the Internet, so you can contact them by e-mail. Information on locating an e-mail address when you know someone's institutional affiliation can be found in the next chapter.

Conducting Personal Interviews

Arrange to interview your experts only after you have done extensive research on your subject. An expert is not a talking encyclopedia and will not know what sort of information you are looking for unless you ask clear, focused questions. Don't arrive at an interview expecting to chat for half an hour and then leave with the information you are seeking. This just doesn't happen.

The burden is on you to move the conversation in the appropriate direction, so have a written list of questions. The list should be longer than you think you will actually need because some of the questions may elicit no response. Either the person being interviewed has no opinion or prefers not to answer certain questions. Be prepared with follow-up questions if you receive yes, no, or single-sentence answers.

You may wish to tape the interview to ensure the accuracy of your direct and indirect quotations. However, always ask the person being interviewed if a tape recorder is acceptable before beginning the interview. Put the recorder on a desk or some other place in plain view. That way, the person interviewed will gradually grow accustomed to it. If you suddenly remember it later, your interview will lose momentum and your subject may suddenly become tongue-tied. In fact, some journalists believe that a tape recorder can ruin an interview and advise against using one.

Conducting Telephone Interviews. The ideal interview is conducted face-to-face, but if your expert lives some distance away, you may have to do the interview over the telephone. Telephone interviews are somewhat more difficult because you are talking to a stranger—eye contact, facial expressions and body language are all absent. You should therefore put even more time into formulating your questions because awkward silences are more common over the phone. You can use your answering machine to record the conversation, but only with your expert's approval.

Interviewing by E-Mail. When your paper is first assigned, you might consider joining an Internet discussion list or listserv group focused on your topic. These groups are discussed in the next chapter. Read the messages that are posted each day; you will soon be able to identify especially knowledgeable contributors. Many list members type their name, title, and the academic institution with which they are affiliated at the bottom of each message.

If you are unable to identify someone on the list with expertise on your topic, you might consider posting a general query to the list. Be specific. Faculty and grad students grow to resent undergraduates who want them to do their work for them.

Once you think you have found your expert on the list, write to his or her e-mail address. Explain the nature of your thesis and the specific information you are seeking. Do not write "tell me everything you know about. . . ." Ask if it would be convenient for him or her to assist you. If this is not the person's area of expertise, you might ask for another recommendation. If you are to correspond with someone else, you will need the complete e-mail address.

Writing Letters. Interviewing an expert by "snail" mail is not as satisfactory as by electronic mail because several days or even weeks elapse between mailing your questions and receiving a response. It also places more of a burden on your expert, who must type a letter, buy a stamp, and take it to the post office or letter box. You may have read that even Bill Gates of Microsoft fame reads his own e-mail; so even well-known people may often respond to an intelligent query. If, however, you cannot locate an e-mail address, you have no choice but to correspond by mail.

Address your letter to a specific person, not to a corporation or agency. Use the organizations listed in the Appendix to identify your expert. When you call or write, ask how to get in touch with the person or persons they suggest. Allow at least a couple of weeks to obtain the information you are seeking, and do everything possible to facilitate the exchange. For instance, enclose a stamped, self-addressed envelope. Some people even send a form with each question followed by several lines for the expert's response. But don't send the form without first having explained your request and given an advance thank-you for whatever information the person can provide.

Researching Public Events

Occasionally you will want to use information contained in a speech, play, public debate, television program, or similar event. Any program appearing on television is, of course, the easiest to deal with because you can videotape it. Later you can advance and back up the tape to note a quotation or describe an event.

It is more difficult to record exact information, however, when you attend an event in person. You may have difficulty hearing every word, or you may be in a darkened auditorium where note-taking is difficult. You can often obtain transcripts of political speeches from the office of your congressional representative, senator, or governor, and campaign speeches may be obtained from a candidate's campaign headquarters. Check your local newspaper for its account of the event. If you quote from the newspaper article as well as your own notes, be sure you make each source clear.

The proceedings of conferences and professional meetings may also be published. Even if these are not available when you're writing your paper, the sponsoring organization probably has a tape or typewritten text they can lend you. In addition, play scripts are often available at your library.

Doing research can be a fascinating experience. In fact, it is often the most enjoyable part of writing a paper. Think of yourself as a detective, searching far and wide for clues that will resolve the mystery. In the next chapter, we will expand our search to cover the entire globe.

Chapter 6

Exploring the Internet

With television, magazines, and newspapers announcing the arrival of the Information Superhighway, one would have to be living on another planet to remain ignorant of recent developments. Although the term has a variety of meanings (including video phones, multimedia, and five-hundred-channel cable) depending on the source, it is the Internet that is causing much of the excitement. Everyone, it seems, wants to be connected to this virtual community. Despite all this attention, you may not be aware that the Internet provides access to thousands of information resources, some of which might be useful for your paper.

Investigating the Internet

When someone asks, "What is the Internet?" the answer may be a confused silence or a long, involved technical explanation. For our purposes, the Internet is a vast, exciting, sometimes confusing world of information that can be transmitted by modem from one computer to another. If you can access the Net, you can travel the world, visiting libraries, talking to interesting people, and tapping into the knowledge held in the world's great universities. On the Internet, you can find books, journals, reference works, and even fascinating conversations.

Twenty-five or so years ago, the U.S. Defense Department began experimenting with a way of linking its computers so that if one location were bombed, the rest of the network would still function. That network, called the ARPAnet, was the beginning of what we now know as the Internet.

Gradually, other networks developed and were linked with ARPAnet, the most important of which was commissioned by the National Science Foundation. The NSFNET allowed large research universities to share supercomputers. Originally, the goal was to move data back and forth, but, human nature being what it is, people were soon sharing recipes and soap opera news as well. In 1995, the number of Internet users topped fifty million.

Understanding the Internet's Organization

A standardized Internet protocol has been devised that allows people using all sorts of computers to communicate with one another. This protocol serves as a universal technical language, making it possible for people all over the world to become one community, using the Internet for business, scholarship, and personal communication. If connected to the Internet, your computer can be linked with computers on every continent just as if you were right next door.

The Internet is actually a web of smaller regional networks linked by a central "backbone" (one of the only Internet metaphors that has nothing to do with transportation). Think of the network as a high-speed interstate highway with many smaller roads leading off from it. The highway or backbone can theoretically move data at rates of forty-five million bits per second, many times faster than the fastest modem. Smaller networks serving the different geographical regions radiate out from the backbone, with even smaller networks feeding off of them. At the lowest level are individual computers like yours.

No central computer or computers run the Internet, so it is almost impossible for the entire Internet to crash at once. A question frequently asked is, "Who owns the Internet?" There is no president or CEO. The Internet, as a whole, is a kind of anarchy. Lots of organizations have their own little piece—their local computer and the workstations that connect to it. Various phone companies own most of the communication lines.

Since no one owns more than a small chunk and there is no central organization running things, why doesn't the whole thing fall apart? The Internet is a unique experiment in cooperation, wherein voluntary governing bodies make global information exchange possible through technology. Membership in these associations is usually open to anyone, including you. In other words, you can help chart the course of the Internet.

Ignoring the Hype

Whether or not you are already connected to the Internet, you may have been bombarded with hype, leading you to think the Net is a magical, mystical experience. In truth, using the Internet requires a sense of adventure and an enormous amount of patience.

Despite the increased availability of user-friendly, graphic interfaces, the Internet requires a willingness to learn and to ask for help. It's like journeying to a foreign country; you can easily become lost. Though the Internet offers much to see and do, you may become frustrated as you search.

Once you master an Internet skill, it seems that everything changes. One site goes out of business and another one appears. A command that worked yesterday gets you nowhere today. The Internet is constantly under construction, and many sites and resources are still experimental. When you connect, don't be afraid to ask for help. No one is watching you and commenting on your ignorance. Each time you log on and haltingly discover a new resource, it becomes easier. Don't get discouraged.

Getting More Information

A number of Internet organizations have assumed the responsibility of organizing the network, developing standards, and providing information to users. Here are a few worth contacting:

- **The Internet Society.** The mission of the Internet Society is "to provide assistance and support to groups involved in the use, operation, and evolution of the Internet."
- **InterNIC.** The Internet Network Information Center maintains lists of systems that provide Internet access. Since it also makes available

introductory information on Internet functions, you might wish to visit their site. Select InterNIC on a Gopher menu.

- **The Electronic Frontier Foundation.** This active group provides numerous documents about Internet history and resources. It is dedicated to promoting academic and personal freedoms in the worldwide computer society.

You can obtain more information about any of these organizations by typing the name into one of the World Wide Web search engines (more about search engines later in this chapter) and following the links.

Observing Netiquette

Since no one owns the Internet, there's no one to police it. Instead, Net users have developed a set of unwritten rules about what constitutes proper behavior. Netiquette guidelines have nothing to do with Emily Post or which fork to use at a formal dinner. Instead, most concern the wise use of the Net's limited resources and consideration for the other people who share them.

When people talk to strangers on the Net, they sometimes fail to realize they are communicating with actual human beings. Since they may feel they are simply typing words into their own computers, they may vent anger and frustration that, under normal circumstances, they would never dream of inflicting on friends or business colleagues. This reaction is called *flaming*.

As you become involved in discussion groups and find yourself writing to other Net users in neighboring towns or on distant continents, try to picture them in your imagination. They are far more than words that appear on your computer screen. Phrase your messages as if you were sitting in the same room carrying on a conversation.

Connecting to the Internet

The key to connecting to the Internet is a modem. As discussed in Chapter 1, modems are translators between computers and the telephone system that convert the digitized information a computer generates into sound waves. If you pick up the telephone while your modem is connected, you will hear these distinctive sounds. At the other end of the line, the sound waves are turned back into digitized information again.

Modems depend on software to tell them what to do. Your software may be specially written for accessing the Net, or it may be a general-purpose communications program that you can also use for connecting with local bulletin boards and sending faxes. Some of these are fairly generic and others work only with a particular Internet provider.

Although you may not realize it, you may already be connected to the Internet through your college or university. Most academic institutions have their own Internet connection node and provide accounts to students. Check with your local computer center. While you're at it, find out whether you can dial in from your home computer or if you must use the machines in the computer lab. If you can call up your college computer from home and connect to the Net, find out what software your lab technician recommends. Your university may even provide you with a free copy.

Understanding Full versus Partial Connections

Your computer center or other Internet provider may have full connectivity, which allows you to use all the tools described below, or it may provide you with only limited access. Large universities very often obtain dedicated network access by leasing special high-speed phone lines. If you have access on-campus to this phone line, you are said to have full connectivity. If, however, you must dial your university computer from home using a modem and normal phone line, you will be more limited in what you can use.

Some universities provide a dial-up connection that requires only a basic communications program. Once connected, your computer seems to go to sleep, and the real communication is between your campus or service provider's computer and the Internet. What you see on your screen is exactly what you would see if you were sitting at the service provider's computer. Other dial-up connections, like those used by the large, commercial on-line service providers, have the appearance of full connection, but they are much slower and can send and receive only smaller bundles of information. Though not the best connections to have, these are usually the least expensive.

A compromise between these two extremes is a SLIP connection. This is not the place for a technical explanation but some Internet providers provide SLIP (Serial Line Internet Protocol) access that allows users to take advantage of most Net facilities. Although the monthly charge is quite a bit higher than for a dial-up connection, you might want to investigate SLIP if you spend a lot of time on the Internet.

A number of academic institutions offer only e-mail. Even e-mail, however, is a wonderfully useful service, and we will spend some time later in this chapter discussing how you can use Telnet, FTP, Veronica, and other useful Internet tools with only an e-mail account.

Exploring Local Access

If your college or university does not offer Internet accounts or if it doesn't provide access to a variety of services, including Telnet, FTP, and the World Wide Web, check into local bulletin boards or service providers. These are usually private undertakings that charge a monthly fee for Internet access. Just be careful that the phone number your modem will dial up is in your local dialing area. It is easy to get caught up in your discoveries and amass huge long-distance charges. The same caution applies to services that charge by the hour. Because so many people are on-line, the Internet can be very slow. You may spend much more time on-line than you realize.

If you don't know how to contact local bulletin board services, ask someone at your college computer center. Most computer techies would be in agony if they could not "surf" the Net.

Using Commercial Services

You may prefer to join a large, commercial computer service, such as America Online, Prodigy, or CompuServe, that offers many resources and activities in addition to Internet access. Most provide access to a variety of Internet tools, although some are more user-friendly than others.

Since you can usually connect to on-line services using a local number, their cost is affordable. Monthly charges average about $10 to $20, depending on time of day and number of hours used. Some services charge a higher rate for time on the Internet than for their other features. Others offer unlimited use of some features but limited Internet use. Still others place a surcharge on use during daytime hours. Read the fine print and compare pricing plans.

Services that may be included in your membership are news, weather, sports, games, and shopping. In addition, databases may include *Associated Press Online*, *Grolier's Academic American Encyclopedia*, *Roger Ebert's Movie Reviews*, *U.S. Government Publications*, *Peterson's College Database*, and many full-text magazines. Public domain software programs can often be downloaded to your own computer. Discussion groups, another enjoyable feature, enable you to talk to people who share an interest in subjects as diverse as religion, history, astronomy, crafts, disabilities, genealogy, photography, and religion. DIALOG databases (discussed in the previous chapter) may be available for an additional fee.

Here are some of the better-known commercial services.

America Online (AOL). AOL is a very popular service, with over two million members. Its Academic Assistance Center may be helpful for some assignments.

Address:	America Online		
	8619 Westwood Center Drive		
	Vienna, VA 22182-2285		
Telephone:	(703) 448-8700	Toll-free:	(800) 881-8961

CompuServe. CompuServe is the oldest of the on-line services for home use.

Address:	5000 Arlington Center Blvd.		
	P.O. Box 20212		
	Columbus, OH 43220		
Telephone:	(614) 457-8650	Toll-free:	(800) 848-8990

Prodigy. Prodigy is a family-oriented service that provides multimedia e-mail. The Homework Helper service, available at an additional charge, offers a variety of reference services.

Address:	Prodigy P.O. Box 191486 Dallas, TX 75219-1486
Toll-free:	(800) 776-3552 (800) 776-3449

Delphi. Delphi allows you to sign up on-line using the toll-free number listed below.

Address:	Delphi Internet Services 1030 Massachusetts Avenue Cambridge, MA 02138
Toll-free:	(800) 365-4636 (Note: this is a communications line, not a voice line) (800) 695-4005 WWW: http://www.delphi.com

GEnie. GEnie offers lower rates for nonprime-time users but may not have a local phone number in your area.

Address:	GEnie c/o GE Information Services P.O. Box 6403 Rockville, MD 20850-1785
Toll-free:	(800) 638-9636 WWW: http://www.genie.com

Which on-line service provider is best for you? Many new computers come bundled with software that lets you try out several of the larger services. They may even give you a free month so you can explore their different features. It is sometimes easier, however, to initiate service than to cancel a subscription. Read the fine print or ask a sales representative about any ongoing obligations.

You will want to choose a service that makes available a local high-speed communications line. Long-distance charges can be much higher than your actual monthly fee, and a very slow line can double or triple the time you spend on-line.

Uploading and Downloading Files

Once you have established your Internet connection, review the basic functions of your communications software. Though you don't have to be an expert, it is important to be able to upload and download files. *Uploading* refers to the process of sending a file from your computer to another computer or system on the Net.

Downloading is retrieving a file from the distant computer and copying it into your own computer. You might think of messages as going *up* to the Internet and *down* to you.

If you are using a commercial on-line service like America Online, user-friendly screens may make these tasks very easy. If, however, you are using a "plain vanilla" communications package to access your university or a local service provider, you will have to do a bit of practicing.

If you are going to send information to another e-mail user, you may want to refresh your memory about the ASCII files discussed in the first chapter. Be sure you know the commands that tell your word processor to save a document as an ASCII or text file. If, however, you and your e-mail correspondent are using the same word-processing program, it may be possible to send the file in the word-processor format as an attachment to an e-mail message.

If you are using a generic communications program, check your software manual to see how files are sent back and forth. Using a dial-up line can be somewhat more complicated because you are using your own keyboard to control a remote computer.

Files are transmitted in a series of bundles or packages. Once a package is sent and received, your computer and the Net system will compare it. If the two pieces aren't exactly the same, it will be transferred again and again until everyone agrees. An *error* message means that a problem has occurred and something is interfering with the transmission. There may be something wrong with the file or the telephone line or one of the computers making the transfer.

When you select a database from your university network menu, you may actually be Telnetting to the remote sight. These connections may be a little primitive, so read every screen carefully. Since you will want to save or print out at least some of the information you find, be sure you have not already bypassed the all-important instruction screen.

Understanding Screen Capture and Logging

Sometimes you discover information that you want to keep. If it's just a few paragraphs, you might save the information on an individual screen or dump it into a file in your computer. If you want to save a lot of information, dumping individual screens becomes cumbersome, but you can set your software program to log and save everything coming in. Until you turn off the logging command, everything that scrolls on your screen is copied into a file like recording on videotape. Experiment with your software program, but check after you're off-line to be sure the information was actually saved to a file.

If you are using a Web browser like *Mosaic* or *Netscape*, saving documents to your own computer is usually very easy and self-explanatory.

Understanding Terminal Emulation

Each time you select a university library or log onto another computer on the Internet, you are usually asked which type of terminal your computer emulates or mimics. *Emulation* has to do with the way a computer displays information on the screen and accepts commands. The response in most cases is *VT100* since almost all communications programs on the market support this standard.

Using Internet Tools

The Internet can provide the researcher with access to a multitude of data sources, and a number of tools exist to help you find what's out there. Though this chapter will not provide all the instructions you will need, it will help you get started. Each Internet site is different, and you will need help from someone in your library or computer center to become proficient at "surfing" the Net.

Exploring the World Wide Web

If you presently have Internet access, you may be familiar with the World Wide Web, which was developed at CERN, the European Laboratory for Particle Physics. A newer, more graphically sophisticated Net program, the Web uses something called *hypertext* to move you from one source to another. Instead of choosing an item on a menu, you use your mouse to click on a highlighted term or topic on a Web "page." If you could see what the program sees, this is what hypertext would look like:

<DT><A HREF="http://www.yahoo.com/Business/Business_Schools/"
>Business School pages (Yahoo)</A>

<DT><A HREF="http://www.cnnfn.com/markets/quotes.html">CNN
Financial Network Quotes</A>
<DD>Stock, Mutual Fund and Money Market Fund current quotes. Requires ticker symbol.

<DT><A HREF="http://edgar.stern.nyu.edu/edgar.html">EDGAR (New
York University)</A>
<DD>Corporation filings (10-K, 10-Q etc.)

<DT><A HREF="http://www.sec.gov/edgarhp.htm">EDGAR (U.S. Securities and Exchange Commission)</A>

<DD>Corporation filings

<DT><A HREF="http://www.financenet.gov/">FinanceNet</A>

<DD>Numerous links to Finance related sites

<DT><A HREF="http://www.finweb.com/">FINWeb</A>

<DD>Finance and Economics Web links

<DT><A HREF="http://www.lib.utexas.edu/Libs/PCL/Government.html">Government Information</A>

<DD>A Menu of Texas, U.S. and International Government information sources

As you can see (if you look closely), the address is a hidden part of the document. Clicking on a term takes you to the hidden address, where you can read more. Hypertext allows you to go in any direction that interests you.

Most Internet providers offer access to Web browsers, graphical interface programs like *Netscape* and *Mosaic* that let you search for interesting sites and set bookmarks so that you can go directly to a site without having to click your way through several dozen screens. Web browsers allow you to print out information or copy it to a file. However, your options will be more limited if you have only partial (dial-up) connectivity.

To get the most out of the Web, you will need a fairly fast Mac or PC with a mouse and good graphics capability. Your academic computer facility must also maintain an expensive dedicated phone line in order to carry all those large graphics files. If you don't have such a computer or if your academic computer center doesn't support a Web browser, you can still use the Web. Lynx is a text-based program developed just for this purpose. There are no fancy graphics, but you still have access to all the same invaluable information.

Search Engines. Sites like *Yahoo!*, *Alta Vista*, and *Web Crawler* provide access to software programs called search engines that create indexes of keywords in the electronic documents they discover. Most search engines provide a box into which you type words to describe your subject. None of these search tools works particularly well. The problem is that they find too much. You will discover that the words you type occur in hundreds of text files. The secret is usually to think of as many keywords as possible and hope that this will bring you closer to finding the specific information you need. It also helps to keep your keywords fairly narrow and focused, so they don't cast too wide a net.

Although students tend to use the Web more than other Internet facilities, you should not assume it is the only source of information. Since most of the documents that would be helpful to your research do not require graphics, they are often available only in older formats like Telnet, WAIS, or Gopher. Although some Web browsers can access Gopher documents, get into the habit of using all the tools you have available. You don't want to miss any good resources.

Interpreting Web Addresses. Web browsers use the Uniform Resource Locator, or URL, a Web site address that may be extremely long and complicated. Even the difference of a period or a slash can keep you from accessing a site. Once you have correctly stored an address in your Web browser, however, you will never have to type it in again, and the computer can remember the longest address without difficulty.

It is not difficult to guess the address of many sites. At least the beginning and ending of most addresses are pretty straightforward. Web addresses begin with the letters "http" often followed by followed by "://www."

http://www

This abbreviation lets the computer know that you're looking for a Web site.

Telnet addresses (discussed below) may or may not begin with the word *Telnet* depending on the software used on your campus. Gopher sites (discussed in the following section) usually begin with the word *Gopher* followed by the *Telnet* address (without the word *Telnet*).

The middle section of a Web address is an abbreviation for a site and is not difficult to decipher. "UMN," for example, is the University of Minnesota; "UNM," the University of New Mexico.

http://www.umn

http://www.unm

The end of the address indicates the country or the type of organization. In the United States, "edu" designates a college or university.

http://www.umn.edu

http://www.unm.edu

http://www.umich.edu

telnet://unm.edu

telnet://umich.edu

gopher://unm.edu

You will come across addresses that end in "org" for nonprofit organizations, "com" for companies or commercial organizations, and "gov" for government agencies. Sites outside the United States usually end in a country abbreviation. For example, British sites end in "uk." British universities end in "ac.uk" (omit "edu").

Complete addresses are often much longer and may include the name of the computer on which a program is loaded. However, by using just these basic elements, you can often get to a menu that gives you the opportunity to select a more specific destination.

Check with your computer center staff for instructions on using the software at your university. For example, on my campus, I would type "open umich.edu" to Telnet to the University of Michigan.

Using Electronic Mail

Most students are familiar with e-mail, and you may be using it to stay in touch with friends at other colleges or to let your family know how you're doing. E-mail is by far the most widely used tool on the Net.

Millions of people around the world have e-mail accounts. Like regular mail, users send messages to other people at unique addresses. Instead of being trucked from post office to post office, the message moves through several computer systems, each one closer to the recipient's address or home computer. E-mail can circulate not only between individuals but among the members of a group. It is also possible to subscribe to electronic magazines and newspapers.

Instead of taking several days or weeks to reach the other side of the world, an e-mail message can arrive in seconds or, to really remote places, in hours. You type your message when it's convenient for you, and the person receiving the message reads it and responds at his or her convenience. If you are nervous about your e-mail skills, you might begin by sending yourself a message. Soon you will have mail waiting for you, and you can practice other skills.

The message you receive may look very different from the one you sent. You will see a lot of indecipherable characters that make up the *header*, which is like a series of postmarks, since each system that routes your e-mail puts its "stamp" on it. Messages go through a surprising number of systems, so you will see messages with lengthy headers. If you do not at first see the actual message, just scroll down until the message appears. Some commercial services move the information in the header to the end of the message.

Even if you pay a fee for Internet access, e-mail is still far cheaper, quicker, and more convenient than using the post office. You can send a message to someone on the other side of the world as inexpensively and as quickly as to a friend across town.

E-mail is the only Internet tool available at some sites, but there's an excellent publication called *Accessing the Internet by Mail* that shows you how to use other Internet search tools like Gopher, Telnet, and Veronica with just e-mail.

Using Telnet

Telnet, one of the most basic Internet search programs, is used for logging onto other computers. By typing the address of a distant computer, you can "Telnet" to that location, search a library catalog, read a journal article, or use a periodicals index as if it were located on your own campus.

Telnet is an older, text-based program that may seem intimidating at first. However, since you are writing a paper, you are probably seeking databases containing large text files. Some databases are available on the Web, but since graphics take up precious storage space, other sites offer only Telnet access. Some library OPAC programs are also not on the Web

During break periods, you may find yourself away from your home campus and want to check your e-mail account. If you can obtain a guest account at a local university or public library, it is usually possible to Telnet back to your home campus and log into your e-mail computer.

How do you use the Telnet program? Some Internet providers have user-friendly software that allows you to choose "Telnet" from a menu and simply type the address you want in the box provided. Other not-so-friendly providers simply give you a blank screen and require that you type a command like *open* and the computer address. Be sure to ask for help if it seems confusing.

Since you are logging into someone else's computer, you may need a password. Not all computers are open to the public. The generic user name and/or password *guest* will, however, get you into many computer systems. If you are trying to connect to a distant library, the word *library* or *opac* may be your "open sesame." The Telnet addresses listed later in this chapter either do not need a password or show the password below the log-in user name.

Understanding Gopher

Until the Gopher program was developed, you could Telnet only to a location whose address you already knew. Gopher is a menu that lets you browse sources all over the world without having to look up their Internet addresses. You also use the same commands to navigate within any Gopher, whether it is located in Sweden or Bolivia. Gopherspace is a safe, secure environment for the novice net surfer. Gopher even warns you when you are about to leave Gopherspace and tells you how to get back if you meet with a crisis.

In addition, Gopher lets you search for information on a particular subject no matter where it's located or what format it happens to be in. You might think of the Net without Gopher as a library without a catalog. All the books, journals, and other materials would be there, but how could you find them? Gopher serves the same function as an OPAC or card catalog.

To get into a Gopher program, you will need to Telnet to your first destination. Thereafter, you need only choose the places you wish to visit.

Jughead and Veronica. Jughead and Veronica are both search tools that help you find information in Gopherspace. Jughead collects searchable menu information from individual Gopher servers. Veronica is somewhat more powerful and can search the actual files, not just the menus. Jughead and Veronica are menu choices on most Gophers, but if you don't see them, you can Telnet directly to them:

> **Jughead:** gopher://liberty.uc.wlu.edu
>
> **Veronica**: gopher://veronica.scs.unr.edu/11/veronica

Understanding Anonymous FTP

FTP (file transfer protocol) is a file transfer program designed for transferring files from one computer or server to another. It is called "anonymous" because you don't need to have an account on the computer where the files are stored. When asked for your user name, you simply type "anonymous." No password is needed.

FTP is sometimes a little more difficult than it looks because the files you request are moved to the computer with the full Internet connection. If you have a dial-up connection, your computer is connected to a computer that's connected to the Net, so FTP is a two-step process. First, you move the file to your college or bulletin board computer, then you move it a second time to your home computer. The first step will be lightning fast. The second may seem to take forever. For large file transfers, it may therefore be more convenient to use the on-campus computer center, with its full Internet connection.

Many computer systems allow you to copy and send lengthy documents to your e-mail address. Though this process is simpler than using FTP, the document may take a few hours to arrive.

Exploring WAIS

WAIS (Wide-Area Information Service) is possibly the best Net program for doing scholarly research, although we don't hear about it as much as some of the other tools. It acts as a subject index, allowing you to search through stored databases within a discipline. Like Gopher, WAIS locates information regardless of where it is actually stored.

Because it is not as popular (no soap operas or football scores), the future of WAIS is somewhat uncertain. However, programs like BUBL, being developed for the World Wide Web, will provide subject access similar to WAIS.

Investigating Discussion Lists

Sometimes called *Listservs* after the computer program that supports them, discussion lists are groups of people who use e-mail to discuss a wide variety—literally thousands—of subjects. There is likely to be a group discussing the subject of your research paper, its participants ranging from undergraduates to scholars in the field.

You can FTP information on these groups by sending a request to the following address:

> Anonymous FTP:
> Address: lilac.berkeley.edu
> Log in: Anonymous
> Choose: Netinfo

You can also send an e-mail request for the complete list of Listserv groups to:

> listserv@suvm.acs.syr.edu

Be forewarned: The list is huge!

It is also possible to search a list of discussion groups on the World Wide Web:

> http://www.nova.edu/inter-links/cgi

If you find a group you would like to join, send the list an e-mail message. Most list addresses begin with the word *Listserv* and then the symbol "@." You are not writing to a person but to a computer, so the message includes only the basic commands. Leave the subject line blank. In the body of the message, type the command "Subscribe," the name of the list, and your real name (not your user name). That's all. Don't add any other information that might confuse the computer.

Many discussion groups are not based in this country, so commands may be different. The British, for instance, use the term *Mailbase* instead of *Listserv*. However, the sign-up information above will work for most of the lists you encounter.

Discussion groups can be very helpful in finding information for your paper. Although members might become irritated if you try to avoid doing your own research, they are always happy to suggest sources and fruitful areas for your investigation.

Understanding Usenet Newsgroups

Usenet newsgroups are similar to the Listserv discussion groups described above. However, when you subscribe to a Listserv group, e-mail messages come directly to your mailbox. Newsgroups are a way to provide similar information but without sending individual messages to each subscriber.

Newsgroups are like a local bulletin board where everyone accessing the board reads the same message. Unlike e-mail, which is usually one person writing to one person, Usenet is more like many people writing to many other people.

Usenet is like an international meeting place where people from all over the world gather. You will find discussions of almost every subject that are similar to those on electronic bulletin boards, known as conferences, forums, or special-interest groups. There are now more than nine thousand of these newsgroups in several different languages. If you join in the conversation, you're judged solely on your own words.

Unlike Listservs, you can't personally sign up for a newsgroup. Your Internet provider does the choosing. Larger providers, naturally, have storage space for a larger number of groups than smaller providers. All, however, try to choose groups that will be popular and heavily used. If you discover a group that you would like to participate in, talk to the staff at your computer center. It is not difficult to add a new Usenet group.

Deja News Research Service is a good source of news about Usenet groups:

World Wide Web:
     http://www.dejanews.com

Getting Net Help

Although many guides to the Net can be downloaded from Net sites, it is helpful to have a real, honest-to-goodness book by your side the first few times you surf. New titles are published daily, but the following Internet guides have been around awhile and are in widespread use:

- *The Internet Yellow Pages*. Organized like the yellow pages of a telephone directory, this large volume lists the most popular sites, where you can find everything from agriculture to zoology. Addresses for fun sites are included as well.
- *The Whole Internet User's Guide and Catalog*. Written by Ed Krol, this book is an excellent introduction to everything you might want to know about the Net. Though sometimes technical, it's well written and easy to follow.

Once you're on-line, you will find many free guides to read, download to your PC using FTP, or have sent to your e-mail address. Here are a few:

- *Hitchhiker's Guide to the Internet* and *Zen and the Art of the Internet*. Both of these excellent guides are available from Yale University:

     Gopher:
          Address: yaleinfo.yale.edu
          Path: Browse YaleInfo
               About the Internet

- *Surfing the Internet*. Brief but excellent introduction to the Net:

     Anonymous FTP:
          Address: nysernet.org
          Path: /pub/resources/guides/surfing*

Gopher:
   Address: nysernet.org
   Path: Special Collections: Internet Help
      Surfing the Internet

- *Roadmap to the Internet.* A set of twenty-seven lessons by Patrick Crispen available by e-mail:

  listserv@ualvm.ua.edu

  Leave the subject line blank. In the body of the message, type only "get map package F=mail." These lessons are also available on the World Wide Web at:

  World Wide Web:
     http://www.brandonu.ca

- *InterNIC Info Guide.* A Web page that provides access to lots of helpful information:

  World Wide Web:
     http://www.internic.net/infoguide.html

- *Entering the World Wide Web: Guide to Cyberspace.* A good, detailed guide to the Web:

  Anonymous FTP:
     Address: ftp.eit.com
     Path: /pub/web.guide/guide.61

  World Wide Web:
     Address: http://www.eit.com/web/www.guide/

- *Let's Go Gopherin'.* A list of Gopher archives:

  Gopher:
     Address: ubvm.cc.buffalo.edu
     Path: /11/internet/info/gophern

- *World Wide Web FAQ.* Frequently asked questions about the Web:

  World Wide Web:
     Address: http://sunsite.unc.edu/boutell/faq/index-html

Locating Internet Sites and Addresses

Since the Internet is always under construction, new resources are appearing and disappearing constantly. Even though it is not difficult to find your own Internet sites, you might take a look at some of the following guides. They have the advantage of including only selected sites—those that have been found to be particularly valuable. The best guides to Internet sites include:

- *Yanoff List of Internet Sites.*

    World Wide Web:
      http://www.uwm.edu/mirror/inet.services.html

- *John December's List of Internet Tools.*

    World Wide Web:
      http://www.rpi.edu/internet/guides

- *Internet Resource Guides.* A group of excellent subject-oriented guides to Internet resources.

    Anonymous FTP:
      Address: una.hh.lib.umich.edu
      Path: /inetdirs/*

    Gopher:
      Address: una.hh.lib.umich.edu
      Path: Inetdirs

- *Clearinghouse of Subject Oriented Guides.* Bibliographies of net resources on any subject.

    World Wide Web:
      Address: http://www.lib.umich.edu/chhome/html

- *Gopher Jewels.* As the title implies, these are all useful Gopher sites. Choose "Other Gopher and Information Resources" from the menu.

    Gopher:
      Address: cwis.usc.edu

Locating Other E-Mail Users

Once you have an e-mail account, you naturally want to locate friends who are also on the Net. Many colleges and universities provide campus directories on their Gopher menus or as links to their World Wide Web home page. If this doesn't work and you know the domain name of a university (for instance, umich.edu), you can often guess at a friend's address. John Smith might be jsmith@umich.edu.

Commercial services maintain their own member directories, but these may be difficult to access if you are not a member. Some, however, maintain Web pages for nonmembers. Here are the domain names of some of the larger services:

America Online   aol.com

CompuServe   compuserve.com

Delphi   delphi.com

GEnie   genie.com

Prodigy   prodigy.com

You may be able to guess at the address of a friend on a commercial service by typing some version of their name plus the domain. For example, jsmith@aol.com or johns@aol.com. The larger services have so many members, however, that they may have dozens of John Smiths.

The "Finger" command is only available on some systems, but it can be helpful in locating addresses since it retrieves information about users registered on a host computer. More information about "Finger" can be obtained from the following:

FTP: FTP//csd.uwm.edu/pub/fingerinfo

and

WWW URL: http://sundae.triumf.ca/fingerinfo.html

New tools for finding Internet addresses are being developed that are more user-friendly than "Finger," so check with your computer center to see which ones are available on your system.

Locating Libraries on the Internet

Most university libraries now have an Internet address. Since their book catalogs are usually on-line, you can search the OPAC of a distant research library just as you would your own local book catalog. If you discover titles that would be useful in your paper, you can request them through interlibrary loan. Just remember that books can't be beamed to you as on *Star Trek*. They must be sent by tediously slow, library-rate mail, so you must allow plenty of time for delivery.

Libraries often maintain full-service Gophers and Web home pages that provide pointers to many useful databases. Some have virtual reference desks with dictionaries, encyclopedias, and other frequently used reference works.

E-Mailing Library Documents. Some sites, such as Ohiolink (the Ohio State Network) and Melvyl (the union library catalog of the University of California system), allow you to e-mail bibliographies and documents back to your e-mail address. The next time you are on-line and discover an interesting text file, see if the options at the bottom of the screen include "mail" or "e-mail." If you choose this option, you will be asked for the e-mail address to which the document should be sent. Insert your e-mail address. Then the next time you check your mail, an article or bibliography will be waiting for you. If you don't see these options on your screen, you might type the letter "m" and see what happens. Some systems do not seem anxious to advertise the service.

Sometimes you can use this service in place of Anonymous FTP. Many sites do not offer FTP, and it can be slow and tedious at others. If you must pay for your on-line time, substituting e-mail for FTP can reduce your cost considerably.

'Access Denied.' Occasionally, just when you have found a useful index or database, you will see the message "Access Denied" and be bounced back to the previous screen. Some publishers charge a subscription fee for their index or database and will permit only library users at that university to access it (naturally, if everyone could use the same program by connecting through the Internet, other libraries would not have to pay a subscription fee and the publisher would go out of business).

Your college or university library may make these same sources available on its public terminals. However, if you think that your library is not adequate for your needs, you might consider contacting a library with good resources and purchasing a library card. If you do so, be sure that your privileges include access to electronic sources.

Some Library Addresses. The following are a few of the many library resources you will find on the Net. Like other Internet sites, they come and go at remarkable speed. By the time you read this section, new resources will have appeared. In all probability, one or more of the sites that follow will have changed its address or limited public access. If, however, you can get into just one library's Gopher or Web site, you will find pointers to many others.

- **CARL.** Based in Colorado, CARL is a network of Colorado libraries. Services include "Uncover," a vast magazine- and journal-indexing and document-delivery service. Library members have access to a number of other databases as well.

  Telnet:
  Address: pac.carl.org

- **Eureka.** Using Eureka, you can search the resources of the libraries in the Research Libraries Group. These include extensive bibliographic files and a document-delivery service.

  Telnet:
  Address: eureka-info.stanford.edu

- **Launchpad.** A service maintained by the University of North Carolina, Launchpad provides access to libraries across the country. Also included at this site is a full-service Gopher with many useful databases.

  Telnet:
  Address: launchpad.unc.edu
  Log in: Launch

- **Library of Congress.** The Library of Congress maintains both an on-line book catalog called LOCIS and MARVEL, a full-service Gopher. When you access the Library of Congress home page on the World Wide Web, you can download thousands of images from the Library's American Memory project.

  Telnet:
  Address: locis.loc.gov

  World Wide Web:
  http://lcweb.loc.gov/homepage/1chp.html

- **Dartmouth College Library On-line System.** Not only an excellent library catalog but many useful databases.

  Telnet:
  Address: library.dartmouth.edu

- **Washington University Services.** Menu interface to university libraries around the world.

  Telnet:
  Address: library.wustl.edu

- **Billy Baron's Library List.** A list of hundreds of libraries and databases around the world.

Anonymous FTP:
    Address: ftp.udallas.edu
    Path: /pub/staff/billy/libguide/*

Gopher:
    Address: nysernet.org
    Choose: Special Collections:Libraries
        Billy Baron List

Or:
    Address: yaleinfo.yale.edu
    Port: 7000
    Choose: Libraries
        Paper List (Barrons' Accessing On-line Bib Dbases)

Locating Books on the Internet

Although the Internet is just a few years old, millions of pages of text have already been typed or scanned into machine-readable formats. Most of the books available on-line are classics, access to which is no longer restricted by copyright laws. Some modern authors, however, choose the Internet as a way of making their work more widely available.

Project Gutenberg. Not only do Netters believe that everyone can work together for the common good without authority figures enforcing rules, but they see the Internet as a democratic way of disseminating the world's scholarship. Project Gutenberg is a volunteer effort to make the world's great literature available on the Net in ASCII format. Most of the titles available are in the public domain (in other words, their copyrights have expired); this means that you can acquire an entire library for the cost of the floppy disks you use to download.

Here are some titles available from Project Gutenberg:

    Moby Dick
    Alice in Wonderland
    Hunting of the Snark
    Peter Pan
    The Federalist Papers
    Roget's Thesaurus
    Paradise Lost

The following addresses will get you to a site where you can download these titles:

Anonymous FTP:
    Address: info.umd.edu

Path: inforM/Educational_Resources/
ReadingRoom/Fiction/*

Or:
Address: mrcnext.cso.uiuc.edu
Path: /pub/etext/etext/*

Gopher:
Address: gopher.umd.edu

Telnet:
Address: info.umd.edu

Bibliographies of Literature. Reading lists and bibliographies on many literary topics are available from the following Carnegie Mellon site.

Gopher:
Address: english-server.hss.cmu.edu
Choose: Books
          Bibliographies

English Server. The Carnegie Mellon site listed above also maintains a collection of texts in English and other languages.

Anonymous FTP:
Address: english-server.hss.cmu.edu
Path: /English Server/*

Index to Literature Servers. You can find links here to most of the literature-related resources.

World Wide Web:
Address: http://www.cs.fsu.edu/projects/group4/litpage.html

Gopher:
Address: english-server.hss.cmu.edu

William Shakespeare. Here you can locate the full text of Shakespeare's plays, poems, and sonnets.

Anonymous FTP:
Address: ftp.funet.fi

World Wide Web:
Address: URL: http://the-tech.mit.edu/Shakespeare.html

Accessing Periodicals

Although practically everything that is happening on the Net is exciting, the advent of electronic journals and magazines deserves special attention. Editors and publishers are finding that they can send information to their subscribers faster and cheaper on the Internet than by distributing printed periodicals through the mail. A number of experiments are underway, some involving traditional printed publications that have added an electronic version and others involving titles that have been developed solely for Internet distribution.

It is difficult to know exactly what the future holds. New informal publications called 'zines are appearing almost daily, and you may enjoy discovering them. Many professional societies are considering major changes in the way they produce and disseminate their journals. The following list will help you find these new electronic periodicals.

The Electronic Newsstand. The following is an address for "one-stop shopping." Most of the magazines and journals on the Net can be found here.

> Gopher:
>> Address: gopher.enews.com
>>> Choose: Magazines, Periodicals and Journals

Journalism Periodicals Index. Produced by the Graduate School of Journalism at the University of Western Ontario.

> WAIS:
>> journalism.periodicals.src

Directory of Electronic Journals and Newsletters. Gives you the latest information about electronic journals available on the Net.

> E-mail:
>> Address: listserv @acadvm1.uottawa.ca
>> Command: GET EJOURNL1 DIRECTRY

On-line Newspapers. Includes USA TODAY and San Francisco Chronicle and Examiner.

> World Wide Web:
>> Address: URL: http://www.nando.net/epage/htdocs/
>> links/newspapers.html

Locating Government Information

In the last few years, the U.S. government has made large quantities of information available over the Internet. This access is possible because most government information is in the public domain, that is, free from copyright restrictions. Government databases on the Net cover the entire spectrum of information. Here are some widely known addresses:

Government Information Sources on the Internet. A list of government databases.

>   Anonymous FTP:
>   Address: ftp.nwnet.net
>   Path:/user-docs/government/gumprecht-guide.txt

>   Gopher:
>   Address: nysernet.org
>   Choose: Special Collections: New York State and Federal Info

> Or:

>   Address: gopher.oar.net
>   Choose: Services and Information Resources on the Internet

Supreme Court Rulings. Cases are available within minutes of their release. Read the "Help" files "info" and "readme.first" before searching for specific cases.

>   Anonymous FTP:
>   Address: ftp.cwru.edu
>   Path: /hermes/*

>   Gopher:
>   Address: info.umd.edu
>   Choose: Academic Resources by Topic
>   United States and World Politics, Culture...
>   United States
>   Supreme Court Documents

>   WAIS:
>   Database: supreme-court

>   World Wide Web:
>   Address: URL: http://www.law.cornell.edu/supct/

Dosfan (U.S. Department of State Foreign Policy Gopher). Foreign policy experts will answer your questions.

Gopher://dosfan.lib.uic.edu

Visiting Museums on the Internet

Many museums around the world have established Web sites at which you can tour exhibits almost as if you were visiting the museum in person. The Smithsonian and the Louvre are just two of the venerable institutions that have electronic counterparts on the Web. Use the following addresses to locate museum exhibits of special interest:

Museums, Exhibits, and Special Collections. A Web page that provides links to museums and collections around the world.

World Wide Web:
Address: http://galaxy.einet.net/gj/museums.html

Museums on the Web. Another Web resource for finding museums and archives including the Hall of Dinosaurs, the London Transport Museum, and the Moscow Kremlin On-line Excursion.

World Wide Web:
Address: URL: http://www.comlab.ox.ac.uk/
archive/other/museums.html

Locating Miscellaneous Sources

Here are some valuable sources that don't quite fit into any of our other categories.

The Writing Lab at Purdue University. Ask your questions about grammar and get help with research papers just by sending an e-mail message.

owl@sage.cc.purdue.edu

The Internet Encyclopedia. Still under construction but an excellent source of information.

http://www.cs.uk.edu/~/clifton/encyclopedia.html/

Anonymous FTP Site List. List of sites where you can FTP both documents and software.

> Anonymous FTP:
>> Address: ftp.shsu.edu
>> Path: /pub/ftp-list/sitelist

Clearinghouse for Networked Information Discovery. Links to any World Wide Web, Gopher, and Archie sites.

> World Wide Web:
>> Address: URL: http://www.lib.umich.edu/chhome.html

Putting It All Together: Let's Surf!

There's no better way to find out what's out there than to take the plunge. Actually, the proper term, as you already know if you have hacker friends, is *surf*. So, let's surf the Net!

Setting a Goal

When you surf, always have a purpose in mind. Otherwise you may go further and further afield, exploring obscure byways until you are totally lost. Let's assume you are looking for information on the subject of illegal immigration to the United States from Mexico. Although a different subject would bring up different sources, the techniques of searching would be essentially the same.

I am going to assume that you have managed to get connected and have mastered the basics of using your software. You will need to be able to save the information you find, so refresh your memory on logging and screen capture.

Browsing the Web

Because the World Wide Web is currently the most popular Internet program, we will spend most of our time there. Then we will try a few Gopher sites so that you can compare the two.

Although I will be using a *Netscape* Web browser, most graphical interface programs for the Web (including *Mosaic*) are quite similar. If you have access to a graphical Web browser, follow my search strategy on your own computer. Since the Web changes so rapidly, you will find different information, maybe even better information. However, you will still be able to follow along. If your Internet provider does not have a Web browser, find out if text-based *Lynx* is available. Though not as attractive, it provides access to the same information.

Netscape automatically takes me to its home page when I log in. I then click on the "Search" button at the top of the screen, which takes me to the *InfoSeek* search program (http://home.netscape.com/home/internet-search.html). It is as good a place to begin as any. I am asked to type several keywords into the box and press the "Enter" key. If you don't see the box, just scroll down until it appears.

Other search programs work the same way. It is best to try more than one since they do not all include the same sites. If you would like to try one now, type in the address at the top of your screen. (All browsers contain a box at the top where the site address automatically appears. Click on it and type in the address you want. Then press the "Enter" key.) Some of your choices are:

Yahoo:

http://www.yahoo.com

WebCrawler:

http://webcrawler.com

Alta Vista:

http://digital.com

Web Directory:

http://webdirectory.com

Entering Keywords

I am going to stay with the *InfoSeek* program and will enter my keywords, which I can do in any order I choose. I type "immigrants Mexican illegal border," which the computer interprets as "immigrants and Mexican and illegal and border." After I press the "Enter" key, my cursor changes to a working (hourglass) symbol, then returns to its normal arrow shape. It doesn't look as if anything has happened. To see the hits my search produced, I have to scroll down to the list. Whenever you think the program has failed to respond to a request, always scroll down past the bottom of the screen to see if the information has been hiding there all the time.

InfoSeek lists the sites it finds in order of relevance. That means the program found the words I typed most often in its first hit and least often in its last. This weighting is extremely important because my search pulled up several hundred sites, most of which were irrelevant to my search. Be sure that whatever search tool you are using weights its results in a similar way. You don't have the time to go through three hundred useless items.

Linking to a Web Site

When I scroll down to the list of hits, I see the title "Immigration and Texas" followed by a paragraph of descriptive information. The title is underlined and in color, which means that if I click on it, I will be taken to the site. When I point my mouse at the title, I see the address box at the bottom of the screen change. It has automatically typed the address for this site, in this case a long one:

http://www.fairus.org/issues/states/tx.html

If I click my mouse, I will be connected. I choose, however, to go on down the list.

As I progress further, I find another title, "Immigration Legislation Introduced in the 105th Congress." The address is similar to the one above:

http://www.fairus.org/legislat/legi.html

I am curious about this "fairus" site so I click on it. I discover that these are resources maintained by a group called the Federation for American Immigration Reform.

For this exercise, I chose the subject *immigration* because it is a controversial one. Many people have strong feelings on the subject and express their views on the Web. You will want to know whether information comes from government sources, from educational institutions, or from groups with a particular agenda. Such groups may be seeking to educate people about an issue or merely to spread biased propaganda.

Most of the books you find in the library have been selected because of their intellectual content and objectivity, but there is no selection process on the Net. Everyone is free to express their views as long as they are not advocating illegal actions. Always check the source of any information you discover.

This particular organization, the Federation for American Immigration Reform, makes it easier for us by providing links on its home page to more information about its work. This includes membership statistics, political philosophy, and organizational goals.

After reading what the organization has to say about itself, I may still want to check further. *The Encyclopedia of Associations,* a printed reference work in the library, lists nearly all organizations in the United States and includes an additional volume on international organizations. Remember, however, that even in this highly respected work, organizations provide the information about themselves. Their avowed purpose may be quite different from their actual intentions.

On their home page, I find a lot of interesting links to other Web resources, such as the Charlotte's Web Immigration Site, phone numbers for contacting members of Congress, and a history of U.S. immigration.

When I am ready to go back to the *InfoSeek* list, I click on the "Back" button at the top of my screen. Although I discover a number of interesting sites, I am not satisfied that I have found the best ones. I might, at this point, try another search tool or take a look at one of the lists of Internet resources, like the December or Yanoff lists (addresses given on page 114).

Fine-Tuning a Search

Although there are a number of techniques for fine-tuning a search, the resources available on library Gophers and Web pages have advantages over those at other sites. For example, they have been selected by librarians using criteria similar to those used in book selection, so when you are dealing with a controversial subject like immigration, you can expect a library site to provide reliable and objective information. Then you can spend less of your time evaluating the credibility of your sources. Even when using library resources, however, you should never suspend your critical judgment.

This time, I add the word *library* to my *InfoSeek* search. I discover that the library at the University of California at Berkeley (http://www.lib.berkeley.edu) has extensive resources on the subject, including the Chicano Studies Library. In fact, I discover a treasure trove of materials for my paper. Had I continued checking the hundred or so sites that my first InfoSeek search turned up, I may have eventually come upon them. However, search programs are not equipped to evaluate quality. They simply count the number of times the words you typed appear in a document.

One of my favorite library sites is the Internet Public Library (http://ipl.sils.umich.edu), an experimental project sponsored by the University of Michigan. The graphics make you feel as though you are in a real library rather than a virtual one. There is even a librarian on duty to whom you can direct your questions.

Dealing with Error Messages

Several times during my search, I was unable to see the document I had selected. Once, for example, a box appeared in the center of the screen with the words "Net Error." Another time I was told that the document did not exist. When such messages appear, back up and try another site. Tomorrow, or even an hour from now, that site may once more be available. For the time being, however, you will have to do without it. If you get frequent error messages, you may have a problem with your connection and need to exit completely out of the program. You may even have to restart your computer.

The Internet is changing so rapidly that it is almost impossible to keep up with new resources. By the time you read this chapter, some of the resources mentioned will no longer exist, while other, more sophisticated ones will have taken their place. Once you have acquired basic Internet skills, however, you will have little difficulty locating the new additions. One discovery leads to another.

Chapter 7

Reading, Evaluating, and Note Taking

As you discover sources of information, you will want first to read and understand the material and then to take notes on what you have read. It is at this point that many potentially good papers fall apart. Your finished paper can only be as good as the notes from which it is created.

Reading Critically

To find the answers you are seeking, you will need to read a lot of material gleaned from a variety of sources. You may already be a good reader, but a research paper demands somewhat different skills from those needed for reading fiction or for understanding a textbook.

Reading for Background Information

The more you know about a topic, the easier it is to understand and digest new information. As you begin your research paper, you may know little about your topic and therefore may find it difficult to plunge right into the professional literature of the field.

Before you delve deeply, find several nontechnical books and articles that contain basic information written in the language of the layperson. This material may not go into your paper, and you may not even take notes on it. Instead, read these sources quickly and casually without struggling to remember specific bits of information or relate it to your outline.

Popular books and magazine articles work better for this purpose than scholarly ones. Immerse yourself in the material and become familiar with its language. In a sense, you want to get on "speaking terms" with the topic. If you encounter points you don't understand, don't worry, and don't pore over the text trying to follow every word. You might think of this as getting the "plot" straight in your mind or exploring the way the topic of your paper fits into the larger discipline.

The sources you use in your paper should be primarily scholarly ones. However, works written for the layperson can form a base on which to arrange the building blocks of information from scholarly sources that are necessary to support your thesis. Try to work your way gradually toward scholarly sources. If you find yourself trying to take notes on information that makes little sense to you, go back to more basic books or articles.

Including information in your paper that you don't really understand is a sure way to ruin it. As you try to put the author's ideas into your own words, you are likely to misinterpret many of them. If you leave the information in the author's words, your paper will become a confusing mass of quotations. The only way to make your prose read smoothly and clearly is to know what you're writing about.

As you begin your research, don't be overly impressed by every book or article you discover. When we know little about a topic, we tend to assume that every author we read has the right answers. Because we know so little, we tend to believe everyone who sounds knowledgeable or impressive. Background reading will not only give you an overview of the topic but will alert you to areas of controversy and to at least some of the opinions of the authorities in the field. When you read a work that runs counter to these opinions, a figurative alarm will sound, triggering your critical faculties.

Reading Scholarly Works

When you read a chapter of a textbook, your object is to understand the information it presents. When you read material for a research paper, you must go a few steps further. For example, you may discover that authorities in the field differ and that some writers are more authoritative than others. One writer may have better credentials; another may have done a more careful study; still another may have relied entirely on secondary sources. You may even encounter misrepresentations of the truth or at least strong prejudice. As you discover arguments among researchers, you may find yourself believing one and doubting another. To present your information as fairly and accurately as possible, you must read source material critically, making decisions about the validity of the evidence the authors submit. Although you are not an expert, you can make informed judgments.

Books look impressive. We tend to think that any information we find in a book must be correct. Coming upon any published book in a library full of scholarly tomes lends an air of authority. Libraries try to select only the best works on a subject; however, many less reliable books also find their way to the shelves. How can you tell whether the information you find is reliable?

Evaluating Information Sources

Novice researchers are sometimes shocked to discover that all the books in the library are not necessarily accurate or authoritative. In the course of your investigations, you are bound to encounter a number of sources that are just plain bad. You will only be misled if you use them in your paper. More often, however, a book or article has merit but appears to contain at least some misinformation. Although you will want to make use of the valuable information it contains, you will need to exert your own critical judgment.

If you ask yourself why you are being asked to write a research paper, you may conclude that the experience will probably improve your writing skills and make you more knowledgeable about the topic you have chosen. However, simply reading and absorbing information without intellectually working your way through it does not really lead to understanding. If you approach your project in a critical spirit, questioning what you read and seeking out your own answers, you will be participating in an inner dialogue with the writer. On the other hand, if you are merely a sponge absorbing information, you will miss much of what is being expressed.

When you read critically, you look for assumptions, key concepts, and justifications. You seek supporting evidence for the author's assertions before accepting them. Instead of passively soaking up whatever comes along, you interpret and assess the material.

How, you may wonder, is this possible? After all, the authors you will be reading know far more about your topic than you do. Yet it is not difficult to master the very same critical skills used by scholars, experts, and other authorities. As you read, ask yourself the following questions:

- **Is the author accurate?** Although it is usually impossible to write a book or an article that is totally free from errors, mistakes, or distortion, a scholar is obligated to strive to be as accurate as possible. Yet both you as the author of the research paper and the authors of the sources you consult must occasionally go beyond that which is known and venture into areas that are less certain. Making mistakes is an essential part of learning, and it is better that both scholars and fledgling scholars make their own mistakes than parrot the thinking of authority figures. As you read a selection, ask yourself whether the author balances the quest for accuracy with the responsibility to stretch beyond established factual information.

- **Does much of the information presented seem vague or ambiguous?** As you read, ask yourself whether the author of a selection makes a consistent effort to be clear and precise in his or her language usage. Although we all occasionally write sentences that are open to more than one interpretation, the practice gets in the way of real scholarship. Since you cannot pin authors down, you cannot verify or check up on their work. The problem may be accidental or deliberate (if they are not sure what they actually mean) but little growth in understanding can occur if all members of the audience are not getting the same information from a passage.

- **Can you analyze or break down the ideas presented into their component parts?** This allows you to examine them in detail and, thus, better understand their essential nature. Often what looks to be reasonable at first glance cannot stand up to closer examination. Once you have looked deeply at an issue or situation, inconsistencies become obvious. We are exposed daily to interpretations, claims, judgments, and theories that may or may not be valid. The sources you use for your paper are no different. Acquiring the habit of analyzing your own ideas and those of others should eventually become second nature.

- **Is the author more concerned with seeking truth or with defending his or her own positions?** When you think of the word *argument*, you probably imagine an angry disagreement or fight. Yet the word has another meaning, and it is this meaning that is crucial to the success of your research paper. Researchers have a responsibility to give reasons to support their views without involving their egos in their reasoning. To argue in this sense is to use logically presented facts to support or refute a point.

If the authors of your sources appear to be involved in a personal struggle to win a point, you might well have reason to question their conclusions. Scholarship should be carried on in a spirit of cooperation and goodwill.

Each of us has a tendency to view everything in relation to ourselves or to confuse our own perception of how things are with reality. It is easy to assume that our own values and beliefs are correct or superior to those of others. This is called *egocentricity* and is a major obstacle in the search for truth. Indulging in self-centeredness results in injecting emotions and feelings such as anger, fear, and jealousy into our writing. Objectivity and reason will inevitably be sacrificed. We want to believe whatever serves our immediate interests and preserves our personal comfort. We try to minimize or overlook inconsistency because it is more comfortable and less stressful to do so. It is also easier to believe what those around us believe and to label those who disagree as "wrong" or "prejudiced." Becoming conscious of these tendencies in yourself and in the sources you consult is an important step in becoming a critical thinker.

- **Does the author make his or her assumptions clear?** An assumption might be defined as a statement that is accepted as true without proof. Once one is aware of one's own assumptions, it is possible to assess and correct them. Assumptions have acquired something of a bad reputation. "Don't assume," we are sometimes told. Yet we must constantly make assumptions. Assumptions are an integral part of all human thought. Otherwise we would keep going back to the beginning and starting all over. Instead of rejecting assumptions, we should be conscious of them, willing to examine and abandon them if they do not stand up to criticism

- **Is the author conscious of his or her own perspective?** As human beings, we always see the world through our own unique point of view. Every author you consult will have his or her own way of looking at things. This is not in itself a reason for criticism. Some distortion nearly always results when one approaches an idea from one frame of reference. Students need not abandon a specific point of view, but rather they should occasionally step aside and examine it. The authors you consult should also have some sense of their own limited horizons.

One should never accept the assumptions that underlie a point of view without question. Since none of us sees the world exactly as it is, writers who are not aware that they do, indeed, have a perspective are deceiving both themselves and their audiences.

In the same sense, all writers have a bias. They will tend to notice some things and not others. However, although this is perfectly natural, blindness or an irrational unwillingness to perceive the weaknesses of their own position is not acceptable.

Bias may also take the form of cultural assumptions or beliefs adopted as a result of growing up in a specific society. Most of us are at least somewhat guilty of accepting a point of view, values, or beliefs because those are the ideas we were reared with. Both you and the authors you consult should be aware of your cultural assumptions and be prepared to examine them critically.

- **Does the author's authority rest with his or her credentials or with the logic and reason of the evidence presented?** Although knowledge and expertise in a field are very necessary, real authority rests on reason and evidence. You cannot suspend your critical judgment simply because an author has the appropriate background to write on a subject. You have both the right and obligation to doubt the conclusions of experts, no matter how prestigious, if reason and evidence are not sufficiently evident in their work.

- **What conclusions does an author draw from the evidence presented?** The conclusion is the last step in a reasoning process; a judgment, decision, or belief formed after investigation. In your opinion, does the author have sufficient grounds or reasons for the conclusions reached? Are conclusions clearly distinguished from evidence? Is the pattern of reasoning that leads from evidence to conclusion evident?

- **Does the author seek to be as clear and easy to understand as possible?** Authors have an obligation to avoid being obscure or confusing their audiences. Without changing the essential nature of the information they are presenting, they should make their work as easy to understand as possible. Occasionally, it seems that an author tries to do just the opposite. Never assume that because passages are difficult to understand their authors must know what they're talking about. In your own writing, you must assume the same obligation. Never make your writing more obscure because you think it sounds impressive.

- **If an author makes judgments or evaluates ideas or evidence presented, is it quite clear what is being evaluated and why?** Does the author establish clear, logical criteria as the basis for the judgments and then apply them accurately and fairly? Is sufficient information available to make informed judgments?

- **Is the writer consistent in his or her ideas? In other words, is one idea consistent with what has already been thought, done, or expressed?** Although life is filled with inconsistencies and contradictions, logical and moral consistency are basic values for which all authors must strive. Similarly, writers sometimes contradict themselves or go against statements they have already made. Although, once again, life contains many contradictions, the work of writers who repeatedly contradict arguments that they have already made in order to support new arguments cannot be considered reliable.

- **Does the author distinguish hard data from the inferences and conclusions drawn from them?** Similarly, does the author make it clear that his or her conclusions are based on observation and experience, rather than on theory? It is a common human failing to distort facts or experiences to support a preconceived theory. You may be surprised at how often you encounter authors who are willing to alter objective findings before they will abandon a cherished theory or belief.

- **Has the author accepted the factual claims of others without fully investigating them?** These may be the author's own claims or those of the authorities he or she consulted. Likewise, you as the author of the research paper have an obligation to ask questions like "How do I know this is true?" The failure to distinguish fact from opinion is another common human failing. We all have a tendency to accept what are really opinions masquerading as facts if they are presented to us in an authoritative manner.

- **When the author presents two or more opposing points of view, does he or she develop each one fully, providing support and raising objections for each? Is one perspective exposed to more intense critical scrutiny than the other?** It is not acceptable to devote one's energy to demolishing or defeating the positions one disagrees with unless the same rigor is applied to the position one supports. In fact, there is a standard in logic called the Principle of Charity that requires that one present the most favorable interpretation of a position that one opposes.

- **Is the author's approach consistent with the subject matter under discussion?** Mathematical thinking, for instance is quite different from historical thinking. The nature of the subject matter should determine the kind of thinking the author displays.

Seeking Out the Opinions of Others

Your own critical skills will serve you well, but you should also get into the habit of finding out what others think about the sources you consult, as well as the qualifications of their authors. The library is the best place to obtain this kind of information.

Locating Book Reviews. A good place to begin is with book reviews. You are, in a sense, inviting someone else to apply these same critical skills. Book reviewers are usually chosen because they possess some degree of expertise on the subject. Reviews vary greatly in length and style. Ideally, a review will discuss the credentials of the author, the quality of the writing, the accuracy of the information, and the importance of the work to society at large or to the scholarly community.

Printed and computerized versions of *Book Review Digest*, *Magill Book Reviews*, and *Book Review Index* are the most commonly used sources of reviews. The on-line version of *Books in Print* also contains reviews, as does EBSCO's *Academic Abstracts*.

In order to find a book review, you will need to know when your book was first published; this information can usually be found on the back of the title page. Look for the copyright date (the date next to the copyright symbol: ©), not the date of the printing. Books are usually reviewed only when they are first published, although later editions are occasionally reviewed as well.

Bear in mind that book reviews do not always agree with one another and, once again, you will need to employ your own critical judgment to choose between conflicting views.

Checking Currency. Even if a book received a favorable review, the information it contains may be out of date. When you discuss your research project with your instructor, ask how recent your sources should be. Every discipline is a little different. Historical materials can often be quite old, while works in the sciences must be more recent. The more frequently new discoveries and other changes occur within a discipline, the more recent your material must be.

Older works of literary criticism, for example, may be just as authoritative as newer ones, depending on the author's qualifications and access to pertinent information. If you are writing about black holes or artificial intelligence, however, much of what was written five or ten years ago may no longer be accurate. Of course, it may be that the older work resulted in a scientific breakthrough, but it is difficult for the novice to tell the difference. If it was indeed a groundbreaking work, its findings will be incorporated into later books on the subject.

Checking an Author's Background. Another way of establishing the authority of a work is to look up the author's credentials. Nearly every discipline has some sort of biographical directory of authorities in the field. Examples are *American Men and Women of Science* and *American Scholars*. More general sources like *Who's Who in America* may also be useful. Although it provides little information besides names and addresses, the *National Faculty Directory* does list the institutional affiliation of faculty members. If your author is on the faculty of a well-known university, you have at least indirect evidence of his or her credentials.

Precisely what sort of information are you looking for? It will vary a great deal depending on the subject matter. If, for example, you are reading a book on early childhood education, you would look for evidence that the author has both practical experience and educational credentials that would qualify him or her as an authority. Possibly the author taught in such a program in the public schools and wrote a doctoral dissertation on state funding of early childhood programs. Since these credentials are directly relevant to your topic, this information would be good evidence that the author has an appropriate background for writing in the field.

Writing Out of One's Field. If your topic concerns high school, however, you might infer that this is not the author's specialty. Remember that a writer who is an expert in one field must write as a layperson when moving into another area. Credentials in a specialty may be impressive, but they do not make a writer more believable in another field.

If you watch television, you have probably seen public personalities giving testimonials in support of commercial products. The sponsor or advertising agency assumes that the public will be more likely to believe something if an authority fig-ure says it is true. But why should a movie star know anything about refrigerators or a sports figure about automobiles? The answer is obvious in these situations, but this is not always the case with scholarly research. The lines separating academic disciplines are getting fuzzy in this era of interdisciplinary studies, so you will need to be cautious in accepting an author's authority.

Checking on the Publisher's Reputation. If you are unable to locate reviews or if your author does not appear in standard biographical sources, you may start to wonder about the credibility of the work. Your next step would be to investi-gate the publisher. Publishers vary greatly in the types of books they publish and the level of scholarship they require. If you discover that the publisher of the book in question has issued other highly regarded works in the same field, you have some assurance of quality. A publisher that has established a reputation in a spe-cific subject area will be anxious to maintain high standards.

University press books are nearly all written by scholars and can generally be relied upon for accurate information. Many commercial publishers also publish works of high quality. At the other end of the continuum are subsidy or vanity publishers that require authors to help pay for the production and publication of their books. Authors are usually unwilling to pay to have their books published unless they have been turned down by commercial or academic presses. Subsidy press books are frequently sent free to libraries and are sometimes added to collec-tions. Most directories of publishers, such as *Publishers Trade List Annual,* exclude vanity presses or place them in a separate section.

If the publisher is neither a university press, a well-known commercial press, nor a vanity press, check some of their other titles using your library's OPAC. Do these titles seem solid and reliable, or do they include bizarre subjects like alien kidnappings?

Checking Journal Articles. Scholarly journal articles usually list the academic qualifications of their authors, and many journals are published by universities. A distinction is made between refereed and nonrefereed journals. Articles in refer-eed journals are reviewed and selected by a panel of experts. To ensure the integri-ty of the process, they are not told the name of the author and the author does not know who is doing the refereeing. Articles in nonrefereed journals are usually selected by the editor or by an editorial board. Although there are many fine jour-nals that are not refereed, overall quality tends to be higher in those which are ref-ereed. Consult *Ulrich's Guide to Periodicals* for a list of refereed journals.

Increasingly, journals are being made available over the Internet. These elec-tronic journals may eventually replace many of the current printed journals. One of the problems with electronic journal publishing is the difficulty in establishing authority. They are so new that they have not established a reputation and their editorial policies are not generally known. Many electronic journals, however, are refereed, and you can establish the credentials of the authors just as you would in the case of a printed article.

Checking Bibliographic Information. An author's strict adherence to bibliographic rules allows a reader to look into controversial findings firsthand. As you write your paper, you will be citing the sources of the information you present. Published writers are expected to do the same. When authors present information that is not simply a statement of fact, they must tell the reader where they found it. Check your sources to see whether documentation is complete and whether potentially controversial information is clearly referenced. Less than responsible authors sometimes appear to be documenting their findings, yet controversial assertions are mysteriously lacking references.

Popular works are more difficult to check, which is why scholarly sources are preferable for research purposes. Although popular works do not usually contain notes or bibliographies, the author must nevertheless provide enough information to allow another investigator to find the source of key statements. For example, if quoting an authority, writers should mention the name and at least some qualifications. The phrase *Authorities say* should be a red flag if the writer does not go on to tell the reader who the authorities are and why they should be believed.

As you take notes, remember that your own readers will want to know this information as well. Include the credentials of the authorities you quote whenever possible.

Taking Notes

Since little can go into your paper unless you have first found the information and recorded it in some way, your notes are vitally important. You will need to decide what to include, how to record this information, and where to store your notes.

Deciding What to Include in Your Notes

Consider this scene from an old Sherlock Holmes movie: Watson, notebook in hand, is reciting the evidence that Holmes has uncovered. Soon, Sherlock will discover one more crucial bit of evidence, and the case will be solved. In much the same way, you are looking for evidence to support a particular thesis. But what kind of evidence? You will need facts and data, of course, but you will also need to record the hypotheses, theories, and conclusions of experts who assist you with your investigation.

The easiest way to decide what to include in your notes is to look at your outline. You will need enough notes to support each of your headings fully, although you may want to stress some points more than others. For example, you may give more attention to a section that your research has revealed to be central. However, in general, you will want to collect about the same quantity of notes to support each heading.

How do you know, like Watson and Holmes, when you have enough evidence to "solve your case"—that is, to support your thesis? Every researcher has a problem deciding how much information to collect and when to stop. A good paper demands that you begin with more information than you will actually use. Some of the information you collect early in your search will no longer seem relevant or worth including when you start writing, and you may doubt the authority of an author after reading more about your topic. At any rate, you will want to have enough notes so that you have the freedom to choose.

On the other hand, your time is limited. If you continue reading and collecting notes on one aspect of your topic after you have found ample information, you are taking time away from other sections. Your paper may become unbalanced, with too much emphasis on one part and inadequate support for the rest. Figuratively step away from your paper every once in a while. Look at it objectively, as if you were the reader rather than the author. Is the paper getting lumpy or lopsided? Are you moving ahead as you planned, or have you gotten side-tracked by irrelevant material?

Recording Information Accurately

Just as important as deciding what to include in your notes is knowing how to record information accurately and efficiently. Since you will be writing many notes, you will want to record information quickly and concisely. Don't worry about style or grammar at this point (unless you are copying a quotation). Clarity is what is important. When you write your rough draft, you will not want to pore over your notes wondering what on earth you meant.

If you are not careful, what may seem perfectly understandable to you as you write the note may sound like gibberish later. Your memory of the book or article will grow faint, so the note must be self-explanatory. As a general rule, be precise but provide more detailed information than you think you will need. Spending a little more time on note taking will save time later, since you will not need go back to the original source to decipher the note.

How often have you diligently read a chapter in your textbook, even used your highlighter generously, yet remembered little of what you read? If your attention isn't focused on the facts and ideas being discussed, then your time is wasted. Don't take notes until you have critically read and thought about the material. You will need to analyze and synthesize what you are reading before it becomes your own.

Summarizing, Paraphrasing, and Quoting. Depending on the type of information you are recording, you might choose any one of three different kinds of notes: summary, paraphrase, or direct quotation.

A summary is a brief overview of what you have read, including all the facts you consider important. Understanding the material before you summarize it will result in clearer, more useful notes and prevent inadvertent plagiarism.

Summary notes are useful in a variety of situations. For example, you may wish to summarize the plot of a literary work. Your own ideas should be recorded just as faithfully as information gleaned from others. Just be careful to make clear which is which.

To *paraphrase* is to restate the words of another author. While a summary condenses a section of text into a smaller space, the paraphrase may not differ significantly in length from the original. Although it is desirable and even necessary to paraphrase some material, it is also dangerous. Suppose a passage contains a useful kernel of information. How do you reword it in such a way that the words are entirely your own, not the author's? When an author's words are in front of you, you may find it difficult to think of others that will not distort the meaning of the passage.

Don't read a sentence or two in the source and then write. Read at least a few paragraphs to distance yourself from the precise wording of the author. It is inevitable that you will use some of the author's phrases, but put quotation marks around even three- or four-word clusters to alert yourself to the danger.

Direct quotations reproduce precisely the words of an author. Students often find quotations easier than using their own words, especially since quoting frees them from the worry of accidental plagiarism or misinterpreting the author. If you have downloaded articles into your computer, it is especially easy to cut and paste sections of text. All you need add are the quotation marks and the source of the quote.

Though you may be sorely tempted, don't rely heavily on quotations. Your readers' attention will flag if they must constantly accustom themselves to a different writing style. Most quotations do not really "fit" and may stick out like a sore thumb.

Quote only the quotable. In order to justify inserting a quotation and trying your reader's patience, a quoted author must have said something memorable, something so unique that the way the idea is expressed is as important as the idea itself. When you choose to quote an author, follow these guidelines:

- Copy the author's words exactly, even the errors.
- Indicate clearly who is being quoted. In an indirect quotation, the source is not the author but someone being quoted by the author.
- Place quotation marks around the entire quotation.

Avoiding Plagiarism.
The word *plagiarism* comes from the Latin word *plagiarius*, meaning "kidnapper." It is defined as using the ideas or writings of another person and representing them as one's own.

You may be aware of widely publicized lawsuits in the musical recording industry charging that the words or music of a song were stolen from the rightful owner. Each of us has a right to our own work. In the case of scholarly writing, we are talking about the theft of someone else's ideas. Stealing someone's research or ideas is just as morally wrong as breaking into a home and stealing someone's belongings. Within academic institutions, plagiarism is seen as one of the worst offenses a student can commit and can carry a penalty as severe as expulsion.

You can, of course, borrow other people's thoughts, but great care must be taken to acknowledge the source. This is one reason documentation plays such an important role in scholarly writing,

Remember, taking a passage and adding or deleting a few words does not make the passage your own. You're still plagiarizing if you don't rewrite it completely in your own words. If you are in doubt as to whether you are stepping over the line, here are some guidelines to help you decide:

- Even though you are writing about the ideas of another, use only your own words.
- Be certain the structure of your sentences is entirely different from the original work. Keeping sentence structure while substituting synonyms for the original words is still plagiarism.
- When paraphrasing text, try not to use any of the words in the original unless they're necessary technical terms.
- If you must use some of the words from the original source, put quotation marks around them even if you're using no more than a phrase.
- Acknowledge the ideas, not just the words, of other writers. If you are stating an idea that is not commonly accepted in a field, the author of the idea should be identified.

Here are some examples of unacceptable and acceptable paraphrasing:

■ Original:
"Washington and almost all military leaders of the war, and many civilians as well, had long felt that the Confederation could never become a respectable government without the power to tax."

■ Paraphrasing that is too close to the original:
Washington and most of the leaders of the war had felt that the Confederation couldn't become respectable without the power to tax.

■ Acceptable paraphrasing:
The power to tax was thought by Washington and many others to be essential to a respectable government.

When writing on a computer, plagiarism is even more of a temptation than with print-based sources because it's so easy to copy and paste someone else's text into your own paper. In fact, many novice writers plagiarize accidentally. Because they cut and paste files carelessly, they lose track of the source of the information. Therefore, be careful in your note taking to distinguish your words and ideas from those of your sources. Otherwise, over time, you're likely to forget which is which, thereby creating a golden opportunity for inadvertent plagiarism.

Storing Your Notes

If you consulted a group of writers, you might find as many ways of storing notes as there were writers. They each have a system that works for them, and they most likely put a great deal of care and organization into the process. There is, however, one common element in their note taking. They probably all take notes that can be separated and rearranged later, either on index cards or on a computer.

Handwritten Note Cards. Handwritten index cards have the advantage of being small and portable and thus easily shuffled into any arrangement you later decide on. If you decide to take your notes on cards, here are some suggestions:

- Use either 4" x 6" or 3" x 5" index cards, depending on how much information you usually include on a card.
- Take notes in pen, not pencil. You may find yourself shuffling your notes like a deck of playing cards. Pencil is easily smudged.
- Write only one item of information on each card.
- Write information relating to only one of your outline headings on each card. If the same information is pertinent to two headings, make a duplicate card.
- Write the source of the information at the top (preferably right-hand corner) of the card. To save time, create an abbreviation for each source. Full information is contained in your bibliography card or record. Note: some writers number bibliography cards and then write the number on the note card. However, this method causes problems if you lose your numbering key or don't have your bibliography cards with you.
- Never write notes from different sources on the same card.
- Write the page number at the top of the card.
- If the note covers information on more than one page, use a slash (/) in the text of the note to indicate the page change.
- Write the heading of your outline where this information is appropriate.
- If note is a quotation, write "QUOTE" at the top of the card. Copy the exact wording from the source complete with the same punctuation, spelling, and capitalization.

- Use only the front side of the card since you can easily overlook information on the back. If you must use the back, write "OVER" to alert yourself to the additional material.
- If one card is insufficient for the note, staple two together.

Treaty of Versailles   Bailey 2

(Quote)   p. 585

"The pact negotiated in Paris but signed at Versailles proved to be one of the most abused and least perused treaties in history."

Computerized Note Card Programs. Many professional writers are finding that the computer can make note taking easier and more efficient, and most newer computers come equipped with a note card program. These programs are user-friendly and allow you to enter information just as you would with real cards. The only problem is that computers are not as portable as note cards. Unless you have a laptop or notebook computer, you will need to type your notes at home or in your campus computer lab.

Include the same information in the computer record that you would if you were writing on an index card, indicating a page change with a slash. The big advantage computer records have over their cardboard cousins is their ability to search every word on every card. We often find ourselves shuffling through our cards for what seems like hours looking for some particular bit of information. The search feature of a software program allows you to locate the information in an instant.

Another useful feature of an electronic note card program is that you need not retype quotations. Depending on the program, a quotation can usually be transferred right into your rough draft. Thus, every word and punctuation mark will be exactly as you typed it the first time. The opportunity for error all but disappears.

Using Other Computer Databases. Just as a wide variety of database programs are useful for maintaining bibliographic information, almost any database can be used for taking notes. *Microsoft Access* or any shareware database would probably work fine as long as you have complete control over the length of the fields you create. You will need to have available several very short fields for the heading, source abbreviation, page numbers, and so on, as well as one very long field for the actual note. Give yourself room for at least 600 characters or about 100 words for this field. If you have already taken some notes, count the number of letters and spaces in a few of them to get an idea of your own note-taking style.

A useful feature in most databases is the macro. Once you create a macro, following the instructions in the program, you can use a single keystroke to type frequently repeated words and phrases, such as an author's name or the title of a book or article.

Using Your Outline. Still other writers store their notes right in their outline. Once again, this means you have to take your notes where you have access to a computer. However, typing notes into your outline lets you structure your paper as you go along, deciding not only which topic the note fits into but reviewing frequently the information you have already stored. Include all the information you would write on a notecard and don't let your notes become larger than note card size. This will make it easy to move them around when you're ready to rearrange them.

You will need two copies of your outline: one in which to keep quotations and one for notes in your own words. Without the two files, it is difficult to keep track of which is which. Since you can actually use any information you type into a computer file without retyping, you must be even more careful that the notes in your own words are absolutely free from any taint of plagiarism.

As you move small chunks of files to appropriate sections, you may forget what you have written in your own words and what you have copied. A separate quotation outline is even more important when working with computer files because the distinction between your own words and someone else's can easily become confused. Here's a technique for keeping it all straight:

- Read the article through.
- Summarize any useful information in your own words. Type right into the article file so that you are able to verify facts easily and spell names correctly.
- Under each note or quote, type a title abbreviation and page number.
- Identify any quotes you may need for your paper and move them to the appropriate heading in your quotation/outline file.
- Move the information in your summary to your notes/outline file.

Concluding Your Research

Though it may sound like an odd question, students often wonder when to stop. When is it time to move on to the actual writing of the paper? Possibly the best way to answer the question is to look at the following checklist:

- Does your research really support your thesis? In other words, will the information you have gathered, together with your interpretations and conclusions, establish conclusively that your thesis is correct?

- Arrange your notes according to the headings of your outline. Do your notes support and develop each of the points you planned to make? Look for holes or missing information.

- Is each note legible? Does each include the source of the information and the page numbers on which it is to be found?

- Did your research uncover other points that should be addressed?

If the questions above did not send you running back to the library, then you are ready to begin your rough draft.

Chapter 8

Writing the Rough Draft

Some students dread the moment when it is time to begin the actual writing of a paper. Many writers, not just students, tend to put off writing, sharpening far too many pencils or engaging in other delaying tactics, such as loading a computer game instead of the word-processing program. Somehow, it seems easier to collect other people's words and ideas than to create your own. You may try to convince yourself that you are not ready to write even though you know that your investigation fully supports your thesis. If you have enough notes to do justice to each topic in your outline, it is time to take the plunge and begin your rough draft. If you discover that a section is a little weak, there is no reason why you can't go back later to do a little more research.

Do be sure, however, that you have explored enough sources and taken enough notes to be fairly certain of the direction you will be taking. Students occasionally begin a rough draft with insufficient information and run out long before the end. Since they did not anticipate having to find and add new information, the first part of the paper often does not connect with the last part. The newly discovered material may fail to support the thesis, or, more often, it redirects the paper, giving your readers a jolt of discontinuity.

Enjoying Your Freedom to Make Changes

A good research paper is actually the result or culmination of many rough drafts. Each draft brings something new to the paper, adding, clarifying, enriching, and distilling. When you use a word processor, drafts are not distinct. They melt into one another. Your paper begins as a rough, incomplete text, and then word by word, phrase by phrase, it evolves into a finished work. Many writers believe that the word processor allows them to produce better work because they feel freer to let their thoughts flow. They know that whatever they write is easily revised.

Writers differ in their work habits, and there is no one right technique. Some write rapidly and produce a very rough draft. The first time around, they try to write as they think, without worrying about grammar, syntax, or spelling. Later they go back and transform their writing into good prose, but while drafting they are interested only in letting their ideas flow. Others write more slowly, thinking not only about their sources and ideas as they write but considering word choices and syntax. Their first draft is usually more finished and requires less revision.

Writing from Beginning to End

Whichever style suits you, stay focused on your outline and try to work your way from beginning to end. Then you can see whether you have actually achieved what you intended and whether you have covered all the points of your argument. Although the computer allows you to skip around, including information as it comes to mind, it is best to keep such digressions to a minimum in the beginning. Informing your readers and convincing them of the truth of your argument require an organized, systematic approach to your topic that can be lost unless you move logically from one point to the next.

Leave plenty of time at the end to revise your work, gather additional information, or rethink a section that doesn't seem to gel. It is surprising how different your paper looks to you after you have had a chance to get away from it for a few days.

Developing Your Paper: Some General Considerations

If you are like most students, you probably have too much information on some topics and too little on others. Even though you were careful to support each of the headings in your outline, you will still have some information, especially notes collected early in your search, that does not really support the development of your thesis. In fact, you probably have some fascinating information that doesn't seem to fit in anywhere.

Although it may be painful, look critically at the notes you have taken. Set aside any that do not directly support your thesis or that seem to take off in a direction you later abandoned. Your argument should move in a clear, logical direction. Eliminate those notes that might weaken your argument and divert your reader's attention with peripheral issues.

A little showing off is perfectly understandable. All writers like to impress their audiences. You would like your instructor to see what a great deal of work you have done, so you might be tempted to include unnecessary material. Including irrelevant or repetitive material, however, weakens a paper. Include only the ideas and information that will help you do what you set out to do.

Putting It All Together

Once you have decided which notes to keep and which to leave out, read over the ones you have kept. Look for new connections between the many bits of information you have collected. Interrelationships among ideas will occur to you, as will new patterns of organization. A research paper should flow seamlessly, without abrupt transitions after each separate thought. If you have not made an outline, be sure you have at least brought related material together under general headings and then under subheadings.

Building Confidence

Once your notes are in order, you are ready to begin. If you are one of those students mentioned above who are reluctant to get started, you may be afraid that what you write will seem foolish or stupid or ignorant. You might be surprised to know that nearly everyone goes through the same self-doubt. Even famous writers find it difficult to put those first words on paper or to type them into their word processor.

Just knowing that this is a first draft and that nothing you write is final may be enough to overcome your hesitation. If you still find it difficult to begin, you may want to try some of the techniques that others have found successful. For example, freewriting can allow words to flow when they seem to be caught in a logjam. Make yourself write about your topic for ten or fifteen minutes or until you are a little tired. Some of what you write will probably be useful in your paper, and, even more important, you will find yourself more relaxed and able to settle down to the task.

If you have been using a journal to record the thoughts that occurred to you as you did your research, you might use it as the basis of your freewriting. Go back to it, look at what you have already written, and write whatever comes into your head about your topic. This exercise will at least get words flowing, and you may well find that some of what you write can be incorporated into the actual paper. Just use sheets of scrap paper, or, if you are comfortable with the computer, type your thoughts directly into your word processor.

Developing Your Writing Skills

Good writing is both an art and a craft. Your main objective is to communicate clearly with your audience, and you will want to express your ideas as smoothly and precisely as possible. It is not enough to have successfully investigated the problem. Now the results of your investigation must be communicated in such a way that your readers can follow the progress of your thoughts. Through your prose, you lead your readers from point to point, making sure they understand each one before you go on to the next.

Remaining Objective

As a researcher, you have an obligation to your reader to present your information objectively and without personal bias. All of us come to a research paper with a lot of preconceived ideas. Unless, however, they are directly relevant to your paper and your research has supported them, they should be excluded. Since your reader is depending on you, be careful that you don't leave impressions or make inferences that could mislead. Avoid unsubstantiated generalizations. Stay away from irrelevant information having to do with age, economic class, sexual orientation, ethnicity, religion, race, or sex.

Following Established Rules

Since your task is not only to find the right words and phrases to express your thoughts but also to communicate them effectively to your reader, you will need to use commonly accepted conventions to avoid confusion. Correct grammar, punctuation, and spelling will all assist you in clarifying your meaning.

Punctuation marks, for instance, contribute to clear communication by showing the relationships between ideas. The reader cannot hear your voice, so punctuation must communicate the information that is lost. It tells the reader where to pause and where to place emphasis. Overusing one type of punctuation is like speaking in a monotone.

Being Consistent with Verb Tense

Although good writing is absolutely necessary to communicate effectively with your readers, the kind of prose used in a research paper is very different from creative writing. Some of the devices you may have learned when writing a short story, for instance, are out of place in a research paper. Unexpected shifts of tense or person, for example, might confuse your readers.

Unnecessary changes in the tense of the verb cause abruptness. Your reader gets a sudden jolt. The present and past tenses are normally used in a research paper. If you need to depart from them for any reason, do so infrequently and come back as quickly as possible. The results of your investigation should be reported in the past tense; your conclusions in the present.

Using the Active Voice

The active voice is the clearest, most direct way of phrasing a sentence. With the active voice, as you will remember from past grammar lessons, the action passes from a doer to a receiver: *Mary threw the ball*. Rarely in normal conversation would you say, *The ball was thrown by Mary*. This passive construction is as uncomfortable in written communication as it is in conversation.

Writers, however, use the passive voice far too often. Because it sounds more formal and less personal, they sometimes choose it as a way of giving a sense of objectivity to their work. Some writers seem to think that such roundabout sentence construction sounds more impressive. Occasionally, the sense of a sentence may be more clearly phrased in the passive voice, but keep these instances to a minimum.

Writing in the First Person

One reason authors used to rely so heavily on the passive voice was that they had to find devious ways around the use of the first-person pronoun *I*. Because formal, scholarly writing should be objective and unbiased, writers in the past considered it improper to inject themselves into their work. They found all sorts of ways to avoid the use of *I* and *me*. Instead of writing *I think* they might substitute *It is thought that*. Another strategy for avoiding the use of *I* was to refer to oneself as *one* or *the author*, as in *the author thinks* or *one thinks*.

This circuitous language makes a writer's prose more difficult to grasp and increases the likelihood of misunderstandings. In general, a research paper is written in the third person, since objectivity is a necessary characteristic of scholarly writing. However, avoiding first-person pronouns does not automatically make your paper more objective. Be careful in referring to yourself as *the writer* or *the experimenter*. Your reader may think you are referring to someone else.

Although the use of the first person has become more widely accepted in scholarly writing, a number of journals still require the third person. Your instructor may think it best for students to be aware of this circumstance and play it safe. If you are in any doubt as to your instructor's preference, it's always best to ask.

Some writers have made their peace with the use of the first person but still feel uncomfortable using the pronoun *I*. Instead, they use *we* in the hope that *we* will carry more clout and acceptance than *I*. If you are referring to yourself and your audience or are working with a joint author, as is common with scientific papers, *we* is appropriate. If, however, you are referring to yourself alone and you have not recently been cloned, use the pronoun *I*.

We is also a poor choice if you really mean experts or researchers, as in the sentence *We classify spiders differently from insects. You* have not done the classifying. Neither has your reader. What you really mean is that biologists have classified spiders. If you are including yourself in a group such as Americans or music lovers, make it clear to whom the *we* refers.

Avoiding Sexist Language and Stereotypes

Until recently, writers used the pronouns *he, his,* and *him* to refer to both men and women: *The student rode his bicycle; The professor entered his classroom.* Feminist scholars, however, made us realize that women were excluded from a great many spheres of endeavor. *He,* we came to understand, really meant *he,* not *he or she,* so writers looked for more inclusive language.

It is no longer acceptable to use a masculine pronoun whenever you don't know the sex of its antecedent. However, our male-dominated language has been evolving over thousands of years and making such a radical change is difficult. The problem does not exist with the plural pronouns *they* and *them,* so in conversation many insert the plural where a singular pronoun is called for (for example, *Each student must turn in their paper by Friday*). Although this has become common in conversation, it is only gradually becoming acceptable in academic writing. Some grammarians still disagree with this solution.

Another solution is to make the antecedent of the pronoun plural. In other words, if your sentence begins *The student checked out his books,* it can be changed to *Students checked out their books* without changing the meaning of the sentence. Some writers transpose a sentence into the passive voice to avoid the problem. Instead of *He threw the ball,* they write *The ball was thrown.* Although grammatically correct, it is roundabout and can lead to confusion.

You may have noticed that this book usually makes the antecedent of the pronoun plural or uses *he or she.* Writing *he or she* each time the situation arises is a frequently chosen solution, but repeated use makes your sentences choppy and awkward. You will also see the form *s/he* used occasionally, but this too produces choppy prose. Since *s/he* is not really a word, the reader's eye must stop and figure it out before continuing.

Another solution is to use roughly the same number of masculine and feminine pronouns in your paper. Just be careful when you are writing about one individual that you are consistent in your use of pronouns. The same student cannot be masculine in one sentence and feminine in the next.

You should also be careful not to inadvertently introduce stereotypes into your paper by designating persons of higher status (doctors or judges for instance) as masculine. Avoid gender-designating nouns like *waitress, mailman, sculptress,* and *chairman.*

Other stereotypes to avoid are those that might be seen as unfair or demeaning to a specific group of people. Look especially at any mention of a minority group such as African Americans, Asians, Hispanics, or Native Americans. Be careful not to single them out in a way that might be considered derogatory.

Quoting Only the Quotable

Imagine your reader groaning every time you insert a quotation into your paper. Think of your own response when you come upon a quotation in a book or article. Quotations often interrupt the flow of a text. You must quickly accustom yourself to the style of another author, and your interest and comprehension suffer as a result.

If you lack confidence in your own writing style, you may think that your readers will prefer the professional-sounding words of others to your own words. In reality, your words are chosen specifically for this paper and are intended to move the reader in one direction. The authors of those quotations had entirely different reasons for their choice of words and, as a result, they may divert your reader's attention. As long as you write clearly in grammatically correct sentences, your reader will much prefer your own possibly less expert style.

A direct quotation is appropriate only when the precise way a writer or speaker has phrased an idea is important. It is a big temptation to copy whole paragraphs into your notes and then, because you are too rushed or too lazy to reword the information, leave it in its original state.

When you're working with a computer, it's all too easy to cut and paste whole sections of downloaded articles into your word-processing document. Instead of summarizing the information, you're tempted to enclose it in quotation marks, document the source, and move on. Look at the text that you're tempted to quote. Could you summarize part of it, integrating a brief quote into the summary? If you summarized the whole passage, would anything of importance be lost?

Although quotations should never comprise more than one-fifth of your paper, fewer is usually better. They should also be fully integrated into the text so that they don't stand out or interrupt the logical development of an idea.

Integrating Quotations into the Text. You have probably read articles in which quotations stood out "like a sore thumb." They seemed to be completely separate from the author's prose. You might have wondered why they were included in the first place. This happens when the author has failed to make the quotations an integral part of the article. Not only is the writing style different, but the quotation seems to be dropped in at random.

Lead into your quotations beforehand, preparing your readers for the information they contain. Let your readers know in advance why you think the quotation is relevant to the discussion. Refer back to the quotation in the text that follows it, pointing out the ways in which the quotation either confirms or argues against the point you are making.

Using Your Own Words. Paraphrasing information in language too much like the source from which it was obtained is a dangerous habit. The dictionary defines *paraphrasing* as restating text in another form. Students, unfortunately, have redefined it to mean copying a passage with only minor changes in the original text. This first occurs as you are taking notes. Instead of summarizing the information presented in an article, you change a word here and another there. The result is a composite of your own words and writing style mixed with those of another author.

When the time comes to write your paper, you may copy your notes, adding or changing only a few words. The next note you use may come from another source, and so the writing style is entirely different. In this way, every paragraph reflects the style of a different author. Your own voice is almost silent, and your writing fails to flow naturally. In addition, you are sailing very close to the treacherous shores of plagiarism.

Some students fail to write in their own voice because they lack confidence in their writing ability. They think they will improve their papers by simulating the styles of published authors. For the same reason, they borrow vocabulary and grammatical constructions they don't fully understand. Trust yourself. If you write clearly, simply, and carefully, you will produce a better paper.

Creating Logical and Grammatically Correct Sentences

Though you may have found the right words, they must be combined in grammatically correct sentences. A sentence is a complete, independent grammatical unit containing a subject and a predicate. The elements of a sentence should be tightly linked together and arranged in a logical way that enables your readers to understand what you are trying to say.

Sentence Length. How long should your sentences be? There is no magic number of words that translates into a good sentence. One fault I find with grammar-checking programs is that their programmers seem to think there is such a magic number. They think they detect an error every time they encounter a sentence that exceeds a certain number of words. It is true that the shorter the sentence, the more likely your reader will be to understand it. Shorter sentences should, therefore, be used whenever possible. However, if the information you wish to communicate can be expressed better in a longer sentence, that should be your choice. One good strategy is to alternate short sentences with longer ones. You might think of it as giving your reader a chance to catch up with you. If you are looking for dramatic effect, a long sentence can build up to a climactic short one.

Conjunctions. Conjunctions can be used to combine short sentences that seem abrupt standing alone. Coordinating conjunctions like *and, or,* and *but* tend to create loose, wandering sentences, so use them somewhat sparingly. Subordinating conjunctions like *since, before, whereas,* and *although* can tighten your sentence structure and emphasize the main clause.

Parallel Construction. When two or more ideas are parallel or serve a similar function in a sentence, they should be expressed in parallel grammatical form. As you write, strive to write sentences that contain similar grammatical constructions for adjacent phrases and clauses. For example:

I am interested in identifying a hawk, a raven, and an oriole.

Note that each of the nouns listed is preceded by an indefinite article. You would not write *a hawk, a raven, and oriole.* In the following sentences, the infinitive verbs are in parallel form:

They gathered to feast and to give thanks.

Her intention was not to discourage him but to help him accept the situation.

Variety. To maintain the reader's attention, vary your sentences as much as possible. Begin them in different ways so that the order is not always subject, predicate, object. Using the same patterns over and over creates monotony. A variety of simple, complex, and compound sentences can also make your writing more interesting.

Occasionally, a writer may repeat the same sentence structure in order to emphasize the connections among the ideas expressed. Although this technique can create a more tightly structured passage, it can become tiring to your readers if overdone.

Creating Cohesive Paragraphs

A paragraph is a group of sentences that express one idea. It is a means of dividing material into units containing tight clusters of ideas. Each paragraph develops a particular point in some detail. Sometimes an author can make a point in just one sentence, but it is more common to use several sentences in each paragraph. The coherence of your paper depends on writing tightly structured paragraphs that connect logically to the ones that come before and after.

The choice of what should be included in a paragraph differs from one writer to another. In fact, the fictional detective Nero Wolfe once solved a case by proving that a suspect had written a book in question. He deduced the identity of the author by the unique way he divided his paragraphs. Writers have very different views on what constitutes a separate idea. The important thing is to divide your material into logical segments that help your reader move from point to point.

Organization. A paragraph should flow logically with some controlling structure. It might move from the general to the specific or from the specific to the general, or it might alternate ideas, comparing and contrasting them. A paragraph can be ordered chronologically, or it might build up excitement, gradually increasing tension by moving from unimportant to climactic events. Another strategy if you are presenting hard-to-understand material is to arrange information in order of difficulty, with easily understood material presented first.

Topic Sentences. Each paragraph should contain a topic sentence. This is the key sentence to which all the other sentences relate. It should present the main idea of the paragraph, setting the tone for the rest of the paragraph. It is normally placed either at the beginning or the end of a paragraph. The topic sentence presents the main idea of the paragraph. If it is placed at the beginning, it sets the tone for what will follow. If it comes at the end, it serves as a conclusion or summary of what has gone before.

Smooth Transitions. A paragraph should follow naturally the one that preceded it. It is helpful to repeat an important word or phrase from the preceding paragraph to make a smooth transition. Not only do sentences have roles within a paragraph but the paragraphs themselves play different roles. The first paragraph in a group introduces the subject while the last one ties together the ideas that have been presented and reemphasizes the most important point.

Dividing the Paper into Sections

A research paper can be divided into three distinct sections: the introduction, the body, and the conclusion. Each serves a distinct and important role.

Writing the Introduction

Since the introduction is the section that first addresses your audience, it should immediately attract their attention. If you think back on books and articles you have read, you probably formed an opinion of them after reading only a very few paragraphs. You may even have decided against reading the rest of a work solely because of those initial impressions. This is obviously not what you want to happen when your audience reads the first paragraphs of your own paper. Instead, your introduction should serve the dual role of preparing your audience for what lies ahead while assuring them that they can expect a well-written and interesting discussion of the topic.

Choosing the Right Approach. Introductions vary widely depending on the writer and the topic. Opening statements differ accordingly and you have a large number of options to choose from.

- **Begin with a succinct statement of purpose.** This is an excellent way to begin for many topics. It can, however, seem a little dull, so be sure you awaken your readers' interest with vivid language and encourage them to continue.

  "Black Power, that is what I would like to talk to you about. When Stokely Carmichael shouted 'black power' in that Mississippi school yard, he performed a mystic function that some poet must always perform at the proper moment in history."

  Richard G. Hatcher

- **Start out by concisely defining the problem.** If you are writing a paper about the environment, for example, this could be an excellent way to begin. Other subjects that lend themselves to an opening definition include social problems like poverty and legal issues.

  "Americans are beginning to realize that the undeveloped countries of the world face an inevitable population-food crisis."

  Paul R. Ehrlich

- **State the key issues you will later address.** Preparing your reader for what is to come is appropriate for many topics. Be careful, however, that you don't dive right into those issues prematurely, omitting the introduction altogether.

  "In a certain sense, we all listen to music on three separate planes. For lack of a better terminology, one might name these: (1) the sensuous plane, (2) the expressive plane, (3) the sheerly musical plane."

  Aaron Copland

- **Whet your reader's appetite with a pithy quotation.** If one of your sources has written something unusually insightful and cleverly worded, a quotation can work well as an opening sentence. It is helpful if the quotation is somewhat dramatic or invites controversy. Be sure, however, that it is clearly related to the subject matter.

> "Wisdom," the Eskimo say, "can be found only far from man, out in the great loneliness."
>
> Loren Eiseley

- **Ask a question that gets your readers thinking about your topic.** A question can be especially useful if your readers already know something about your topic. If we are to be perfectly honest, we are all more interested in our own ideas than any others. There is no point, however, in asking a question about which your readers have no opinion.

> "Unjust laws exist: shall we be content to obey them, or shall we endeavor to amend them . . . ?"
>
> Henry David Thoreau

> "Who are you? You singly, not you together. When did it start—that long day's journey into self? When do you really begin to know what you believe and where you're going?"
>
> Marya Mannes

- **Begin with an illustration.** Since we all enjoy being told a story, this is an especially effective method of quickly getting your readers' attention. If you are writing about an individual, a humorous or touching incident from his or her life might be appropriate. If you are writing about a social problem, a story about a real person who has suffered as a result of the problem will make your paper more real and compelling to your readers.

> "I travel with a great deal of gear, but don't go away, because herein lies a tale."
>
> William F. Buckley, Jr.

> "Let us now imagine that the dolphin is swimming along in a bay and that there is a flat surface on the water from which his call will be reflected."
>
> John C. Lilly

Avoiding Poor Beginnings. Don't begin by apologizing for your material or your writing. You want to encourage your audience to read on, and apologizing is certainly not going to inspire confidence or fill anyone with enthusiasm. Neither is the introduction the place for plunging into a detailed account of your material or for presenting a lot of self-evident facts.

Deciding What to Include. As you write the introduction, consider the following questions:

- What is the point of the paper?
- How will the information you are about to present contribute to your reader's understanding?
- Why is this information important?
- How will an understanding of your investigation enrich or enlighten your reader? In other words, how will your reader be better off after having read your paper?
- What do you plan to do? What can the reader expect?
- What methods will you use to develop your argument?

Now is the time to decide upon a final version of your thesis statement, which answers at least some of these questions. Traditionally, the thesis statement is the last sentence of the first paragraph.

Establishing a Relationship with Your Audience. The introduction is also the place to establish your relationship with your audience. This is your first meeting, and you want to get off on the right foot. It is important to focus on the audience and the way they will approach your topic. Of course, with the exception of your instructor, you know almost nothing of the readers who comprise your audience. You have made some general assumptions, such as whether they are specialists or laypersons, but you can't know them individually. They will, however, have somewhat similar needs and expectations when it comes to reading your work. They will need a "hook" in the form of some connection to their own lives to awaken their interest. The introduction is a good time to relate your topic to something the readers already know about and are interested in. Maybe the hook has to do with a recent national event or a widely held concern about marriage, family, home, friendship, government, or even personal happiness. Whatever the hook, it must cause individuals in your audience to think, "This paper has something to say to me."

In the following example, A. H. Maslow "hooks" his readers with an irresistible appeal to their curiosity:

"Something big is happening. It's happening to everything that concerns human beings. Everything the human being generates is involved. . . ."

Telling the Reader What You Plan to Do and How You Plan to Do It.
Your readers want to know what to expect. Will this be a scholarly treatment of the topic or a popular one? Do you plan to exhaust all the literature on the topic

or only a small sample? Have you consulted primary sources or relied entirely on secondary ones? Which aspects of the topic will you consider in depth and which will you treat as peripheral? You will be the one setting down the playing rules. By telling the readers what to expect, you protect yourself from failure to meet their unwarranted expectations. However, although you have a lot of freedom in this regard, once you commit yourself, your readers will expect you to follow through. You have made a pact with them, and you now have an obligation to do as you promised.

Providing a Road Map. Some research papers are sufficiently complex that your readers can easily become lost. This is sometimes the case if you are discussing research findings or technical subjects. If you think your paper might be difficult for a lay audience to follow, you can do them a much-appreciated service and ensure that they stay focused on your material by providing them with a road map. A road map is simply a brief but precise explanation of exactly what you plan to accomplish in your paper. Road maps allow your readers to anticipate the twists and turns you will take and to follow your line of reasoning. Just as a real road map lets you know your geographical location, an introductory road map helps your readers know where they are in the discussion or development of your thesis.

The concept of the road map can work for nontechnical papers as well. There's nothing wrong with letting your readers know exactly what they can expect to find when they read your paper.

Writing the Introduction Last. Some writers recommend writing the introduction last, so you can see what you have actually written. On the one hand, writing the introduction first can impose discipline that you may really need. It can provide guidance as you later decide what to include and what to leave out. However, a paper takes shape as you write. Although you have done your research and taken voluminous notes, you rarely know at the beginning just how the paper will turn out. You may feel that writing the introduction first locks you into a plan that you may later want to abandon. There's no reason why you can't change your introduction at that point, but you may feel you have wasted too much of your time. Whichever choice you make, be sure your introduction is not filled with vacuous generalities and clichés. Whether you write it before or after the body of your paper, the introduction is not the time to "fudge" or be evasive about what follows. It must, instead, have something clear, definite, and interesting to say.

Keeping the Introduction Brief. Despite the many functions the introductions serves, it should not be long-winded. You do not want to bore your reader before you have even started. Once you have the attention of the reader and have indicated what to expect in the sections that follow, you are ready to move on to the body of the paper.

Writing the Body

If you made an outline, you have a head start on this section. You already know how the body of the paper will be organized and are ready to start fitting in the information you have gathered. Research papers differ considerably in the way they are structured, but all must have some organizing principle.

Defining Key Terms. Most of your paper will be spent developing and defending your thesis statement, but where do you begin? Before you get too deeply involved in these tasks, you will want to define the terms you will be using and show how they relate to the material. You might think of yourself as providing your readers with tools—in this case, an understanding of terminology—that will make it possible for them to fully comprehend the information you present.

Using a Chronological Approach. Some papers lend themselves to a chronological organization. This method is obviously appropriate for historical topics, but it has other applications as well. Complex scientific topics can sometimes be made simpler and clearer by presenting the information chronologically in small, manageable chunks. Instead of hurling all the information at your readers at once, they can follow along and observe the gradual day-by-day or year-by-year investigation of a problem. Social problems may be best understood by describing their origin and how they have escalated over time.

Asking Questions and Providing Answers. Another way of presenting your information is first to ask a question and then proceed to answer it. Just as a question can pique the reader's interest in the introduction, the same technique can also maintain interest throughout the paper.

Exploring Cause and Effect. Still another approach is to discuss a problem in terms of cause and effect. What caused the situation you are describing? How did the problem occur? What factors or variables were responsible? Then, after you have made the reader aware of the causes, explain the impact or the effect the problem has had.

Presenting a Problem and Offering a Solution. You might begin by defining a problem and showing how it came into being. Convince your readers that this is a serious, even an urgent problem. Are there potential dangers or consequences that will result if no action is taken?

Next, propose a solution or a plan of action that seems to be the best way to proceed. How would it be implemented? Why should your readers support such a solution? Would it be difficult to achieve or are there easy steps that could be taken with presently available resources?

What objections might your readers raise to your proposed solution? Should you try to deal with every one of them or focus only on the more important ones? If you are aware of other solutions, why is yours better? Can any of these alternate solutions be incorporated into your solution? As you seek to refute these objections, try not to attack anyone. Rely on the soundness of your arguments, not on empty rhetoric.

Comparing and Contrasting. The method you choose for organizing your material depends, for the most part, on the type of information you wish to communicate. If you are advocating a change or a policy, you might compare situations in which the policy has been implemented to others in which it has not been implemented. Compare the old with the new; compare the policies of one administration with those of another; compare the way people lived before and after the invention of some labor-saving machine.

Proceeding Logically. Whichever approach you choose, develop your argument logically, gradually working in the various details without allowing them to distract from the unity of the whole. Each step of the way, you must keep your readers with you. Each assertion must be based on a solid support structure that you construct.

Achieving a Sense of Balance. As you write, maintain your sense of perspective, giving more time and attention to important issues. Lesser issues should occupy a correspondingly less prominent place. Make a conscious decision on what aspects you wish to emphasize, and don't allow your decision to be overly influenced by what you happen to have the most material on. Each main idea should be developed separately and fully. Make your main ideas clear to your readers, and don't let them get lost in the text.

Writing the Conclusion

Many people find conclusions difficult to write. They tend to write until they have run out of material and then stop. A research paper should not stop when the writer has run out of steam but rather when the problem has been fully and completely dealt with. A conclusion should thus provide the following:

- A restatement of the thesis
- A summary of the author's conclusions
- A solution to the problem if this is the writer's intention

You might want to restate the seriousness of a problem, summarize your proposed solution, recap the most important points, or bring a chronologically organized paper up to the present and suggest future directions. What conclusions can be drawn from the previous discussion? Is it appropriate to summarize the individual points that were introduced earlier? It might even be effective to end with some questions addressed to your readers, encouraging them to continue thinking about the issues you have raised in your paper.

The conclusion should be brief and to the point. A conclusion is not the place to bring in arguments you forgot to incorporate in the body of the paper. As a general rule, do not include references in the conclusion that were not discussed previously.

The conclusion should not apologize for doing a poor job of presenting the material. Neither should it be used to qualify or blunt the impact of points made earlier. Occasionally, writers reread what they have written and are assailed by doubt. Fearful that they have been mistaken, they may try to limit negative criticism with wishy-washy disclaimers. This is not the time for an attack of nerves. Neither is it a time for afterthoughts or minor details.

A good conclusion tends to have a certain dramatic quality. Some writers become uncomfortable, even a little embarrassed when they feel they are expected to produce high drama for the grand finale. In their embarrassment they may take refuge in a series of meaningless clichés. Although a little excitement at the end can be useful, what the writer must provide is a sense of closure, saying, in effect, "This is what I set out to do (thesis statement), and this is what I did."

Avoiding Clichés. Even good writers sometimes find it difficult to come to the end, so they're tempted to add something that sounds good but means nothing. Some of us use clichés and empty phrases when we're tired. We just want to get through. If you find yourself doing this, take a break or work on a less demanding section of your paper. Since a good conclusion requires at least a pinch of inspiration, you might want to take advantage of any inspired moments while you're working on the body of your rough draft. You may have one of those rare experiences when everything seems to come together and you are clearly aware of the larger implications of your topic. Write down those momentary inspirations so that you can later incorporate them into the conclusion.

Choosing a Title

Have you thought of a good title for your paper yet? A title should tell your reader what your paper is about, while at the same time adding an element of interest. Clever plays on words have become popular in recent years, but you should avoid overly cute titles for an academic paper. Make your title as brief as you can while still getting across the basic idea. Sometimes a brief title followed by a lengthier subtitle is effective.

If you were actually publishing your paper, you would want potential readers to find it easily. That means including keywords in the title or subtitle that clearly describe the subject matter. Remember how you searched the library's OPAC using keywords? Other readers do the same. Avoid adding extra words to the title that serve no real purpose except to take up space. Words like *study*, *investigation*, and *method* add little and are not useful as keywords.

Getting the Most from Your Computer

The computer allows you to type almost as fast as you can think. There is no paper to insert and advance; there is no need to worry about errors. Typos are so easily deleted and text reworded that you can concentrate almost entirely on what you want to write. Even if you are a poor typist, your fingers may fly across the keyboard as you struggle to put your ideas into words. Since taking time out to check the dictionary or reword a phrase can interrupt the flow of thought, wait until later to do your editing. If you can't remember a name or date, just make a note to yourself to check it later. You can do this right in the text like "John Mc?????" or "19??." Work out your own system for letting yourself know what's missing. Of course, you have to edit carefully later, but it's worth it. Your text will flow; your sentences will be more cohesive; and your thoughts will be expressed in a natural, logical way.

Navigating On-Screen

When you write or type on paper, you can not only see the whole page but can leaf through the other pages you have written to see what you have already covered and where. The computer screen doesn't allow you to do this easily. You can see only a fraction of a page at one time, and when you scroll up or down, you can no longer see the section you have been working on. Therefore, without the structure of an outline, you may tend to get lost.

Despite the fact that most word-processing programs show the page and line numbers at the bottom of the screen, you may still feel disoriented. Because it is difficult to see how the lines you are writing relate to the lines you can't see, it is easy to repeat yourself or to leave out important information. An outline can give you a sense of where you are and what material you should be covering at this particular point.

For storing new ideas, the computer has an enormous advantage over pencil and paper. You are able to locate the appropriate section and incorporate information exactly where it is needed. Those handwritten notes could be edited and copied into the text of the rough draft, recopied as part of interim drafts, and finally retyped into the final draft.

The most efficient way to write your rough draft, using a computer, is to type it right into your outline. Begin with a file that contains only a copy of your outline and allow your paper to grow out of it.

This idea comes as a shock to many people since one would never dream of doing such a thing with a typewriter. When you use a typewriter, you type slowly and carefully, because correcting errors is difficult. Everything you type will remain as it is since there is no easy way of erasing or deleting text. With a word processor, however, you can leave your outline right in the paper while you write your rough draft. It serves as a kind of skeleton. As you write your paper, you can clothe the skeleton with words, fleshing it out and turning it into a fully developed work.

Incorporating the outline into your rough draft allows you to work on different sections as inspiration strikes. While you are working on the first section, you may have a sudden thought, a point that should be included in the third section. If you were working with paper and pencil, you might tear off a sheet of paper and head it "Notes for Historical Section" or some other heading from your outline. When you type directly into a computer, you will need some other way to store these inspirational thoughts, for fragments can easily become lost. When you store a finished paragraph or two in a section of your outline, you will never need to retype it unless you wish to make changes. If you are satisfied with this bit of prose, it can stay just as it is and ultimately become part of your final draft

When you are far enough along that the paper's organizational structure is obvious and you no longer need the outline, you can simply delete it. As long as your outline is easy to distinguish from the text of your paper, it takes only a few moments to remove. Just be careful to make your outline stand out. The best way to do this is probably to type it all in capital letters although some writers use a different type font or size.

Acknowledging Your Sources

To avoid losing track of important bibliographic information, you should acknowledge your sources while composing your rough drafts. In the past, researchers used footnotes and endnotes to give credit for other people's words and ideas. Although you may not be aware of it, however, something wonderful has happened to the research process in the past few years. The Modern Language Association (MLA), the American Psychological Association (APA), and many other professional bodies that publish guidelines for citing bibliographic information have all but abandoned footnotes and endnotes. If you are new to writing research papers, you might not understand that this is cause for rejoicing.

Your own instructor may have horror stories about painstakingly retyping page after page because she forgot to insert a footnote on the proper page and ended up one line short after trying to sneak it in. How well I remember my inadequate typing skills and the way the typing paper flipped loose at the bottom of the sheet as I tried in vain to rescue a page over which I had labored. Today much of the old drudgery is gone, and researchers can devote more of their time to the interesting tasks of research and writing.

Scholars used footnotes because simply including a reference list or list of "Works Cited" at the end of a paper was not enough to locate the source of the information. The "Works Cited" list may let your readers know what materials you consulted, but it tells them nothing about what information was found in which source. A method is needed to connect the information to the source. Footnotes satisfied this need by repeating the same bibliographic information that would later appear in the "Works Cited" list. Fortunately, this time-consuming system has been replaced by simple references of no more than a few words in the body of the text.

Using Parenthetical Citations MLA Style

Whenever you use someone else's words or ideas, let the reader know their source. You need only insert a brief acknowledgment immediately following the material. Here is an example of the MLA style, which, in most cases, consists simply of enclosing the author's last name and the page number in parentheses:

> Medicine has long been under pressure to present a unified theory of disease (Thomas 16).

This reference will mean nothing, however, unless it is linked to full bibliographic information on the book being cited. This information appears in the list of "Works Cited" that follows the text of your paper. There, the reader should find the following entry:

> Thomas, Lewis. <u>The Medusa and the Snail</u>. New York: Viking, 1979.

Although parenthetical documentation is a far simpler system than its predecessors, you must still take care that the reader is not misled. Here are some basic MLA guidelines for creating meaningful parenthetical references:

- The reference must clearly point to one specific source on the "Works Cited" list.
- The reference must begin with the same name as the one used on the "Works Cited" list, for example, the author, editor, translator, or narrator.
- If the "Works Cited" list contains only one work by the author, the last name and page number are sufficient:

(Smith 93)

- If the list contains more than one author with the same last name, include the author's first initial:

(T. Smith 125)

- If the list contains more than one author with both the same last name and first initial, include the author's first name:

(Henry Smith 287)

- If two or three names begin the entry, include them in the reference in the same order:

(Smith, Wilson, and Jones 342)

- If the work has more than three authors, use the same form as the bibliographic entry (either the first author's last name followed by "et al." or all the authors' last names):

(Wilson et al. 176–77)

- A corporate author may be a corporation, association, government agency, or other group. If the work has a corporate author, use either its complete name or a shortened version:

(UNESCO 223–32)

- If the work has no author given and is listed by title, use the full title or a shortened form of the title (be sure to begin with the first word of the title as given in the "Works Cited" list):

(<u>King and Country</u> 187)

- If the list contains two or more works by the same author, add the shortened title after the author's name:

(Wilson, <u>Hard Times</u> 17)

- If the list contains more than one volume of a multivolume work, cite the volume. Separate volume and page numbers with a colon (:) and a space:

(Smith 3: 37–44)

- Omit page numbers when citing complete works or alphabetically arranged reference works:

(Smith)

- When citing a literary work, include any needed additional information such as stanza, act, or scene. Type the page number, then a semicolon (;) followed by additional information with appropriate abbreviations:

(Trollope 19; ch. 4)

Using Parenthetical Citations APA Style

Although the APA style is similar to MLA style, page numbers are usually not included in the reference, while the date of publication is. Full citations are included in a "References" section at the end of APA papers. Here are some basic APA guidelines for reference citations in text:

- If the reference list contains only one work by one author, include only the last name and the date of publication, separated by a comma:

(Harvey, 1990)

- If the work has two authors, include both names each time you cite the work. If the work has three, four, or five authors, cite them all the first time you refer to the work and after that include only the last name of the first author followed by "et al.":

(Martin, Abrams, Wilson, & Sorenson, 1992)

A later citation would simply read:

(Martin et al., 1992)

- If a work has six or more authors, cite only the last name of the first author followed by "et al." and the year of publication for all citations. (Note: the names of all authors should be included in the reference list.)
- Spell out the names of most corporate authors each time you cite them:

(National Endowment for the Arts, 1995)

- In some cases, if the abbreviation is easily understood, you may abbreviate the corporate name after the first citation:

(NEA, 1995)

- If the author of a work is given as "Anonymous," use this term in the citation:

(Anonymous, 1990)

- If the work has no author, use the first few words of the entry in the reference list. These are usually the title:

(<u>U.S. Military</u>, 1992)

- If the list includes works by two authors with the same last name, include each author's initials in all citations.
- If you wish to include two sources within the same parenthetical reference, give the authors' names in the same order in which they appear in the "References" list. If the works are by the same author, arrange the works by year of publication:

(Benson, 1982, 1992)

- If more than one work with the same date and the same author are cited within a parenthetical reference, add a suffix "a," "b," or "c" to the date, both in the citation and in the "References" list:

(Wellnitz, 1994a, 1994c)

- If the works of more than one author are cited in the same parenthetical reference, list them in alphabetical order. Separate the citations with semicolons (;):

(Jones, 1991; Wasserman, 1990)

- If a work has no publication date, cite it by the author's name followed by a comma and "n.d.":

(Bentham, n.d.)

- If you are citing a very old work, cite the year of the edition or translation you used:

(Aristotle, trans. 1922)

- If you are citing a quotation, give the page number on which it appears. Use the abbreviation "p" to denote page number:

(Sternberg, 1992, p. 220)

- If you are citing a specific section, indicate the chapter, figure, or table:

(Chwalek, 1989, chap. 6)

- Personal communications (letters, telephone conversations, messages, and so on) are not included on the "References" list because the reader cannot look up the source. Since, other than in the text, the parenthetical reference is the only place it is mentioned, more complete information is needed:

(John R. Hansen, personal communication, October 12, 1996)

Citing Electronic Sources

More and more frequently, researchers are citing electronic sources like discussion groups, bulletin boards, and database files. These sources are discussed in detail in Chapter 10 in sections dealing with "Works Cited" and the "References" list. For parenthetical documentation, however, these sources differ little from print sources.

It is important, however, to distinguish between publicly accessible sources— that is, sources the reader will be able to locate on the Internet or by using a service like Dialog or America Online—and personal communications, such as e-mail, bulletin boards, and discussion groups. Even though the latter categories may not be sent directly to you, they will be deleted soon after they have been posted. It is unlikely that your reader could ever locate them. In this case, treat such sources as personal communication.

Improving Your Writing

Both the MLA and APA systems of parenthetical documentation save time, space, and frayed nerves. However, those are not their only advantages. They also make the text more readable, since the reader's attention is not constantly diverted by references at the bottom of the page or the end of the paper.

As a writer, you want your audience to stay focused on the ideas you are communicating. By carrying the new system one step further, you can integrate the references more fully and retain even more of your reader's attention. Look at the following statement with a parenthetical reference:

APA: Directors share an admiration for Italian neorealism (Tudor, 1974).

MLA: Directors share an admiration for Italian neorealism (Tudor 98).

However, the same information can also be worded:

APA: Tudor (1974), in his work on film theory, describes the directors' admiration for Italian neorealism.

If you were using the MLA style, the page number would be inserted in parentheses rather than the year of publication.

MLA: Tudor (98), in his work on film theory, describes the directors' admiration for Italian neorealism.

APA permits you to go one step further and omit the parentheses altogether:

APA: Tudor, in his 1974 work on film theory, describes the directors' admiration for Italian neorealism.

Here the sentence becomes more readable. We do not insert parentheses in our conversation, so we don't quite know what to do with them when we encounter them in text. Such elements interrupt the natural flow of language. The sentence above contains all the information the reader needs without distracting from the point the sentence is making.

Using Footnotes

Although they constitute an all but extinct species, footnotes are still appropriate in some situations. It is occasionally useful to add information that amplifies a point in the text. Interrupting the text to add it, however, would distract from the point you are making. Such information can be placed in a note at the bottom of the page. Keep the information in such a note to a minimum. If you find yourself writing long notes, it would probably be better to create an appendix at the end of the paper to present the additional material.

When might you add a footnote? Perhaps you came across an author who disagreed with the point you are making. It may seem like a petty objection or you have reason to doubt the reliability of the source. However, honesty demands that you let your readers know that such an objection exists. You might also have some information to add to the discussion that seems so detailed that your readers could lose the train of thought. Yet the information might be helpful if they want to delve more deeply into the question. Footnotes are best used for information that is helpful but not essential, information that relates to the point you are making but is not really central to it.

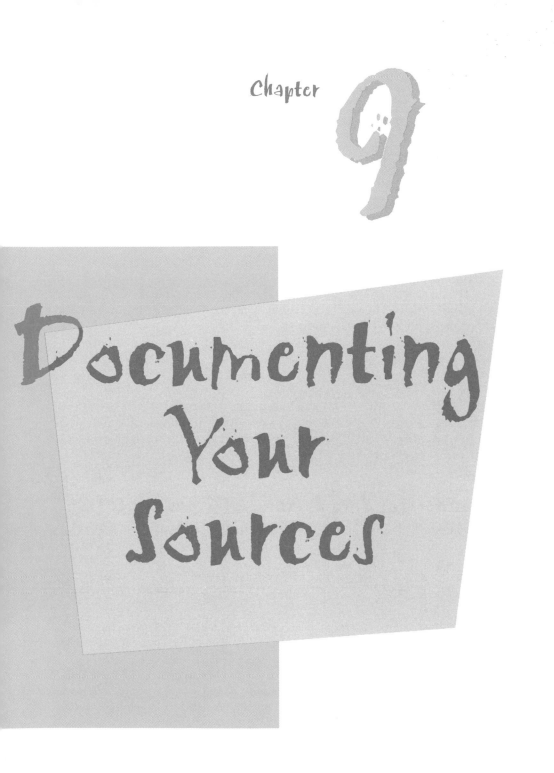

Chapter

9

Documenting Your Sources

The main characteristic that distinguishes a scholarly or professional work from a popular one is its extensive use of documentation, a kind of shorthand that tells readers where writers found their information. For a contribution to be accepted by the professional or scholarly community, authors must prove that what they have written constitutes new knowledge or a different viewpoint. To do so, they must make it possible for their readers to check their findings and make certain that they have fully investigated the related literature and interpreted it correctly.

If, in the past, you have found documenting your sources a frustrating experience, you are not alone. However, as a responsible investigator, you must let your readers know what information you obtained from other sources. Knowledge is not something "out there." Others have painstakingly built up the base bit by bit and are entitled to have their work acknowledged.

For your readers to know whether your evidence is reliable and to be able to check it themselves, they will need the correct page numbers of the actual books or journals from which it was taken. In the case of electronic and other hard-to-find sources, you will need to include even more information about the path you took when you made your discovery. Though most readers will not actually check your sources, you must give them the opportunity, or you cannot ask them to accept your work as valid.

When you acknowledge your sources using parenthetical citations, as discussed in Chapter 8, be careful not to confuse your reader. If you cite a source in the body of the paper, there must be a corresponding citation at the end. Otherwise, you have in a sense cheated, making it impossible to check your reference.

Understanding Systems of Documentation

Academic disciplines differ in the kinds of research performed and in the types of sources used. For example, a documentation system that works well for literary critics may not be appropriate for engineers. Therefore, professional associations, such as the Modern Language Association (MLA), the American Psychological Association (APA), and the American Chemical Society (ACS), have developed bibliographic styles for use by members of their professions.

In addition, there are style manuals developed by publishers. For example, the *Chicago Manual of Style*, developed by the University of Chicago Press for use by writers whose works it publishes, is also used by many researchers with no connection to the University of Chicago. At the end of this chapter, you will find a section on writing across the curriculum that describes some of the differences between research carried out in a variety of fields and the documentation systems most often used.

If the research paper you have been assigned is for an English class, you will probably be asked to use the MLA style. In other classes, however, your instructor may request that you use another system. This chapter will cover the MLA and APA system in some depth and will briefly introduce the *Chicago* style.

Whichever bibliographic system you use, follow it exactly, even if it seems time-consuming to proofread each bibliographic citation again and again. Don't mix up two systems, using one method for citing joint authors and another for conference proceedings. It would be like alternating French words with English ones in conversation. Your audience would not know what you were talking about. To communicate, a language must be known by both writer and reader, and even small changes in format can cause misunderstandings.

Understanding MLA Documentation Style

The bibliographic style developed by the Modern Language Association is a widely used, consistent, and easily understood system of documentation. Every formal research paper written in the MLA style concludes with a section entitled "Works Cited." As the title states, this list includes only those works actually cited in the body of your paper. In other words, each bibliographic citation corresponds to one or more parenthetical references.

If there are sources you don't cite that you feel would be helpful to your reader (or if you want your instructor to know how diligent you were), you may wish to add a second section titled "Works Consulted." In most cases a "Works Consulted" section is optional, while the "Works Cited" section is required.

MLA has developed a number of guidelines for listing sources in the "Works Cited" section. The most important guidelines are:

- Position the "Works Cited" section at the end of the paper.
- Begin the "Works Cited" section on a new sheet of paper.
- Continue the page numbering from the beginning of the paper throughout the "Works Cited" section.
- Type page numbers in the upper right-hand corner, flush against the right margin, half an inch from the top. Center the title "Works Cited" one inch from the top.
- Begin each entry flush with the left margin, then indent succeeding lines one-half inch or five spaces.
- Double-space all entries, and do not add extra space between entries.
- Make your citations as brief as possible but include all information your reader needs to locate the source.
- List the author's name as it appears in the parenthetical reference.
- Type the author's name as the first word of a citation and arrange the entries alphabetically so that your reader can quickly locate a source.
- If your sources include two or more works by the same author, list them alphabetically by title. First list the works written alone, followed by those written with other authors.
- Alphabetize works written by corporate authors by the first main word of the group name (ignoring *the* and *a*).

- Alphabetize books with no author (including those listed as anonymous) by title.
- Check to be sure that each parenthetical citation has a corresponding entry or citation in the "Works Cited" section.

Understanding MLA Format for Books

Although the citations of some books include more information than those of others, present the information in the following order:

Author's name

Title of a part of the book

Title of the book

Name of the editor, translator, or compiler

Edition used

Number of volume used

Name of series

Place of publication

Name of publisher

Date of publication

Page numbers

Additional bibliographic information

Annotation

Authors' Names. Give the authors' names as they are listed on the title page. Give the first author's name in inverted order (last name first):

James, Sharon R.

Give a second author's name in normal order:

Montoya, William P., and Harold R. Jones.

If three authors are given, list the last two in normal order:

Swanson, Mary B., James M. Garcia, and William Otto.

If there are more than three authors, list only the first one, inverted, followed by the Latin abbreviation *et al.*

Jones, Sharon R., et al.

If there are more than three editors, the entry would look like this:

Jones, Sharon R., et al., eds.

If the full names of the authors are not listed on the title page and you think this information would be helpful, you may supply it using square brackets:

Winston, R[aymond] B[ernard].

Titles. Capitalize all main words in title and subtitle.

Real Estate: A Bibliography of the Monographic Literature.

The Real Estate Industry: An Information Sourcebook.

Place of Publication and Publisher. If the city is well known, it is not necessary to list the state. If more than one city is listed, give only the first one. Publishers' names can be shortened. For example, omit the words *Press, Inc.,* and *Co.* Include enough for the reader to identify the company by looking it up in a standard reference work like *Books in Print.* For example, *Harcourt, Brace* may be shortened to *Harcourt.*

Garden City, NJ: Doubleday.

New York: Harcourt.

Missing Information. Occasionally you will encounter a book or journal that does not provide complete bibliographic information. When this happens, you can use the following abbreviations:

- **No Date.** If you know only the approximate date, type the letter *c* and a period before the date [c.1993]. If you are unsure of the date, type a question mark after it [*1993?*]. If you have no information at all, use the abbreviation *n.d.*

Dickens, Charles. <u>Oliver Twist</u>. London: Ward, Lock, [1900?].

Dickens, Charles. <u>Barnaby Rudge: and The Mystery of Edwin Drood and Other Stories</u>. New York: William L. Allison, n.d.

Leffmann, Henry. <u>The Jews of Dickens' Novels</u>. [Philadelphia?]: Havelock, [c.1893].

Dickens, Charles. <u>The Personal History of David Copperfield</u>. Boston: DeWolfe, Fiske, [18??].

- **No Place of Publication or Publisher.** Use the abbreviation *n.p.* where the place or publisher would usually be typed.

Rekela, George. <u>Sports Great Anfernee Hardaway</u>. N.p.: Enslow, [c.1995].

Lurie, Jon. <u>Beginning Snowboarding</u>. Minneapolis: n.p., 1996.

Dickens, Charles. <u>The Uncommercial Traveller</u>. Centennial ed. Charles Dickens Complete Works Ser. N.p.: Edito-Service, 1970.

- **No Page Numbers.** Use the abbreviation *n. pag.*

Dickens, Charles. <u>The Adventures of Oliver Twist: Pictures from Italy and American Notes</u>. New York: William L. Allison, [c.1838]. n. pag.

Sample Entries for Books

The following are the situations that will most frequently arise as you collect your sources. If you encounter a problem with an unusual or complicated citation, consult the most recent edition of the *MLA Handbook for Writers of Research Papers*.

Author, Anonymous.

<u>Space Flight: The First 30 Years</u>. Washington, DC: United States Office of Space Flight: National Aeronautics and Space Administration, 1991.

Author, Corporate. *Corporate* means only that a group or organization, rather than an individual, is responsible for the work.

> National Institute of Mental Health. <u>Marijuana and Youth: Clinical Observations on Motivation and Learning</u>. Rockville, MD: GPO, 1982.

Author, Single.

> Sirotzki, Len. <u>The Bensenville Home: A Caring Community for Children and Old People</u>. Schaumburg, IL: Communities of Learners, 1995.

> Walsh, David Allen. <u>Selling Out America's Children: How America Puts Profits Before Values and What Parents Can Do</u>. Minneapolis: Fairview, 1994.

> Paxton, L[ew] P[rice]. <u>Creating and Using the Native American Love Flute</u>. Garden Valley, CA: Author, 1994.

> DeServille, Paul. <u>Tubbo: "The Great Peter's Run."</u> New York: Oxford UP, 1982.

> Easton, Susan M. <u>The Problem of Pornography: Regulation and the Right to Free Speech</u>. London: Routledge, 1994.

> Feuchtwanger, E. J. <u>From Weimar to Hitler: Germany, 1918–33</u>. New York: St. Martin's, 1993.

Authors, Joint.

> Fontana, Vincent J., and Douglas J. Besharov. <u>The Maltreated Child: The Maltreatment Syndrome in Children: A Medical, Legal, and Social Guide</u>. 5th ed. Springfield, IL: Thomas, 1995.

> Baruth, Leroy G., and M. Lee Manning. <u>Multicultural Education of Children and Adolescents</u>. 2nd ed. Boston: Allyn and Bacon, 1996.

> Kvaerne, Per, et al. <u>The Bon Religion of Tibet: The Iconography of a Living Tradition</u>. Boston: Shambhala, 1995.

Graham, Claudia, June Biermann, and Barbara Touhey. <u>The Diabetes
Sports and Exercise Book: How to Play Your Way to Better
Health</u>. Los Angeles: Lowell House, 1995.

Inciardi, James A., Ruth Horowitz, and Anne Pottieger. <u>Street Kids,
Street Drugs, Street Crime: An Examination of Drug Use &
Serious Delinquency in Miami</u>. New York: Wadsworth, 1993.

Book in a Series.

Chan, K. M., ed. <u>Sports Injuries of the Hand and Upper Extremity</u>. The
Hand and Upper Extremity Ser. 12. New York: Churchill
Livingstone, 1995.

Dourley, John P. <u>Jung and the Religious Alternative: The Rerooting</u>.
Studies in the Psychology of Religion Ser. 6. Lewiston, NY: Edwin
Mellen, 1995.

Toner, Sheila C. <u>George Washington: America's First Strategic Leader</u>.
USAWC Strategy Research Project Report No. AD-A309 270.
Carlisle Barracks, PA: U.S. Army War College, 1996.

Blackman, Steve. <u>Space Travel</u>. Technology Craft Topics Ser. N.p.:
Watts, 1993.

Book Introduction.

Yamaguchi, Harrison P. Introduction. <u>To Rise from Earth: An Easy to
Understand Guide to Space Flight</u>. By Wayne Lee. Austin, TX:
Texas Space Grant Consortium, 1993.

Book Published before 1900. The publisher's name may be omitted.
Substitute a comma for the usual colon after the place of publication:

Wilson, James Macdonald. <u>The Art of Michelangelo</u>. New York, 1884.

Weems, M[ason] L[ocke]. <u>The Life of George Washington: Together with
Curious Anecdotes, Equally Honourable to Himself, and
Examplary to His Young Countrymen: Embellished with Six
Engravings</u>. Philadelphia, 1834.

Conference Papers.

Factor-Litvak, P., J. Kline, and J. Graziano. <u>Blood Lead and Blood Pressure in Children Aged 5.5 Years</u>. 34th Annual Meeting of the Society of Toxicology, Mar. 5–9, 1995, Baltimore, MD. Reston, VA: Society of Toxicology, 1995.

Ellis, M. M. <u>Examining the Visual Perception Skills of Japanese and American Children</u>. 104th Annual Meeting of the Ohio Academy of Science, Apr. 28–30, 1995, Westerville, OH. Bowling Green, OH: Ohio Journal of Science, 1995.

Oller, D. K. <u>Early Speech and Word Learning in Bilingual and Monolingual Children: Advantages of Early Bilingualism</u>. American Association for the Advancement of Science Annual Meeting, Feb. 16–21, 1995, Atlanta, GA. New York: Harcourt, 1996.

Essay in a Collection. Begin the citation with the author of the essay you are citing, followed by the title of the essay. Follow with the title of the volume in which the essay appears and its editor:

Wilson, Joseph R. "As America Viewed the Potato Famine." Ed. Lindsay Rothberg. <u>Immigration as a National Experience</u>. New York: Dodd, 1994. 154–87.

Pamphlets. Pamphlets are cited exactly as if they were books.

<u>The Problem of Space Travel</u>. Washington: NASA, GPO, 1995.

Republished Book. Give original publication date after the title, and then the reprint date at the end of the citation:

Lawrence, Bruce B. <u>Defenders of God: The Fundamentalist Revolt Against the Modern Age</u>. 1989. Studies in Comparative Religion Ser. Columbia, SC : U of South Carolina P, 1995.

Ley, Willy. <u>Rockets, Missiles & Space Travel</u>. 1991. N.p.: Buccaneer, 1994.

Translation.

Schleiermacher, Friedrich. <u>On Religion: Speeches to its Cultured Despisers</u>. Trans. Richard Crouter. New York: Cambridge UP, 1996.

Semelin, Jacques, and Suzan Husserl-Kapit. <u>Unarmed Against Hitler: Civilian Resistance in Europe, 1939–1943</u>. Trans. Suzan Husserl-Kapit. Westport, CN: Praeger, 1993.

Understanding MLA Format for Periodicals

When citing articles in periodicals (journals, magazines, and newspapers), include the following elements if relevant:

Author's name

Title of the article

Name of the periodical

Series number or name

Volume number

Issue number

Date of publication

Page numbers

Supplementary information

Sample Entries for Periodicals

Editorials.

Stewart, Mitchell A. "All of Us Must Remake the Federal Government." Editorial. <u>Cleveland Times</u> 8 April 1995, late ed.: A12.

Journals Using Continuous Pagination. Scholarly journals are often paginated (page numbers assigned) continuously. Numbering begins with page one in the first issue and continues through the last issue of the volume. In other words, the first page of the second issue continues the numbering instead of starting all over again, and the volume is treated as one work rather than several separate ones. If a journal has continuous pagination, you do not need to list the issue number:

Stoddard, Jeffrey J. "Health Insurance Status and Ambulatory Care for
Children." New England Journal of Medicine 330 (1995):
1421–25.

Hooker, Ann. "The International Law of Forests." Natural Resources
Journal 34 (1994): 823–77.

Garstang, M., et al. "Atmospheric Controls on Elephant
Communication." Journal of Experimental Biology 198.4 (1995):
939–51.

Journals Paginated by Issue. Popular magazines and many scholarly journals
begin each issue with page one. The reader thus needs not only the volume number but also the issue number to identify the source. In the citation, the issue number follows the volume number, separated by a period:

Miller-Hewes, Kathy A. "Making the Connection: Children's Books and
the Visual Arts." School Arts 94.2 (1994): 32–34.

Romer, Paul M. "Economic Growth and Investment in Children."
Daedalus 123.4 (1994): 141-54.

Kishton, Joseph M., and Ashley C. Dixon. "Self-Perception Changes
Among Sports Camp Participants." Journal of Social Psychology
135.2 (1995): 135–143.

Kershaw, Ian. "'Working Towards the Fuhrer': Reflections on the Nature
of the Hitler Dictatorship." Contemporary European History
(Great Britain) 2.2 (1993): 103–18.

Tchamba, M. N., et al. "Some Observations on the Movements and
Home Range of Elephants in Waza National Park, Cameroon."
Mammalia 58.4 (1994): 334–48.

Journals with Only Issue Numbers. A small number of periodicals do not use
volume numbers at all. Treat the issue number like a volume number.

Rosse, Richard B., et al. "The Relationship Between Cocaine-Induced
Paranoia and Compulsive Foraging: A Preliminary Report."
Veterans Affairs Medical Center Journal 1048 (1994): 241–72.

Magazine, Weekly. Whether or not a weekly magazine contains a volume or issue number, the date is sufficient to identify it:

> "Children's Literature (book review)." <u>Economist</u> 10 June 1995: 79–80.

> Oliver, Andrew. "Marijuana: The Forbidden Medicine." <u>National Review</u> 29 May 1995: 65–66.

Newspaper. Since different editions of a newspaper may contain different information, specify the edition when available. Also specify the section if it is applicable. If the article is continued on nonconsecutive pages, indicate with a plus sign (23+). As in the following example, begin an anonymously written article with the title:

> "Child Pornography Probe." <u>Washington Post</u> 18 February 1995, capital ed.: A4.

> Biskupic, Joan. "Court Backs Child Pornography Law, Lets Video Retailer's Conviction Stand." <u>Chicago Tribune</u> 30 November 1994, final ed.: A19, 22.

> Day, Kathleen. "Service Calls FBI on Child Pornography: America Online Says Photos Transmitted." <u>Washington Post</u> 10 January 1995, metropolitan ed.: D4.

Understanding MLA Format for Theses and Dissertations

Theses and dissertations are usually written as a requirement of graduate programs in higher education. In undergraduate research, you will be more likely to come across an abstract or a published work, than an unpublished dissertation or thesis. It is important that you make clear the source of your information.

Sample Entries for Theses and Dissertations

Dissertation Abstracts.

> Newman, Lynn R. "The Paradox of the Mystical Text: Immanence and Transcendence in Medieval English Literature." Diss. U of Chicago, 1992. <u>DAI</u> 53 (1992): 1524B.

Published Dissertation. A dissertation may be published and distributed as a book, or more commonly, made available in microfilm. Treat each format as a published dissertation, that is, as if it were a book, indicating, however, that it is a dissertation and listing the degree-granting institution. If the dissertation was published by University Microfilms International, give the order number:

> Immel, Andrea L. Little Rhymes, Little Jingles, Little Chimes: A History of Nursery Rhymes in English Literature Before "Tommy Thumb's Pretty Song Book." Diss. U of California, Los Angeles, 1994. Ann Arbor: UMI, 1995. 5739626.

Unpublished Dissertation. Unpublished dissertations are written, bound, and placed in the library of the university at which they were written. Place quotation marks around the title (do not underline it), and then type *Diss.* Then type the name of the degree-granting institution, a comma, a space, and finally the year:

> Schroth, Randall Evans. "A Pantheon of Dragons: Images of Vermicular Monstrance in English Literature from 'Beowulf' through 'The Cantos'." Diss. U of Colorado at Boulder, 1994.

> Henningfeld, Diane Andrews. "Contextualizing Rape: Sexual Violence in Middle English Literature." Diss. Michigan State U, 1994.

> Baugh, Harvey Francis. "The Placement of the Creoles of Louisiana in American Literature Through the Novels and Short Stories of George Washington Cable, Kate Chopin, and Grace Elizabeth King." Diss. U of Virginia, 1930.

Understanding MLA Format for Government Documents

Cities, counties, states, and nations all publish huge quantities of documents dealing with every conceivable subject. Some of the works you consulted in the reference collection, circulating stacks, or government depository may have been government documents. The government agency that issued the document is usually cited as the author, and the following abbreviations are used:

Congressional Record	Cong. Rec. 23 Mar. 1993: 4265–72.
Senate Bills	S 44
House Bills	HR 53
Senate Resolutions	S. Res. 32

House Resolutions	H. Res. 103
Senate Reports	S. Rept. 14
House Reports	H. Rept. 106
Senate Documents	S. Doc. 329
House Documents	H. Doc. 33

Sample Entries for Government Documents

Documents from the United States Federal Goverment.

United States. Cong. House Committee on Commerce. <u>Hearings</u>. 105th
    Cong., 1st sess. Washington: GPO, 1996.

United States. Dept. of State. <u>United States Contributions to
    International Peace</u>. Washington: GPO, 1995.

United States. Cong. House Committee on Public Works and
    Transportation. Subcommittee on Aviation. <u>To Repeal Section 29
    of the International Air Transportation Competition Act
    (Pertaining to Commercial Airline Operations at Love Field,
    Dallas, TX): Hearing before the Subcommittee on Aviation of the
    Committee on Public Works and Transportation</u>. 102nd Cong.,
    1st sess. HR 858. Washington: GPO, 1992.

McCracken, Janet Brown, ed. <u>Helping Children Love Themselves and
    Others: A Resource Guide to Equity Materials for Young
    Children</u>. Washington, DC: The Children's Foundation: Women's
    Educational Equity Act Program, U.S. Dept. of Education: U.S.
    Dept. of Education, Office of Educational Research and
    Improvement, Educational Resources Information Center, 1990.

United States. General Accounting Office. <u>Early Childhood Programs:
    Parent Education and Income Best Predict Participation</u>.
    Washington: GAO, 1994.

Documents from Other Countries.

Great Britain. Parliament. House of Commons. <u>Report of the Select
    Committee on European Union</u>. London: HMSO, 1995.

European Foundation for the Improvement of Living and Working
Conditions. <u>Monitoring the Work Environment: Report of
Second European Conference</u>. N.p.: Eur. Communities Official
Pubns. Office, 1994.

United Nations Documents.

United Nations. Economic Commission on Central Europe. <u>Regional
Development Plan for Central Europe</u>. New York: United
Nations, 1995.

State and Local Documents.

Fuller, Sharon. <u>The Gun Control Debate: An Update</u>. Informational Bul.
Ser. 94-3. Madison, WI: Wisconsin Legis. Ref. Bur., 1994.

Understanding MLA Format for Reference Works

Encyclopedias.

Bleznick, Donald W. "Cervantes." <u>Encyclopedia Americana</u>. 1995 ed.

Other Reference Works.

"Gingrich, Newton Leroy (Gingrich, Newt)." <u>Who's Who in America</u>.
24th ed. 1995–96.

Understanding MLA Format for Audiovisuals

Not all the information you discover will be found in books and journals. You may
have viewed a video program, listened to a cassette tape, or attended a film. No
matter what the format, your goal is the same: to enable your reader to identify and
locate the same information you found. This may mean including additional information if you think the source may be difficult to locate. You may also need to
consult the *MLA Handbook for Writers of Research Papers* for unusual audiovisual
formats. If you are still unable to find an appropriate example, it is not incorrect
to improvise. Just make sure you have followed the MLA models as closely as possible and that you consistently follow your own model. The important thing is to
inform, not confuse, your reader.

Television Programs. If you are citing a television program, include the title of the episode, program, and series if available. Also include the name of the network and the call letters of the local station. Information about the participants in the production is also useful.

> "Ulysses S. Grant." <u>Civil War Journal</u>. Narr. John Henderson. Dir. William Hurt. Arts and Entertainment Network. 7 Nov. 1995.

> <u>Wednesday's Children</u>. By Susan Silverberg. Dir. Rachel Hardy. 3 episodes. Masterpiece Theatre. Introd. Russell Baker. PBS. WGBH, Boston. 23 May–12 June 1994.

Sound Recording.

> Davis, Miles. "Silhouette in Blue." Rec. 20 June 1950. <u>The Best of Miles Davis</u>. Audiocassette. Columbia, 1990.

> <u>It's a Wonderful Life</u>. Soundtrack. Dir. Frank Capra. Perf. James Stewart, Donna Reed, Lionel Barrymore, and Thomas Mitchell. 78-rpm disc. RKO, 1946.

Understanding MLA Format for Electronic Sources

Many references that researchers now cite are not books or printed journal articles, and some sources may never have appeared in paper at all. Examples include on-line and CD-ROM sources as well as Internet-based sources. Tracking them down can be considerably more difficult than locating a book.

Since these formats are so new, they pose special problems to the researcher who is trying to cite them. Bulletin boards, Web pages, and FTP sites come into and go out of existence with distressing rapidity, and no one organization is responsible for keeping track of all the research and discussion that appears on the Internet. As a rule of thumb, include more bibliographic information when citing an electronic source than a printed one because of the difficulty of finding the reference months or years later. For example, electronic sources cannot be looked up in *Books in Print*, *The National Union Catalog*, or your local library catalog.

Another difficulty is that electronic sources can easily change. Information can be added or removed, so when you cite your source, you want your reader to be able to retrace your steps and find the same document that you consulted.

Understanding MLA Format for On-Line Sources

Traditionally, the information in a bibliographic citation refers to a physical object you can hold in your hands. But terms like *volume* and *page* lose their meaning when you are referring to text on a computer screen. Since it is sometimes not possible for the reader to consult the same electronic source that you did, whether because of cost or restricted access, a reference to the printed journal or index is preferable to the electronic one. In some cases, however, an electronic journal or index may have no printed counterpart. You must, therefore, cite the source as you actually found it. The following are general guidelines for citing on-line sources:

- Use the date of publication or the most recent update. It is also helpful to include the date of your own search.
- Instead of the publisher and place of publication, substitute a statement of availability that includes enough information for your reader to locate the document.
- If the information was found on the Internet, specify the tool used, such as FTP, Gopher, or World Wide Web. Include the path and directory information.
- If found on a commercial service, give the name of the service.
- If available both on-line and on CD-ROM, specify "On-Line" or provide full information on both formats.

If you found information on a CD-ROM or on a commercial on-line database service like DIALOG, that information will probably still be available when your reader wishes to find it. If you found your information in a document on the Internet, the chances are that the information may have disappeared. It has been estimated that the average document remains on the Internet for only forty-four days. Although scholarly resources maintained by universities and professional organizations remain available for a longer period, you should anticipate that your readers will have difficulty in obtaining an Internet document.

Internet sources run the full gamut from totally useless and even misleading to highly reputable and scholarly. Generally, it is unwise to use an electronic source unless you can establish its authorship and reliability. Since making such a judgment can be difficult, it is preferable to use resources that come from widely known and respected individuals and organizations. No matter what the source, you will want to be as helpful and informative as possible, but if you are citing a little-known source, your obligation to your reader is even greater. Always remember that the whole point of the MLA style is to inform readers of the existence of resources and provide sufficient information to enable them to locate these resources. If at all possible, try to identify individuals or professional organizations that your readers might contact if they are unable to find documents. If you can include e-mail addresses as well, do so. E-mail addresses also change, but at least you are providing two opportunities for your readers to locate the documents in question.

Since new scholarly publications appear daily on the Internet, you might consult the printed reference work *Directory of Electronic Journals, Newsletters, and*

Academic Discussion Lists. When citing a source found on the Internet, you may find it provides more information than the actual Internet document.

On-line services offer such large databases that today's student reads more abstracts than in past years. These abstracts are valuable even if you do not read the entire article, but you must make the source of your information clear.

Sample Entries for On-Line Sources

Document Originally Published in Print.

> Tallant, Matilda. "Nuclear Waste on Local Beaches." New York Times 11
>   Nov. 1995, late ed.: C2. New York Times Online. Online. Nexis.
>   22 Apr. 1996.

> Martinez, Diego. "Guidelines for Early Childhood Recreational
>   Activities." Urbana: ERIC Clearinghouse on Elementary and
>   Early Childhood Educ., 1994. ERIC. Online. DIALOG. 28 Mar.
>   1996.

Document with No Print Source.

> Beneditti, Horace. "Successful Telecommuting: Some Basic Guidelines."
>   National Business Employment Weekly. Online. Dow Jones News
>   Retrieval. 12 Mar. 1994.

> "Mental Measurements Yearbook." The Merck Index On-line (DRUG4).
>   Online. Knowledge Index. May 1995.

Electronic Journals, Newsletters, and Conferences.

> Workman, R. S. "The Liberal Arts in the University." Humanist 7.0176
>   (24 Apr. 1994): 12 pp. Online. Internet. 28 Mar. 1996.

> Agonito, John. "An Essay in Understanding." Postmodern Culture 1.4
>   (1993):36 pars. Online. Internet. 22 Nov. 1995.

Electronic Texts.

> Austen, Jane. Sense and Sensibility. Ed. Ruth M. Scanlon.
>   Harmondsworth: Penguin, 1969. Online. Oxford Text Archive.
>   Internet. 15 Feb. 1996. Available FTP: etext.virginia.edu.

E-Mail. You may subscribe to a discussion group and discover that a member is knowledgeable about your subject. You may then become involved in a fascinating conversation, at least some of which can be used for your paper. If such an e-mail message has a subject, use it in place of a title:

> Woodward, Suzanne. "Greetings from Ohio." E-mail to John Williams. 20 Apr. 1996.

> Romero, Leo. "Causes of the Revolution." E-mail to Lois Winthrop. 15 Dec. 1995.

Documents on the Internet.

> Clinton, Bill. "Bill Clinton on the Bosnian Peace Accord." 1995. On-line. Internet. Available FTP: Hostname: nptn.org Directory: pub/clinton/bosnia.dir File: c89.txt. Also available WWW: http://www.vc1.umn.edu/pub/clinton/bosnia.html.

> Kehoe, B. P. "Zen and the Art of the Internet." 2nd ed. 1992. On-line. Internet. Available FTP: Hostname: quake.think.com Directory: pub/etext/1992 File: zen10.txt.

> Williams, Stanley. "Guide to Sending Inter-Network Mail." 1995. On-line. Internet. Available E-mail: LISTSERV@MASSVM Message: Get MAIL GUIDE.

Internet Sites—World Wide Web. Occasionally, you may want to make reference to a Web site or "home page" rather than an actual document. This is sometimes necessary if the resource pages are not titled. Provide as much information as you can.

> "Families USA Foundation." On-line. Internet. Available: http://epn.org/families.html. Contact Webmaster Martin Hogan. E-mail: mhogan@uiuc.edu.

> "Yahoo!—Society and Culture." Yahoo! Corporation. On-line. Internet. Available: http://www.yahoo.com/Society_and_Culture/.

> "United Nations Conference." United Nations Conference on Trade and Development. On-line. Internet. Available: http://gatekeeper.unicc.org/unctad/.

"Federation of Students." Federation of Students (FedS), University of Waterloo. On-line. Internet. Available: http://waterv1.uwaterloo.ca/~fedintrn.

Boyle, Brian, comp. "American Civil War, 1861–1865." On-line. Internet. Available: http://www.access.digex.net/~bdboyle/sw.html.

Newsgroups and Listserv Discussions. Even though your reader will probably be unable to locate the posting, provide as much information as possible:

Worlitzer, Hans. "Do We Have a Common Language?" 23 Feb. 1996. Online posting. Newsgroup comp.edu.languages.natural. Usenet. 3 Nov. 1996.

Understanding MLA Format for CD-ROMs and Other Portable Sources

Unlike the on-line source, a CD-ROM disk is a physical object like a book. Publishers usually produce multiple copies of a disk to sell to libraries or individuals. Like a book, the disk can be updated and new editions or versions produced.

When you are citing a CD-ROM disk, remember that the information provider and the vendor or publisher may be different. For instance, the Modern Language Association produces the contents of the MLA *International Bibliography*. However, Silver Platter and other software companies produce and distribute the CD-ROM version of that same source. Since the information provider may have leased electronic versions of their data to more than one vendor, you need to let your reader know which one you used. The different versions may not be identical.

When you use a CD-ROM title in a library, you may not see the actual disk and printed material that accompanies it. However, the vendor's name usually appears on the title screen. Your library may own a reference work entitled *Gale Directory of Databases* that gives the name and address of both the information provider and the CD-ROM vendor. If you don't see it, ask a librarian for help.

CD-ROM programs that cover periodical literature are usually updated several times a year. The newspapers or journals on the disk also have their own publication dates, so cite both the date of the disk and the date when the information was first published. For example, the *New York Times* is published daily in paper. CD-ROM vendors collect these daily issues and publish a new disk every few months. At the end of the year, they may produce another disk that supersedes earlier ones and that covers the entire year. When you cite a *New York Times* article that you located on a CD-ROM disk, cite both dates.

Sample Entries for CD-ROMs and Other Portable Sources

CD-ROMs with No Corresponding Printed Source. Not all CD-ROM disks are merely electronic versions of printed works. However, learning whether a printed version is available may be difficult. If you don't have complete information, cite whatever is available:

> United States. Dept. of State. "Industrial Outlook for Coal Products." 1995. National Trade Data Bank. CD-ROM. US Dept. of Commerce. Dec. 1996.

> "Sara Lee, Inc.: Company Report." 14 Sept. 1995. General Business File. CD-ROM. Information Access. Dec. 1995.

> English Poetry Full-Text Database. Rel. 2. CD-ROM. Oxford: Oxford UP, 1992.

Occasionally, an electronic publication is sold in a package containing more than one type of media. For example, both a CD-ROM disk and a diskette may be supplied, or a video cassette may accompany the program. In such cases, provide information on the entire contents of the package to help your reader locate the program you actually used.

Nonperiodicals. Some CD-ROMs are issued only once, and others are updated infrequently. Encyclopedias are an example of this type of publication:

> The Oxford English Dictionary. 2nd ed. CD-ROM. Oxford: Oxford UP, 1992.

Periodicals.

> Martinson, Sonya B. "Educational Opportunities for Immigrant Families." Urbana: ERIC: Clearinghouse on Elementary and Early Childhood Educ., 1995. ERIC. CD-ROM. Silver Platter. June 1996.

Williams, Henry R. "Mexican Immigrants Find New Home." <u>New York Times</u> 26 Aug. 1995, late ed.: C2. <u>New York Times Ondisc</u>. CD-ROM, UMI-Proquest. Dec. 1995.

Russo, Natalie. "Toward a Historical Understanding of Immigration." <u>DAI 56</u> (1996): 2546A. U of Virginia, 1995. <u>Dissertation Abstracts Ondisc</u>. CD-ROM. 1996.

Publications on Diskette. Since a computer disk is limited in its storage capacity and usually holds just one program or file, the bibliographic citation looks much like that of a book:

Rodriguez, Jose. <u>Twilight of History</u>. Diskette. Ypsilanti: Southwark, 1995.

<u>Alpha Four</u>. Ver. 4.0. Diskette. Burlington: Alpha, 1995.

Sample MLA Research Paper

The following paper illustrates the MLA style of documentation. Each page of the research paper should carry your last name and the page number in the upper right-hand corner, one-half inch from the top and one inch from the right margin. The first line of the text on each page should be one inch from the top of the page. The *MLA Handbook* recommends double-spacing the entire paper.

Martinez 1

Ronald Martinez

Dr. William Skeats

Introduction to Composition

1 June 1996

Each page should have a running head that includes your last name and the page number. The running head should be one-half inch from the top margin and one inch from the right margin.

William Penn: His Life and Role in the

Creation of the Colony of Pennsylvania

As William Penn wrote a petition to the English Crown in June of 1680, asking that he be given land in America, he signaled the start of a new era for English nonconformists, the birth of what would become Pennsylvania. This action heralded the end of his unsuccessful efforts in England in support of religious liberty and the beginning of a new and fateful endeavor (Miller 132). The land that was awarded to Penn by King Charles II gave new hope to Englishmen, whose lives had become objects of persecution.

MLA does not require a title page. Instead, type your name, your professor's name, the course, and the date, as shown. Your name should be one inch from the top margin. Center the title of your paper.

As a Quaker, or member of the Religious Society of Friends, Penn had spent nearly all of his thirty-seven years in search of God in the form of the "inner light." One aspect of this sense of inner or Divine direction was a search for social justice. Central to any account of Penn and his role in the colony of Pennsylvania is the seeming contradiction between the aristocrat who maintained strong personal ties with the English King and the Whig-Quaker

Martinez 2

preacher who actively opposed his government's suppression of
nonconformist religious beliefs and individual liberty. Alvera
writes: "In his zeal, Penn openly denounced the Church of
England, and was despised by many" (65). Since he spoke his
views in public and wrote pamphlets expressing them, he made
numerous enemies (Leslie 26-66) and was frequently thrown into
jail. So strong was his conviction that when offered release
during his imprisonment if he would publicly repent, he stated ".

Because two
works by
Penn are
listed in the
"Works Cited"
section,
parenthetical
references to
either of the
works must
include a brief
version of the
title to identify
which book is
being cited.

. . my prison shall be my grave before I will budge a jot" (Penn,
Passages 326). He then spent nine months in prison and was
finally released. English hatred and abuse of Quakers and other
nonconformists continued unabated. The death of Penn's father
and his marriage to Gulielma Springett occurred soon after one
another, and he found himself the recipient of an unpaid debt
that Charles II had owed to his father, an admiral in the British
Navy (Giscardi 96). This debt amounted to six thousand pounds
but William asked that the debt be repaid with land rather than
money. Fontana and Kvortes make it clear that the acquisition of
the land that was to become Pennsylvania was important to Penn
not because of its material value but rather its spiritual worth
(101). It was soon to become a home where Quakers could
practice their beliefs unhampered by the prejudices of others.

The land Penn received lay north of Maryland, south of

Martinez 3

New York, and west of Delaware. At that time, approximately three thousand English Quakers as well as Dutch and Swedish immigrants occupied the area (Fontana and Kvortes 143). With his cousin William Markham, Penn dispatched a proclamation from the king announcing that he would be their governor. Penn accompanied the proclamation with a letter assuring them that their well-being had not been handed over to a tyrant (Penn, Papers 198). He later sent three commissioners to help Markham, who was to be his deputy governor, and added a letter addressed to the Indians who inhabited the area. In this letter, Penn wrote, "I have great love and regard for you and desire to win and gain your love and friendship by a kind, just, and peaceful life . . ." (Penn, Papers 218). In 1682, Penn, together with his friends Algernon Sydney and John Locke, wrote The Frame of Government for Pennsylvania, designed as Penn put it "to leave myself and successors no power of doing mischief, so that the will of one man may not hinder the good of a whole country" (Penn, Papers 224). On 30 August 1682, shortly after the death of his mother to whom he had been greatly attached, Penn left England for the new land.

Sailing on the small ship Welcome, Penn and the more than one hundred colonists who accompanied him filled the ship to

The top, bottom, left, and right margins are all one inch.

Martinez 4

bursting, bringing with them nearly three hundred tons of cargo (Rustokowski et al. 87). This weight was made up almost entirely of the equipment needed for the setting up of the colony. Walters notes that one colonist brought a mill, and Penn brought horses (213). Penn noted in his papers that a tragic outbreak of smallpox had resulted in the death of thirty-one colonists by the time the ship reached land on 27 October (170). The colonists were met by Markham at the small Dutch town of New Castle. It was there that Penn presented to the people of the three counties that made up the Duke of York's territories, which later became the state of Delaware, the deeds to their land. The territories were subject to his authority but were not to become part of Pennsylvania (Alvera 111).

Choose a clear, easily readable typeface. Start with a new printer ribbon or toner cartridge. Print on only one side of the paper.

The Welcome sailed twenty miles up the Delaware River to the Swedish town of Upland. Here Penn held his first "meeting for worship," renaming the town Chester. Next, Penn sailed by barge up to the high ground that lay between the Schuylkill and the Delaware Rivers. Although only one house known as the Blue Anchor Tavern marked the spot, he decided to build what he called a city of brotherly love: Philadelphia. Penn was actually a pioneer in the field of city planning and laid out a rational checkerboard pattern that could accommodate the rapid growth

Martinez 5

of the city that was to follow (Miller 140).

For the next month, he oversaw the realization of his plans for Philadelphia and met with the local Indians. During this period, he also began construction of his own home, Pennsbury Manor, where he planned to live with his wife Gulielma. In November, Penn met with three Indian tribes to negotiate a treaty among them. Present were the Lenni Lenape, the Mingoe (a branch of the Iroquois), and the Shawnee from the Susquehanna region (Penn, <u>Papers</u> 289). The two groups made speeches and pledged, in the Quaker tradition, their good faith to each other. The event was recorded with a wampum belt, and the treaty was long upheld. Penn was called "Onas," the Indian word for quill, and was treated with admiration and affection throughout his life.

On 4 December, Penn oversaw the first Assembly, which lasted four days. During the Assembly, the members banned "superfluous and tedious speeches," admitted the three lower provinces into Pennsylvania at their request, and created a code of seventy laws, forty of which were already contained in Penn's charter (Miller 140). Four days later, Penn set out for Maryland to meet with Lord Baltimore in order to clear up a dispute over the hazy border between the two states. As Alvera writes: "The

The first line of every paragraph is indented one-half inch (or five character spaces).

Martinez 6

charter of each governor gave him rights to territory also

included in the other's charter, probably the result of . . .

inaccurate maps and land surveys" (275). Although they were

unsuccessful in resolving the dispute, they remained civil to one

another and promised to meet again to take up their

deliberations in the spring.

Ellipses (three spaced periods) indicate words that have been omitted.

  Philadelphia grew quickly, and twenty-three ships of

colonists arrived before the summer of 1683. The city saw the

birth of its first native child to the Key family who became

known as First-Born Key although his given name was actually

John. Penn celebrated the event by giving the child a plot of

land in central Philadelphia. The Assembly met again in March,

merely making the previously revised <u>Frame of Government</u> into

a constitution and reducing the weight of the Governor's vote

from that of three persons to one (Alvera 267). Penn met once

again with Lord Baltimore in May but with no more success than

was the case with the first meeting. He also negotiated with the

Indians for as much land as a man could cover, walking for

three days from Neshaminy Creek. However, after walking with

tribal leaders for one and a half days, he decided that that was

sufficient for the colony's needs for the time being. Penn's time

was divided between Pennsbury Manor and his home in

Philadelphia. On 20 August 1683, Thomas Lloyd, a Welsh physician, and Francis Daniel Pastorius arrived with the intention of buying fifteen thousand acres. Both became close friends of Penn and active participants in the new colony (Giscardi 243).

A cloud seemed to pass over Pennsylvania and matters took a turn for the worse. News came that Lord Baltimore had left for England to bring his border claims to the attention of the king. In the meantime, General Talbot seized land near New Castle, building a fort and commanding the local residents to pay taxes to Lord Baltimore (Walters 278). Penn decided that he must go as well in order to uphold Pennsylvania's claims. On 12 August 1684, Penn sailed on the <u>Endeavor</u>. Forty-seven days later, he arrived at Sussex, just six miles from his home. Four months after his arrival, Charles II died and was succeeded by James II, an old friend of Penn's father. Although the king met with the two governors and split much of the disputed territory between them, the border between Pennsylvania and Maryland would only be settled with the establishment of the Mason-Dixon line in 1762 (Alvera 301). The royal patronage that Penn enjoyed during this period came to an end with the Bloodless Revolution of 1688. In the meantime, however, Penn was able to secure the release of all religious prisoners, including fifteen thousand Quakers, some of whom had not been free for over fifteen years. Penn also traveled in Germany and Holland to spread the news of Pennsylvania. When William of Orange and Mary assumed the throne, Penn was seen as a suspicious character because of his ties to the former king. He was arrested again and again but on each occasion he was able to prove his innocence.

While still in England, Penn ordered that a public school be built and appointed George Keith its first master. This school, Penn stipulated, was to be available to Quakers and non-Quakers alike (Penn, Papers 376). Families were to pay whatever they could and even the children of families who could pay nothing could attend. The founder of Quakerism, George Fox, died on 13 January 1691, deeply shaking the Quaker community. Just before Penn and his family were to sail for Pennsylvania, he was charged with treason. Although he was later freed of charges, the Crown took away Penn's position of governor and news came from the colony that George Keith had instigated religious strife among the Quakers. Closely following came the death of his wife Gulielma.

In August of 1694, however, the colony was returned to Penn and his cousin William Markham was once again made

Martinez 9

deputy governor. On his arrival at Chester, he was given a
festive welcome although the celebration was dampened when a
boy lost his arm while firing a cannon. Going on to Philadelphia,
he found that much had changed during his absence and strife
and anger were dividing the colony. Slaveholding was creeping
into the colony despite Penn's resistance. Colonists divided into
two groups: Quakers and the Church Party (Alvera 359).

Word came in 1701 that a bill had been raised in
Parliament that would take all proprietary governments away
from their owners and return them to the Crown. Once again
Penn had to return to England in order to save the colony. A
newly elected Assembly met and established a third charter with
some changes. One of these specified that Pennsylvania and the
territories could separate whenever they wished as long as due
notice was provided. The other difference allowed the Assembly
to propose laws. Appointing Andrew Hamilton as deputy
governor, Penn and his family sailed for England on 3
November 1701 on the ship <u>Dalmahoy</u>. Although Penn was able
to halt the threatened legislation, he was never to see
Pennsylvania again. Strife once again broke out among the
colonists and the territories split away from Pennsylvania, calling
themselves Delaware.

Martinez 10

Although Pennsylvania's problems were far from over and Deputy Governor Hamilton was discovered to be secretly working against the colonial government, conditions gradually improved. The Assembly elected in 1710 was more sympathetic to Penn, and Deputy Governor Charles Gookin proved to be an intelligent, responsible administrator (Rustokowski et al. 299).

Penn retired to a productive life in England, where he lived with his second wife and their children, writing a number of religious works. In 1712, he suffered a stroke from which he failed to recover. Thus passed a remarkable life of achievement. Through his relentless work, even in the face of disaster, William Penn surmounted incredible obstacles to meet what seemed impossible goals. The results of his work in support of religious toleration and human rights continues to be visible, even in the present day. The Constitution of the United States is to some extent a testimony to his efforts. Americans can do no better than adopt William Penn as a role model in their efforts to achieve social justice. Although Penn failed in many of his struggles, we would do well to follow his example and strive in our own time to surmount the evils that plague our own world.

Martinez 11

Works Cited

Alvera, Hermina B. <u>The Colony of Pennsylvania: A Study of the Influence of William Penn</u>. Boston: Allyn, 1978.

Fontana, Ingrid, and Sharon Kvortes. <u>William Penn and the Religious Society of Friends</u>. Studies in American Religion Ser. Syracuse: Atherton, 1987.

Giscardi, Maria. Introduction. <u>The Penns of Pennington: Their Domestic and Religious Life</u>. London, 1893.

Leslie, Charles. <u>Primitive Heresie Revived in the Faith and Practice of the People Called Quakers Wherein All is Shewn in Seven Particulars</u>. 1698. London: Macmillan, 1982.

Miller, Susan R. "William Penn and the Founding of Philadelphia." <u>Daedalus</u> 123.2 (1994): 131-42.

Penn, William. <u>The Papers of William Penn</u>. 1746. Philadelphia: Mellon, 1976.

---. <u>Passages from the Life and Writings of William Penn</u>. Ed. Earl Patterson. New York: Doubleday, 1954.

Rustokowski, Martha, et al. <u>A History of the Quakers of Chester, Pennsylvania</u>. Philadelphia: Livingston, 1933.

Walters, Henry R. <u>The World of William Penn</u>. New York: Harper, 1986.

"Works Cited" always begins on a new page. The heading is centered one inch from the top of the page. The entire page is double-spaced, with no extra space between entries. Entries are alphabetized.

The first line of each entry is typed at the left margin; subsequent lines are indented one-half inch or five spaces.

Two works by the same author. Note the use of three hyphens in place of the author's name.

Underline book and journal titles, and capitalize all important words.

Understanding APA Documentation Style

The system of documentation developed by the American Psychological Association is widely used for psychology as well as for other social and behavioral sciences. In some ways, it varies little from MLA. However, be alert for differences and follow the rules precisely if you are asked to use this style for the paper you are writing.

Instead of a list of "Works Cited" at the end of the paper, APA uses a list of "References" that includes full bibliographic information on each source. Be sure that each parenthetical reference in your text has a corresponding entry in the "References." Conversely, sources on the reference list should be cited in the body of the paper.

Understanding APA Format for Books

Select the bibliography cards or records for sources you have referred to in the body of your paper and alphabetize them by author. One way APA differs from MLA is the way authors are cited. Give the names of all authors (not simply the first) in inverted order. Use a comma after each name and an ampersand (&) before the last name:

Pritchard, J. B., & Brown, S. R.

Williams, B. T., Smith, J. B., & Wilson, C. R.

The following are general guidelines for citing sources in the APA style:

- All entries should be double-spaced. The first line of each entry should be at the left margin; runover lines should be indented three spaces.
- Author's name should be shortened by using initials instead of given names.

Romero, R. P.

James, T. R.

- Two or more works by the same author should be listed chronologically, with the older work being listed first:

Hardy, T. (1891). Tess of the d'Urbervilles.

Hardy, T. (1895). Jude the obscure.

- Two or more works by the same author that are published in the same year are alphabetized and annotated with lowercase letters:

Terwilliger, M. (1995a). <u>Under the elm tree</u>.

Terwilliger, M. (1995b). <u>The tree of life</u>.

- Capitalize only the first word of the title, the first word of the subtitle, and any proper nouns. The entire title should be underlined.

<u>The problem of pornography: Regulation and the right to free speech</u>.

- Use the post office abbreviation for the state if the city is not well known (the abbreviation that is used with the zip code).

Morristown, NJ

Shelby, NC

- Do the same for foreign countries.

Reims, FR

- Volume numbers should be given in Arabic numerals, not Roman.
- Alphabetize entries with numerals as if the numerals are spelled out.
- When typing the name of most publishers, do not include words like *Company, Publishing,* and *Inc.;* instead, use a shortened form—for example, Scribner's or Van Nostrand. In the case of academic publishers, however, do write out the full name, for example, University of Chicago Press, Columbia University Press.

To save space, APA uses abbreviations whenever possible. Frequently used abbreviations include:

chap.	chapter
ed.	edition
Rev. ed.	Revised edition
2nd ed.	second edition
Ed. or Eds.	Editor or Editors
Trans.	Translator(s)
n.d.	no date

p. or pp.	page or pages
Vol.	Volume (as in Vol. 4)
vols	volumes (as in 4 volumes)
No.	Number
Pt.	Part
Tech. Rep.	Technical Report
Suppl.	Supplement

Sample Entries for Books

Although the following examples cover most of the works students frequently encounter, you may occasionally find yourself citing a different type of source. If you are in doubt, consult the latest edition of the *Publication Manual of the American Psychological Association*.

Author, Anonymous.

> Marijuana, the national impact on education. (1982). New York: American Council on Marijuana and Other Psychoactive Drugs.

> Exoatmospheric & space travel. (1994). N.p.: Systems Co.

Author, Corporate.
Since the author of the book is also its publisher, substitute the word "Author" for the publisher's name:

> University of South Alabama Archives. (1994). Index to divorce cases of the Thirteenth Judicial Circuit Court of Alabama, 1816-1918. Mobile, AL: Author.

Author, Single.

> Ittyerah, M. (1994). Laterality in blind children. Delhi: University of Delhi.

> McCourt, K. (1977). Working-class women and grass-roots politics. Bloomington: Indiana University Press.

> DeServille, P. (1982). Salinger's vision of the twentieth century. London: Routledge.

Feuchtwanger, E.J. (1993). <u>From Weimar to Hitler: Germany, 1918–33</u>. New York: St. Martin's.

Authors, Joint.

Mayer, H., & Wade, R. C. (1969). <u>Growth of a metropolis</u>. Chicago: University of Chicago Press.

Clayton, R. R., & Estep, W. (1995). <u>Marijuana in the "third world":</u> <u>Appalachia, U.S.A.</u> Boulder, CO: Reinner.

Book in a Series.

Rogers, F. (1994) <u>Divorce</u>. Let's talk about it series. New York: G. P. Putnam's.

Toner, S. C. (1996). <u>George Washington: America's first strategic leader</u>. USAWC strategy research project series. Carlisle Barracks, PA: U.S. Army War College.

Books—Date in Question.

Dickens, C. (1900?). <u>Oliver Twist</u>. London: Ward, Lock.

Dickens, C. (n.d.). <u>Barnaby Rudge: And the mystery of Edwin Drood and</u> <u>other stories</u>. New York: William L. Allison.

Dickens, C. (c.1838). <u>The adventures of Oliver Twist: Pictures from Italy</u> <u>and American notes</u>. New York: William L. Allison.

Dickens, C. (18??). <u>Barnaby Rudge: A tale of the riots of "Eighty."</u> Boston: DeWolfe, Fiske.

Conference Proceedings.

European Foundation for the Improvement of Living and Working Conditions. (1994). <u>Monitoring the work environment: Report of sec-</u> <u>ond European Conference</u>. Paris: European Communities Official Publications Office.

Factor-Litvak, P., Kline, J., Slavkovich, V., & Graziano, J. (1995). Blood lead and blood pressure in children aged 5.5 years. <u>34th Annual Meeting of the Society of Toxicology, Baltimore, MD, 5–9 Mar. 1995.</u> Reston, VA: Society of Toxicology.

Ellis, M. M. (1995). Examining the visual perception skills of Japanese and American children. <u>104th Annual Meeting of the Ohio Academy of Science, Westerville, OH, 28–30 Apr. 1995.</u> Bowling Green, OH: Ohio Journal of Science. New York: Harcourt, 1996.

Oller, D. K. (1995). Early speech and word learning in bilingual and monolingual children: Advantages of early bilingualism. <u>American Association for the Advancement of Science Annual Meeting, Atlanta, GA, 16–21 Feb. 1995.</u> Washington, DC: American Association for the Advancement of Science.

Edited Book.

De Silva, R. S. (Ed.). (1991). <u>Treating the marijuana-dependent person.</u> New York: American Council on Marijuana and Other Psychoactive Drugs.

Essay in a Collection.

Wilson, K. B. (1995). Early Years of the College. In Jack W. Berryman, <u>Out of many, one: A history of the American College of Sports Medicine.</u> Champaign, IL: Human Kinetics.

Later or Revised Edition.

Haman, E. A. (1994). <u>How to file for divorce in Florida: with forms</u> (3rd ed.). Clearwater, FL: Sphinx.

Translation.

Bergaust, E. (1985). <u>Wernher von Braun: The authoritative and definitive biographical profile of the father of modern space flight.</u> (Cheryl R. Northridge, Trans.) Washington: National Space Institute. (Original work published 1976)

Semelin, J., & Husserl-Kapit, S. (1993). <u>Unarmed against Hitler: Civilian resistance in Europe, 1939-1943</u>. (Suzan Husserl-Kapit, Trans.) Westport, CN: Praeger.

Works with More than One Volume.

Guell, A. (1993). <u>Physical countermeasures to be applied during long-term manned space flight</u> (Vols. 1–2). Noordwijk, The Netherlands: European Space Agency, 1993.

Understanding APA Format for Periodicals

Here are some general guidelines for citing articles from periodicals using APA style:

- Capitalize only the first word of the title and the subtitle of the article as well as any proper names.
- Do not underline the article title or enclose it in quotations.
- Capitalize all important words of the journal title.
- Underline journal title and volume number.
- Enclose any information needed to identify the article that is not a routine element of a citation in brackets, for example, [Editorial] or [Letter to the editor].

Sample Entries for Periodicals

Although the following examples cover most of the information needed to cite periodical literature, you may occasionally be uncertain as to the correct format. If you are in doubt, consult the most recent edition of the *Publication Manual of the American Psychological Association*.

Journals Using Continuous Pagination. Many scholarly journals number pages continuously for all issues in a single volume. In other words, if the first issue of a volume ends with page 224, the next issue will begin with page 225. In such cases, only the volume number and page numbers are needed:

Luepker, R. V. (1995). Reducing blood cholesterol levels in children. <u>The Journal of the American Medical Association, 273</u>, 1461–1463.

Garstang, M., Larom D., & Raspet, R. (1995). Atmospheric controls on elephant communication. <u>Journal of Experimental Biology, 198</u>, 939–951.

Hooker, A. (1994, Fall). The international law of forests. <u>Natural Resources Journal</u>, <u>34</u>, 823–877.

Journals Paginated by Issue. In some journals, every issue begins with page 1. Therefore, the issue number is needed to find the article cited. In such citations, the issue number is placed in parentheses and follows the volume number:

Caputo, M., & Ostrom, B. J. (1994). Potential tax revenue from a regulated marijuana market: A meaningful revenue source. <u>American Journal of Economics and Sociology</u>, <u>53</u>(4), 475–484.

Davidson, E. S., & Schenk, S. (1994). Variability in subjective responses to marijuana: Initial experiences of college students. <u>Addictive Behaviors</u>, <u>19</u>(5): 331–344.

Kershaw, I. (1993). Working towards the Fuhrer: Reflections on the nature of the Hitler dictatorship. <u>Contemporary European History (Great Britain)</u>, <u>2</u>(2):103–118.

Tchamba, N. M., Bauer, H., Hunia, A., De Iongh, H. H., & Planton, H. (1994). Some observations on the movements and home range of elephants in Waza National Park, Cameroon. <u>Mammalia</u>, <u>58</u>(4), 334–348.

DeFrances, Carol J., & Smith, Steven K. (1994, Summer). Federal-state relations in gun control: The 1993 Brady Handgun Violence Prevention Act. <u>Publius</u>, <u>24</u>, 69–82.

Letter to the Editor.

Postrel, Virginia I. (1995, April 30). Reawakening to Waco: Does the federal government understand the message it's sending? [Letter to the editor]. <u>Miami Herald</u>, pp. C3, 11.

Magazine, Weekly.

Minard, Lawrence. (1995, June 19). Battling affluenza (rearing rich children). <u>Forbes</u>, <u>96</u>, pp. 10–11.

Cockurn, Alexander. (1995, May 29). Harvard and murder: The case of Carlos Salinas. <u>Nation</u>, <u>104</u>, pp. 747–748.

Newspaper. When an article is continued on nonconsecutive pages, list all page numbers separated by commas.

> Day, Kathleen. (1995, January 10). Service calls FBI on child pornography: America Online says photos transmitted. The Washington Post, pp. D4, 6.

Newspaper, Anonymous Author.

> Around the nation: Child pornography probe. (1995, 18 February). The Washington Post, p. A04.

Newspaper, Single Author.

> Biskupic, Joan. (1994, November 30). Court backs child pornography law, lets video retailer's conviction stand. The Washington Post, p. A19.

Understanding APA Format for Theses and Dissertations

A thesis or dissertation must be completed as part of the requirements for a graduate degree in many universities. Students are required to submit copies of their work to the university library of the degree-granting institution and an abstract or brief description of the work is also sent to *Dissertation Abstracts International* (*DAI*). The thesis or dissertation may also be made available in microform by University Microfilms or may be published in paper by a book publisher.

Sample Entries for Theses and Dissertations

Dissertation or Thesis in Dissertation Abstracts. Include the volume and page numbers of *DAI*. If microfilm was used, include the University Microfilms number:

> Spellman, Leslie L. (1992). Date rape and sexual aggression by college males: Incidence and the involvement of impulsivity, anger, and hostility. Dissertation Abstracts International, 52, 3542A. (University Microfilms No. 92-05,121)

> Palczewski, Catherine Helen. (1994). The feminist anti-pornography movement and the rhetorical construction of social knowledge. Dissertation Abstracts International, 54, 4453A-4454A. (University Microfilms No. 94-12,105)

Unpublished Thesis.

Baugh, Harvey Francis. (1930). <u>The placement of the Creoles of Louisiana in American literature through the novels and short stories of George Washington Cable, Kate Chopin, and Grace Elizabeth King</u>. Unpublished master's thesis, University of Virginia, Charlottesville.

Swann, Israel. (1995). <u>George Washington: The making of an American legend</u>. Unpublished master's thesis, California State University, Dominguez Hills.

Note: Published theses and dissertations are treated like books.

Understanding APA Format for Reference Works

Bennett, T. R. (1994). Asteroid. In <u>Encyclopedia Americana</u> (Vol. 3, pp. 548–551). Danbury, CT: Grolier.

Understanding APA Format for Government Documents

Many useful publications in the social and behavioral sciences are available from the government. However, state and local as well as foreign governments also produce material. The following are some general guidelines for citing a government publication:

- All government documents available from the Government Printing Office (GPO) should show this office as the publisher.
- When citing ERIC (Educational Resources Information Center), give the ERIC number in parentheses at the end of the entry.
- If a report is available from a document deposit service like NTIS or ERIC, enclose the document number in parentheses at the end of the entry. Do not use a period at the end of the document number.
- List the name of the specific department, office, or agency that published or produced the document exactly as it appears.
- If the office that produced the report is not well known, give the higher or umbrella department or agency.

For statutes, include the source and section number. In parentheses give the publication date of the statutory compilation, which may be different from the year in the name of the act.

Sample Entries for Government Documents

Documents from the U.S. Federal Government.

To repeal section 29 of the International Air Transportation Competition Act. . . : Hearing before the Subcommittee on Aviation of the Committee on Public Works and Transportation, House of Representatives. H.R. 858, 102d Cong., 1st Sess. (1992).

National Institute of Health. (1995). Adverse reactions to HIV vaccines: Medical, ethical, and legal issues (DHHS Publication No. BRT 95-2411). Washington, DC: U.S. Government Printing Office.

Harriman, C. J. (1994). Assessing the role of passive smoking in cardiovascular disease (NIH Publication No. 94-1365). Washington, DC: U.S. Department of Health and Human Services.

O'Neill, Tip. (1978). The office and the duties of the Speaker of the House of Representatives (95th Cong., House Document 354). Washington, DC: U. S. Government Printing Office.

Haworth, T. R. (1995). Teacher preparation in early childhood programs (Report No. NCRTL-FF-95-5). East Lansing, MI: National Center for Research on Teacher Learning. (ERIC Document Reproduction Service No. ED 456 104)

Swenson, R. T. (1996). Perspectives from space: NASA classroom information and activities. (NTIS No. PB 95-123 234/AS)

Americans with Disabilities Act of 1990, Pub. L. No. 101-336, § 2, 104 Stat. 328 (1991).

Documents from Other Countries and International Organizations.

European Foundation for the Improvement of Living and Working Conditions. (1994). Monitoring the work environment: Report of second European Conference, November 11-12, 1992. Papers of the conference held in Dublin, Ireland. N.p.: Eur. Communities Official Pubns Office.

State Documents.

Fuller, Sharon. (1994). <u>The gun control debate: An update</u>. Madison, WI: Legis. Ref. Bur.

Understanding APA Format for Audiovisuals

If you are citing a source like a television broadcast or a musical recording, here are some general guidelines:

- Give the names of all the primary contributors like the producer, director, or recording artist if they are available. List their function in parentheses after their names.
- If it is not clear from the citation, specify the medium in brackets immediately after the title.
- List the location and name of distributor or broadcast station.
- Place the name of the scriptwriter or songwriter in the author position.

Sample Entries for Audiovisuals

Hobart, W. (Producer). (1994). <u>Slowly changing ways: The Amish in America</u>. [Film]. (Available from Learning Modes, Inc., 300 Madison Avenue, New York, NY 10023)

Mayo, R. (Producer). (1995, November 14). <u>Far and away</u>. [Television program]. New York: WNET.

Schoenfeld, H. (Speaker). (1995). <u>Changes in our attitudes toward mental illness</u>. (Cassette Recording No. 243-233-66B-C). Washington, DC: American Psychological Association.

Understanding APA Format for Electronic Sources

Electronic information sources are still very recent and new formats are still appearing. Therefore, the correct way of citing electronic information will continue to evolve. Luckily, works like *Electronic Style: A Guide to Citing Electronic Information*, by Xia Li and Nancy B. Crane, have taken much of the guesswork out of constructing citations. If your paper includes many electronic references, check to see if your library has any of these titles in its collection. Since electronic sources are so varied, you may find that you need a more complete treatment of the subject.

Sample Entries for Electronic Sources

As a rule, electronic information sources are considerably more difficult to locate than printed ones. Few bibliographic tools exist to identify electronic information. Some information is only available through fee-based services that your reader may be unable to access. Other information may be found only on the Internet and may disappear weeks after you have discovered it. Whenever possible, cite only Internet sources that are available through a professional or scholarly association. The best rule to follow is: provide as much information as possible. In this uncertain period, the precise format for an electronic source is less important than doing all in your power to ensure that your reader can locate your sources.

Entire Works.

Kirk-Othmer online (4th ed.) [On-line]. (1993). Available: Dialog File: Kirk-Othmer On-line (CHEMS)

Mental measurements yearbook [On-line]. (1995, May). Available: Knowledge Index File: The Merck Index On-line (DRUG4)

Gillen, Shawn, & Barasch, Sam, eds. (n.d.). Highbeams. [On-line serial]. Available http: http://stu.beloit.edu/~highbe

ANU Student Association's survival handbook [On-line]. (n.d.). Student Association, Australian National University. Available http: http://student.anu.edu.au/SSH

1492: An ongoing voyage: Europe claims America [On-line]. (n.d.). Library of Congress. Available http: http://sunsite.unc.edu/expo/1492.exhibit/e-Eur.claims.amer/eur.claims.amer.html

Boyle, B., comp. (n.d.). American Civil War, 1861-1865 [On-line WWW]. Available: http://www.access.digex.net/~bdboyle/sw.html

Clinton, B. (1995). Bill Clinton on the Bosnian peace accord [On-line]. Available FTP: Hostname: nptn.org Directory: pub/clinton/bosnia.dir File: c89.txt

Kehoe, B. P. (1992). Zen and the art of the Internet (2nd ed.) [On-line]. Available FTP: Hostname: quake.think.com Directory: pub/etext/1992 File: zen10.txt

Note: the Kehoe document can be obtained using file transfer. The one that follows can be obtained by sending an e-mail request.

> Williams, S. (1995). Guide to sending inter-network mail [On-line].
> Available E-mail: LISTSERV@MASSVM Message: Get MAIL
> GUIDE

The document cited below can be accessed via Telnet.

> Periodic table of elements [On-line]. (1994). Available Telnet:
> gopher2.tc.umn.edu Directory: Libraries/Reference Works File:
> Periodic Table of Elements

Journal Articles.

> Fondas, N., & Steward, R. (1994). Enactment in managerial jobs: A role
> analysis [CD-ROM]. Journal of Management Studies, 31(1), 83-103.
> Available: UMI File: Business Periodicals Ondisc Item: 94-12654

> Wellnitz, H. B. (1992). Testing children with Down's Syndrome.
> Exceptional Children [On-line serial], 58, 327-332. Available: DIA-
> LOG File: Health Periodicals Database (149) Item: 1532652

> Coleman, W. E. (1991). The time trap—the new version of the classic
> book on time management. Personnel Psychology [On-line serial], 44.
> Available Telnet: gopher.tc.umn.edu Directory: Libraries/Newspapers,
> Magazines, and Newsletters/Psychology

Part of a Work. Both of the following works can be accessed via Telnet:

> Pedagogy. (1992). In Oxford English dictionary (2nd ed.) [On-line].
> Available Telnet: UWIN.U.WASHINGTON.EDU Directory:
> I/REF/OED File: pedagogy

> Harrelson, Ralph E. (1995). Space flight. In Grolier's online encyclopedia
> [On-line]. Available Telnet: UWIN.U.WASHINGTON.EDU
> Directory: I/REF/GROL File: space

Internet Sites—World Wide Web. Occasionally, it is necessary to refer to a
site rather than to a specific document. This can happen when Web pages are
untitled or when information is spread over a number of pages.

Families USA Foundation [On-line WWW]. (n.d.). Available:
http://epn.org/families.html

Yahoo!—Society and culture [On-line WWW]. (n.d.). Yahoo!
Corporation. Available: http://www.yahoo.com/Society_and_Culture/

United Nations conference [On-line WWW]. (n.d.). United Nations
Conference on Trade and Development. Available:
http://gatekeeper.unicc.org/unctad/

Federation of students [On-line WWW]. (n.d.). Federation of Students
(FedS), University of Waterloo. Available:
http://watserv1.uwaterloo.ca/~fedintrn

Sample APA Research Paper

The following paper illustrates the APA style of documentation. The *Publication Manual of the American Psychological Association* recommends double-spacing the entire paper. APA style also requires a title page that signifies what the identifying running head will be in the paper. Each page should then carry that running head for purposes of identification. In general, the running head should be an abbreviated form of the title. APA style also calls for an abstract.

Stereotypes 1

Per APA form, all pages, even the title page,
are numbered and carry a running head
(page header), which is positioned one-half
inch from the top of the page and one inch
from the right margin.

Stereotypes: A Discussion of their

Effects on African-Americans

Laura Wood

English 101

Professor Rider

March 28, 1996

All material on the title page should be
double-spaced. Include information about the
course, along with your name and the date.
The title is typed in uppercase and lowercase
letters and is centered on the page.

The abstract is typed on a
separate page (page 2). Like the
rest of the paper, it is double-
spaced.

Abstract

Stereotypes are great levelers. They exaggerate and
exploit a few seemingly unusual attributes of a group of people,
assert Geist and Jimenez (1994), and apply them to all the
members of that group. They focus on these differences and try
to dehumanize their target. To endow that group with too much
variety in appearance or actions might well make them seem
too real or too human (Bakarric & Robbins, 1995). Prejudice
loses its force when a real human being lives and works with
another. Prejudice flourishes when individuals are dehumanized.

Negative stereotypes of African-Americans abound. From
pre-Colonial days to the present, misconceptions about African-
Americans continue. African-Americans feel the effects of these
views in a variety of ways, from justifications for slavery to
segregation and job discrimination. These effects lead to
continued racism and discrimination, thereby perpetuating the
stereotypes.

Stereotypes: A Discussion of their Effects
on African-Americans

Black stereotypes were developed by individuals and
groups who focused on superficial characteristics and
exaggerated them. First and most obviously, Blacks have been
set apart by their color. White people who immigrate to this
country have the opportunity to avoid negative stereotypes by
blending in. Some change their names in order to be less
conspicuous, and if they become fluent in English, they are
almost indistinguishable from other White Americans. Blacks
have no such choice. Color will always make them stand out.
Then they are prey to all the stereotypes about their race.
(Almaguer, 1995).

Stereotypes are strengthened by ignorance. Most
Americans and Europeans know very little about African-
Americans. Direct contact with Blacks was not a part of the
experience of most Europeans. Thus from the earliest periods,
Williams (1995) writes, "White men and women relied on a
relatively small number of observers who wrote travel accounts
which tended to focus on the facets of African life and culture
which seemed most unusual from their European perspectives."

Stereotypes 4

Stereotypes about Blacks were produced by Whites for a primarily White audience. There was no opportunity for a Black person to point out that such descriptions were not accurate. Unfortunately, too many White Americans still obtain their most important impressions of Black Americans through such misrepresentations. Even now, jobs are segregated, neighborhoods are segregated. White contact with people of color is usually as subordinates, not as friends, or even equals.

Beliefs Surrounding Blackness

Some stereotypes about African-Americans also come from cultural beliefs about Blackness. According to Winthrop Jordan in <u>White over Black</u> (1992), the color Black was a cultural symbol of baseness and evil long before Europeans had any contact with Africans. These unconscious views of Blackness helped to insure that Black people would be treated poorly by Europeans (Geist & Jimenez, 1994).

West (1995) considers the Marxist belief that racism has its roots in the rise of modern capitalism. However, it can easily be shown that although racist practices were shaped and appropriated by modern capitalism, racism itself predates capitalism. To Europeans, non-European Black, brown, yellow, and red people personify "otherness" and embody alien

APA papers frequently use headings. First-level headings are centered and typed in uppercase and lowercase letters. No extra space is used above or below headings.

Stereotypes 5

All three authors are listed the first time the Yomsdoblich source is cited. Subsequent references (see below) will carry only Yomsdoblich's name and "et al."

"difference" (Yomsdoblich, Henry, & Silver, 1994).

Even Europe's Christian heritage appears to contribute to a negative image of Blackness. For example, there is the Biblical account of Ham who looked upon his father, Noah's, nakedness and failed to cover him. Ham received divine punishment in the form of the blackening of his progeny. In this highly influential narrative, Black skin is a divine curse, punishing disrespect for and rejection of paternal authority (Yomsdoblich et al., 1994).

The Effects of Stereotyping

Ignorance about African-Americans affects not only the uninformed but even educated people in many different disciplines, including film, literature, and philosophy. Postmodern writers seem not to know that Black women exist. They fail to even consider the possibility that they might have something significant to say and should be listened to, or that they might be producing art that should be seen, heard, and approached with intellectual seriousness (Burton, 1995). Many third-world scholars passively absorb White supremacist thinking and, therefore, never notice or look at Black people on the streets or at their jobs. They do not see Blacks as individuals but only gaze at them through the distorted lens of somewhat more sophisticated stereotypes. Sociological scholarship

Stereotypes 6

produced under such circumstances is not likely to produce liberating theory that will challenge racist domination. Nor will it promote a breakdown of traditional ways of seeing and thinking (Williams, 1995).

<u>Sexual and Violent Stereotypes</u>

The combination of ignorance and cultural prejudice towards Blackness led to many stereotypes (Blake, Garcia, & Marticello, 1994). Some had to do with the association of Black with evil and sexuality. Non-Europeans became associated with acts of bodily defecation, violation, and subordination (Sniderman, Margolis, & Pollwitz, 1995). Black sexuality was seen by Whites as wanton, uncontrollable, and insatiable. According to the stereotypes, Black men lusted after White women, and Black women were willing temptresses (Geist & Jimenez, 1994). Fiction abounds with the stereotype of the dangerous, rebellious man who wants to rape White women (Burton, 1995).

Typical stereotypes also addressed the need of slave owners to give reasons for slavery. Sambo, with his mindless frolicking, intense loyalty to the master, and childlike need for protection and guidance is a good example (Jordan, 1992). Sambo needed his master as much as his master needed him.

Second-level headings are typed at the left margin and underlined. Again, no extra space is used above or below headings.

Choose a clear, easily readable typeface. Start with a new printer ribbon or toner cartridge. Print on only one side of the paper.

Stereotypes 7

To enslave another race requires some justification (Geist & Jimenez, 1994). "Other good Blacks were always loyal. Mammy was the fat, jolly, motherly cook; Uncle Tom was her husband, an older Black who served competently and faithfully, worked at light tasks, and entertained with tall tales" (Geist & Jimenez, 1994, p. 133). Both are content with their position, having accepted the family's values. Both love their masters.

Following the horror of the Holocaust, the U.S. government began to legislate against racist behavior at home (Bailey, 1996). Legal barriers supporting segregation were torn down. Jobs in the rust-belt industries of auto and steel increased Black social mobility and a significant middle class of peoples of color came into existence (Bailey, 1996; Williams, 1995). Overt racist language, even under the Reagan administration, became unfashionable (Geist & Jimenez, 1994).

Children of the poor, however, include, to a disproportionate extent, people of color, and the underclass of Black and Brown working and poor people at the margins of society has grown (West, 1995). As Bakarric and Robbins (1995) explain the problem: "Despite a change in language, [racist] ideas still flourish in a more coded way; expressions of hostility to affirmative action, busing, and special interests . . .

If the same information is contained in two or more works, they are listed alphabetically according to the last name of the author and separated by a semicolon.

have now replaced overt racist discourse" (p. 144). At the same time, the federal government is cutting back federal payments to the needy and diminishing occupational health, safety, and environmental protection (Bailey, 1996). The number of low-wage, service sector jobs is rapidly increasing. Those most adversely affected by these policies have been blue-collar industrial workers and the poor, particularly women and children (West, 1995). These children then go into an impoverished educational system and face unequal opportunities when they enter the labor force.

Conclusion

"Though Black people all face oppression because of the color of their skin, there are multiple experiences of Black identity. . . . Class mobility has altered collective Black experience so that racism does not necessarily have the same impact on our lives. . . . (There are) multiple Black identities, varied Black experience. . . . Colonial imperialist paradigms of Black identity . . . represent Blackness one-dimensionally in ways that reinforce and sustain White supremacy " (Williams, 1995, p. 571).

Stereotypical views of African-Americans reinforce these negative images and thereby contribute to the further intensification of racism and discrimination.

Stereotypes 9

The "References" start on a new page. The heading is centered and positioned one inch from the top margin. All entries are double-spaced. No extra space is included between entries.

| (arrow marker)

Capitalize the first word of the title and subtitle as well as all proper nouns.

Underline book and journal titles.

The first line of each citation is flush left; subsequent lines are indented three spaces.

References

Almaguer, C. C. (1995). Exploitation and sterotyping: Mapping
the course of racism. American Ethnologist, 22(1), 176-
198.

Bailey, T. I. (1996). Racism and the color of welfare. Ethnic and
Racial Studies, 19(2), 243-266.

Bakarric, B. R., & Robbins, M. V. (1995). The creation of ethnic
categories: Ethnicity in the United States and Great Britain.
Rural Sociology, 60(1), 132-166.

Blake, S. R., Garcia, P. N., & Marticello, D. (1994). Origin of
racial imagery in modern society. American Sociological
Review, 59(3), 223-243.

Burton, V. R. (1995). Human differences: Their use and abuse in
literary works. American Sociological Review, 60(1), 654-
669.

Geist, R. N. (1994). The economic impact of stereotyping.
Capital and Class, 49, 123-143.

Hooks, G. R. (1995). Stereotyping and the problem of Black
identity. [On-line WWW]. Available: http://vt1su.uwater-
loo.ca/hooks/nt.html.

Jordan, W. R. (1992). White over Black: Historical processes
and stereotyping. Contemporary Sociology, 21(2), 154-
168.

Stereotypes 10

Kowalski, R. P. (1994). Stereotyping and the Black experience.
American Journal of Sociology, 100(4), 226-243.

Sniderman, R. R., Margolis, G. K. , & Pollwitz, B. H. (1995).
Sociology and the influence of stereotypes. Annals of the
American Academy of Political and Social Science, 540(3),
186-208.

West, V. R. (1995). A socio-historical interpretation of stereotypes. American Journal of Economics and Sociology, 54(3),
14-44.

Williams, R. E. (1995). Historical origins of White supremacy.
Contemporary Sociology, 24(3), 567-579.

Yomsdoblich, H. T., Henry, B. D., & Silver, J. K. (1994). Prejudice
and the invention of the White race. Journal of American
History, 81(4), 145-176.

Works are listed alphabetically by the name of the first author. The names of the other authors follow in the order in which they are given on the title page of the work cited.

Understanding Chicago Documentation Style

Initially, the *Chicago* style was developed by the University of Chicago Press for their own authors. It, therefore, is not limited to one discipline but may be used for documentation in the humanities and the social, biological, and physical sciences. Your instructor may prefer that you use it rather than the MLA or APA style. The *Chicago Manual* recommends an author-date system of parenthetical documentation followed by a reference list very much like the APA style. There are, however, differences between the two styles. Since the *Chicago* style is used in a wide variety of disciplines, authors are encouraged to adapt it to their needs. For example, the reference list is sometimes titled "Literature Cited" or simply "References."

Here are some basic guidelines for using the *Chicago* style:

- Place the reference list at the end of the work. Put appendixes before the reference list.
- As with the MLA style, only the first author is listed, last name first, when two or more authors are responsible for a work.
- The year of publication immediately follows the author's name. Unlike APA, it is not enclosed in parentheses.
- The second and following lines are indented two spaces from the left margin.
- Authors' names may be given in the form in which they appear on the title page or the given name may be abbreviated.
- Titles of book chapters and periodical articles are not enclosed in quotations. Titles of books and periodicals are underlined.

In general, the University of Chicago Press prefers more complete information than APA, including full names, full titles, and full publication facts. However, it recognizes that different disciplines have their own conventions. It may be this openness that is responsible for its increasing popularity and wider use.

Sample Entries for Chicago Style

Jones, Ronald M. 1994. <u>The Behavior of Bats</u>. Cambridge: Harvard University Press.

Norko, Juliet M. 1993. Hawthorne's love letters: The threshold world of Sophia Peabody. <u>American Transcendental Quarterly 7</u>, no. 2:127–39.

Marvin, R. P., and J. L. Robbins. 1994. Galaxies by the thousand: New Hubble discoveries. <u>Nature</u> (London) 274:276–83.

Bernstein, Sandra. 1995. Mandela forever. Harpers (March): 47–63.

New York Times. 1995. Editorial, 12 March.

Horowitz, S. R. 1994. Bloodbath in Bosnia. Charlotte Observer, 22 January, final edition.

U. S. House. 1995. Committee on Commerce. Ryan White CARE Act Amendments of 1995. Report to accompany H. R. 1872. 104th Cong., 1st sess. Committee Print 23.

Writing across the Curriculum

The first time you use this book will very likely be in a freshman composition class in which you may write the first of many college research papers. If you plan to continue on to graduate school, the number and complexity of your research assignments will increase, but the basics will remain the same. Techniques you have learned in this course will serve you well no matter what sort of research project you undertake. However, certain differences exist in the way different disciplines conduct research.

Writing in the Humanities

Research techniques used in the humanities have been emphasized in this book. The following are some of the conventions of style and format found in a humanities paper:

- Internal headings are less common because the paper is seen as a whole, with paragraphs closely connected both to the thesis and to one another.
- Both topics and style tend to be less formal than in the social, biological, or physical sciences.
- A paper may be directed at a lay audience, which is usually not the case with a paper in a scientific discipline.
- Clarity is especially important, and writers should refrain from the use of excessive jargon.
- Writing in the first person is acceptable when you're expressing your own views and reactions. However, third person is more appropriate for an objective tone.
- Typical areas for research in literature include the way the work is constructed, the effect of structure on the author's purpose, or the work's plot, characterization, or use of imagery. Literary analysis can take many forms, such as psychoanalytical, historical, and economic.

- English papers use the MLA style although scholars in history, philosophy, and music favor the *Chicago* style. *The Handbook of the Linguistics Society of America* is the choice of most scholars in linguistics, although the APA style is also used.

Writing in the Social Sciences

Research in the social sciences, some of which are anthropology, economics, education, political science, psychology, and sociology, is not very different from the humanities in introductory courses. As students advance to upper division courses, however, they will notice marked differences.

Here are some of the common characteristics of research in the social sciences:

- Papers tend to be more formal.
- The style of a paper conforms to the particular objective of the project. A paper may be descriptive, explanatory, exploratory, or evaluative,
- Descriptive and explanatory formats are the most common for presentation of information in psychology, sociology, anthropology, and political science. Such papers accurately describe individual patterns and provide explanations of the dynamics of a group or organization.
- A paper typically begins with an abstract followed by a literature review.
- Descriptions of research methods, findings, and discussion comprise the remainder of the paper,
- Technical vocabulary is more frequently used than in a humanities paper. Your audience consists of specialists, so it is important that you use the language of the field.
- The case study is a common format. It describes the problem at hand and presents solutions or treatments.
- Other papers in the social sciences follow a similar format, stating the problem, providing background information concerning the problem, methods or processes used to solve the problem, and finally conclusions and recommendations,
- Charts, figures, graphs, maps, and photographs are commonly included. Numerical data is often presented in a table.
- The use of standard statistical terms such as means, percentages, chi squares, and other terms found in statistical analysis are common. You must, however, explain clearly what these statistics have to do with your project.
- Internal headings are necessary to separate the sections of the paper. Typical headings might be "Statement of the Problem" or "Conclusions."
- Each section is written as a complete and separate entity from beginning to end. The reader should be able to read it separately out of context and still make sense of it.

Writing in the Natural Sciences

Research in the physical and biological sciences is carried out in still other ways. The following are some of the characteristics of scientific writing:

- Typical forms of scientific writing include literature reviews and reports of scientific experiments. The latter include detailed descriptions of the procedures and materials used so they can be replicated and contain the empirical results of the experiment and their implications.
- Although a scientific paper may be persuasive, it tends to be more objective and expository in nature.
- Research is usually performed by collecting data through observation or experimental research.
- Accuracy, more than writing style, is of prime importance in the reporting of observations and experimental data.
- Results are usually tabulated and presented graphically. Tables and figures should be numbered and labeled clearly and placed as close to the discussion of their contents as possible.
- In addition to experimental data, scientific research requires extensive searches of the relevant literature in the library.
- Most scientific disciplines have their own style guidelines. Even individual journals within a discipline may vary.
- Many standard bibliographic formats have been developed by professional societies. For example, electrical engineers use the format of the Institute for Electronics and Electrical Engineers. Chemists use the form developed by the American Chemical Society, and physicists, the American Institute of Physics.
- The passive voice is often used to emphasize the tasks themselves rather than the person performing them.
- Avoid the second person *you*, and do not give instructions and directions in a scientific paper.
- The first person *I* or *we* is acceptable when writing about one's own experiment.
- Since readers may be scientists in other disciplines, style should be clear and self-explanatory.
- Though technical terms must be used for accuracy, avoid overreliance on them.
- Scientific papers are typically divided into four main sections: introduction, methods, results, and conclusion, preceded by a title page and abstract.
- The introduction should identify the question, formulate a testable hypothesis, state the purpose of the investigation, and mention the general method of investigation that will be used.

- The methods section normally lists the equipment used and describes chronologically the steps of the experiment.
- In the results section, clearly describe the data you collected. Raw data such as printouts may be presented in the appendices.
- In the conclusion, discuss your results and their importance. Compare them with those discussed in the literature. Explain how your observations support or undermine the theory.

Chapter 10

Revising Your Paper

Now that you have finished your rough draft and documented your research with parenthetical references and a "Works Cited" page, it is time to fine-tune your work. Very likely, if you are using a word processor, you have been doing some revising as you went along. The word processor makes it so easy to make changes that we tend to add a bit here and delete a word there every time we read over what we have written. That is quite different, however, from a systematic revision.

It is helpful to have a cooling-off period after you finish the rough draft, when you can get away from the paper completely. If you are not rushed and if you can put the paper aside for a few days, you will be more likely to see it as if it were someone else's work. Though perhaps difficult, it is important that you look at the paper objectively. While you were working on it, you may not have noticed that you didn't explain something fully. Because you have been immersed in the topic for so long, you may have forgotten that your reader does not share your information and point of view. It may be necessary to add a sentence here and there or even an additional paragraph to clarify your meaning.

You may discover, if you can distance yourself, that your transitions are too abrupt or that the paper does not flow smoothly in some places. It is also helpful to your reader, especially if your material is somewhat difficult, to give examples to illuminate the points you are trying to make. These can be added during the revision process.

Another big advantage of putting your rough draft aside for a few days before beginning the revision process is that it saves time. You can accomplish more in less time because needed changes jump out at you. There is no need to struggle to locate them.

Going Beyond Fiddling

Revising is not the same thing as tidying up. Your goal is not to trim a loose end here and correct a spelling error there. Peter Elbow writes in his excellent book *Writing with Power* that, in the beginning, your revising tool should not be a touch-up brush but a chain saw.

At the same time, you must take care that you don't over-revise or make your work worse rather than better. You will want to leave your good passages little changed. It is not at all unusual to clarify and elaborate and explain until your reader has fallen asleep. Although most students spend too little time on revising, it is nevertheless possible to spend too much time. If you lack confidence in your writing ability, you may get bogged down editing the same few pages of draft text, rather than devoting more of the time available to expanding and developing your rough draft.

Working with Other Students

Your fellow students can be extremely helpful in spotting problems with your paper. They can also stop you before you go too far with the chain saw. Since they have not been staring at your rough draft for the last few weeks, they can bring a whole new perspective to the editing process. If it is possible to join a study group organized for this purpose, consider doing so. If no such group exists, you might exchange rough drafts with another student in your class or ask your roommate to read over your paper. You will probably find that you do a better job when you are editing someone else's paper. Since these are not your own painfully wrought words, it is not as difficult to trim down excessive verbiage. When your student editor does the same, don't allow yourself to become defensive. Evaluate the recommendations as objectively as possible. None of us enjoy criticism, but there is no point in wasting this opportunity to improve your work just because of a tender, easily wounded ego.

Taking Advantage of your Campus Study Skills Center

Most colleges and universities maintain a center to which students can go to get help with their research papers. It is surprising how few students take advantage of this opportunity. Trained tutors and professional staff members are available to work with you, pointing out problems and giving you ideas for developing and fine-tuning your paper. Tutors are often English majors in their junior or senior year of college. Since they are not experienced teachers, you may have to encourage them to explain themselves more fully. Don't allow them to make changes in your paper unless you fully understand why the change is needed. This is your paper, not theirs. You are in charge, and you alone know what you want to say. Their help can be very valuable as long as you remain in the driver's seat.

Reading for First Impressions

Many students find it helpful to read their rough drafts quickly from beginning to end before they actually change a word. Their goal is to get an overall impression and a sense of the paper's strengths and weaknesses. This is not possible unless you have been able to put the paper aside for several days and can approach it critically and objectively. Although you will want to make notes on parts of the paper that don't seem to come together, this does not mean that you are looking only for problems. Seek out and make note of particularly well-written and expressive sections. Some pats on the back are certainly not out of order. Don't let yourself get bogged down in specific wording. Instead, try to keep the whole paper in the forefront of your thoughts. It should move steadily forward, developing and defending your thesis. Here are a few general questions you might consider while you are reading:

- **Is your subject really interesting?** You're probably not going to be able to answer this question honestly unless you have been able to get away from the paper for a few days. Otherwise, you may be feeling tired of writing and maybe even a little negative.

- **Is your paper directed toward your audience?** Have you kept your readers clearly in mind while you wrote?

- **Is your language vivid?** Does it entice your readers and help to maintain their interest? Although the language you use in a research paper will be quite different from that used in an adventure novel, it need not be bland and boring. Your tone and choice of words should let your readers know that you are enthusiastic about your topic and want them to share your enthusiasm. As you read through the rough draft, ask yourself whether this sense of vitality comes across. Later you might consider adding specific words and details that will help your readers picture the situations or conditions you are describing.

- **Were you consistent in the organizational scheme you chose?** In other words, if you began by organizing your material chronologically, did you abandon this plan in the middle and choose another organizational strategy?

- **Is the subject well-focused?** Does the paper stay clearly on the topic and the thesis with no diversions into information you have discovered in the course of your research that is not central to the discussion.

- **Have you made the controlling theme clear to your audience?** This question is related to the one above. The controlling idea might be compared with a center of gravity around which your paper revolves. In later readings, you will want to go back and remove information that distracts your readers but for now make note of any tendencies you may have had to wander from your theme or purpose.

- **Does reading the draft bring to mind any new ideas?** Sometimes, the experience of reading a rough draft in its entirety gives rise to a new understanding or perspective. Don't stifle such ideas in your haste to finish. They may be just the small additions your paper needs to progress from just adequate to superior.

- **Are you, and therefore your reader, left with unanswered questions that should have been addressed?** By the time you reach the conclusion, such questions should have been resolved.

Controlling Your Inner Demons

Some students have a hard time getting started. Filling those first empty computer screens with words seems an insurmountable task, but once they have conquered the blank page or blank screen and have produced some sort of rough draft, revising it is relatively easy. For other students, the rough draft may hold no terrors because they know it is not final or irrevocable. Instead, it is the process of revising that brings out their worst fears. When they first read over their rough draft after having spent some time away from it, they are dismayed. It sounds awful. What they remembered as an "okay" paper has somehow turned into an embarrassment. The thought of people reading such worthless trash fills them with horror. This reaction can be quite as devastating as the stage fright that grips some of us at the beginning of the writing process.

Probably the best way to deal with these fears is to anticipate them. Just as you eventually managed to convince yourself as a child that there was really no ghost in the closet, you will have to convince your adult self that there is no basis for such devastating self-doubt. If you have been conscientious and followed most of the advice given in previous chapters, your rough draft is probably quite satisfactory and will soon become much better.

Being Willing to Throw Your Words Away

If you are a student for whom writing is a slow and time-consuming process, you may want to preserve every word, phrase, and sentence you type. Unfortunately, good editing means being willing to keep what is good and discard what is not really needed or does not achieve the purpose you intended. Nothing is more painful than abandoning a page that took you an hour or more to write and yet sometimes it must be done.

Make your rough draft longer than the length you anticipate for your final paper. It will be less painful to part with hard-wrought prose if you have prepared yourself in advance. Of course, your paper may actually grow as you discover sections that need more explanation or development. Don't count on it, however. The ideal mental state, as you sit down to revise your paper, is a detached, objective outlook that allows you to freely let go of any text that does not enhance your work. Knowing that you have that cushion of additional pages does much to make such an outlook possible.

Editing for Content, Organization, and Style

Editing a research paper is not done in one pass but in many separate readings. You simply can't do everything at once. The first time you reread the paper, search out problems with content and the clear expression of your ideas. Read over your work to see if it makes sense, if your argument develops logically and if you have fully supported each point. At this point, don't fret about whether your punctuation is correct. Concentrate on one thing at a time. Don't worry about mechanical errors or style until later unless they happen to pop out at you. In later readings, you can address these details individually.

Becoming Comfortable with the Revision Process

You have a decision to make at this point. Will you be more comfortable working with a printed copy of your rough draft or can you revise your work just as well— or better—by working directly with the computer? Obviously, the cut-and-paste functions of word-processing software make revising for content and organization much easier than the old scissor-and-glue method. If you are an inexperienced computer user, you may want to print out your rough draft, make your corrections on it, and then type them into the computer later. This way, you can see your paper as it will actually look. Since you have been accustomed to reading words printed on paper most of your life, you may have difficulty applying your critical faculties to a computer screen.

However, if you can work comfortably with computer text and have discovered that it is as easy to find and correct errors on the screen as on paper, you have an advantage. You can make much more extensive changes because the computer does it so readily. It is easy to be daring and to try out different ways of saying the same thing. If it doesn't work, you can change it back.

If you are unsure, why not compromise. Begin by editing your text on the computer screen. Then, just before you are ready to print your finished paper, print out a working copy. You may notice problems that you did not see before. You will also be able to see if your page numbers are printing correctly, and whether spacing and margins look the way you expected them to. Even if you are an experienced computer user, it is helpful to print out just one page to see if everything looks right.

Be sure that you know how to move around efficiently in your document. The *find* command is especially important. Research papers can become so long that you forget what you wrote five pages back. This may make your prose seem to ramble, and you can find yourself repeating information you have already discussed. By using the *find* command, you can search the text for a word or phrase and then move easily to that location, discover whether you are repeating yourself, and pull related information together.

You will also want to move quickly. Delay may cause you to forget what you were looking for or that great idea you had for the conclusion. Check your word-processing manual to learn how to move from the top of your document to the bottom, from the beginning of a paragraph to the end, and even from the beginning of a sentence to the end. As these skills become second nature, you will begin to feel as if you can see and work with your whole paper, not just the few sentences that appear on your computer screen.

Making a Plan

Because you will be going through your draft several times as you edit, it is easy to forget what you have already done and what changes remain to be made. It is helpful, therefore, to jot down a plan with each stage of the revision process listed. Your plan should be based on the tasks listed in this chapter. As you complete a pass through the text, you can mark it off on your plan, giving you a sense of accomplishment and saving you unnecessary repetition. The plan will also let you know when you can safely call your paper complete or finished.

Revising with a Word Processor

More sophisticated word processors often include a revision feature that may or may not assist you in editing your paper. If you choose to invoke the revision command, you can see both your original draft and any changes you have made. Changes usually appear in a different color from the original text, and deletions show as being crossed out. This can be helpful if you are reluctant to part with text you have already written but would like to experiment with possible improvements. Seeing both the original and the revised text on your computer screen can be confusing. It is usually possible to remain in revision mode yet see only your revised text. That way, if you later have a question, you can return to the view that includes both texts.

Editing for Content

The content of your paper should reflect a unified whole, with every sentence and paragraph making a contribution. Does every section of your paper support your thesis? Did you end up including irrelevant information just because you happened to come across it and it looked interesting? Possibly you ran out of material and had to pad a too-brief paper with peripheral material. If this is the case, you probably failed to develop fully the various headings of your outline. Go back and take a look at it. What did you forget?

Students occasionally find themselves with too little material and too many pages to fill. If they pad their writing with unnecessary words and phrases, they can turn good writing into bad. Good writing requires economy of expression. Use only the words you really need. Unnecessary verbiage gets in the way of communication between you and your reader.

When writing a long paper, it is easy to become redundant. Be sure you frequently reread what you have already written to avoid repeating yourself. Say what you mean as quickly and clearly as possible without beating around the bush. Weed out overly detailed descriptions and don't elaborate on the obvious. Also, eliminate irrelevant observations or asides.

Incorporating Graphics. If you did not already do so when writing your rough draft, now is a good time to add relevant graphics to your paper. Some topics lend themselves well to the use of charts, tables, graphs, diagrams, drawings, and other illustrations. Technical subjects, especially, can be made clearer with the thoughtful use of visual materials. If you are writing about population, for example, you might want to use a statistical table to show how certain populations have changed over a span of time. The same technique might be used to show how taxes or the number of people living below the poverty line have increased. A paper about space flight might be more readily understood if you included a diagram of a space shuttle.

Use the following guidelines to ensure that your visuals enhance, rather than detract from, your paper:

- Make your illustrations as simple and brief as possible.
- Be sure the information in a table or chart is accurate.
- Present the information in a way that is easy to interpret.
- Always write a caption to describe your visual.
- Number tables and illustrations (referred to as "Figures") consecutively. Do not mix the two.
- Capitalize titles and the words "Table" or "Figure."
- Double-space above and below each table or illustration.
- Place the graphic as close to the text in which it is discussed as possible but not before you first mention it.
- If the table or illustration is large, place it on a separate piece of paper.
- When you refer to the table or illustration in your text, let your reader know why the information it contains is important, but do not repeat the information.
- Don't repeat statistics in the table in such a way that your reader must continually page back and forth from text to table.
- If table and text are not on the same page, give the page number when you refer to the table in your text.
- Refer to table or illustration number, not "the following table" or "the illustration below."

If charts, graphs, and diagrams are important to your paper, you may wish to use a computer graphics program. They are easy to use and can produce professional results. *Harvard Graphics*, for example, produces mainly statistical charts, while *Corel Draw*, *Microsoft PowerPoint*, and *Paintshop* produce drawings, diagrams, and other illustrations.

These programs can add a lot to your paper as long as they are not overused. You may have seen the comic strip in which the little boy has spent so much time creating an extravagant multimedia book report that he never got around to reading the book. Graphics programs can divert your attention from the real task in much the same way.

If you are inputting statistical information into a program, be sure you know how you want the program to display your data. Most instructors have seen beautifully produced charts in which all the data are in the wrong place. Look carefully at any chart produced by a graphics program and make sure it conveys the information you intended.

Although high-end word-processing programs can often produce excellent graphics, you may need a separate graphics program. Many graphics programs can export the illustrations they produce directly into your word-processing program so that graphics and text are all stored in the same file and printed out together. If your software cannot do this, you may have to print out your graphics separately and insert the pages into your final printed paper.

Sophisticated desktop publishing programs like *Pagemaker* can take output from different sources and combine them, creating an attractive, polished document. These programs are often available in campus computer centers, and experienced computer users sometimes use them to "spiff up" their final papers. Although they do make a paper look professional, they are far from necessary.

Editing for Organization

A research paper's content is obviously important, but the significance of *what* you say may be lost if the paper is not organized clearly and logically. Compare your paper with your outline:

- Did you develop your points in the same order?
- Did you provide basic or introductory information before you asked your reader to understand more difficult material?
- Did you build a firm foundation of fact before making inferences?
- Did you develop each point fully before you moved on to the next?

Writing Clearly. Though not an expert, you know a lot about your topic that your readers don't. They are being exposed to the information for the first time, so you must take care to present it so that each idea follows the last one in a clear and orderly way. Good writing depends as much on clarity as it does on content.

In order for your reader to stay with you, the concepts you present must flow logically and seamlessly from the opening statement to the conclusion. If you misplace words or phrases, your reader can easily become confused. Be careful of the sequence in which you present your ideas. Irrelevancies can mislead readers, and excessive wordiness can cause them to lose the thread of the argument. If you feel you are getting bogged down, consider condensing or eliminating unnecessary information. Add more information if it will better prepare your readers for what follows.

Creating Transitions. Making a paper flow smoothly, both within and between paragraphs, is one of the most difficult aspects of the writing process. You may feel as if you have a thousand separate puzzle parts, and you may wonder how you will ever manage to fit them all in. Transitional words and phrases help to provide continuity, making it possible for the reader to move from one idea to the next. Some of these transitional words include *then, next, after, while,* and *since.*

Transitions can show logical relationships. For example, a transition can introduce another item in a series as in *furthermore, in the second place,* and *similarly.* It can introduce an illustration with words such as *specifically, for example,* and *namely* or a conclusion with words such as *altogether, clearly,* and *to sum up.* Transitions that show temporal relationship (time) can indicate frequency, as in *hourly, often,* and *occasionally.* They can also show duration, as in *briefly* and *during,* or they can indicate the beginning, middle, or end of something, as in *at first, in the meantime,* and *afterwards*. Finally, there are transitions that show spatial relationships. Closeness might be expressed by *near, next to,* or *alongside*; distance by *far, beyond,* and *away*; direction by *above, below,* or *inside*.

To help a paragraph follow naturally the one that precedes it, repeat an important word or phrase from the preceding paragraph to make a smooth transition. Within paragraphs, using pronouns can help achieve smooth transitions. For instance, you might use a pronoun in one sentence to refer to a noun mentioned in the preceding one. Just be sure it is clear to whom or to what the pronoun refers. Having someone read over your paper can be useful in this regard. They are more likely to discover abrupt transitions since they are reading the paper for the first time.

Learning to Move, Cut, and Paste Text Effectively.
The word processor enables you to move information around far more easily than was possible with typewriters. If you write or type a sentence or paragraph on a piece of paper, it must remain there permanently unless you erase and retype it in a different section of your research paper. This might discourage you from making major changes.

When using a word processor, it couldn't be easier to select a few lines of text and move them to a place where they are more appropriate, enabling you to organize information in the most logical way. If you find a section of your rough draft confusing, analyze it. Number the paragraphs in the order in which they appear and jot down a few words from the topic sentence beside each number. Is this really the most logical order, or would it be helpful to move one or more paragraphs to create a different logical sequence? Once you have made your decision, simply highlight or mark the paragraph to be moved and reposition it. The same technique can be used for moving sentences within a paragraph.

If both the text to be moved and the new location are visible on your screen, it is normally possible to use the drag and drop feature to move the text with your mouse. *Drag and drop* is the term used for holding down the mouse button while you "drag" a highlighted piece of text or a graphic around the screen. If the old and new locations of the text to be moved are not both visible on your screen, it is probably best to use another common word-processing technique called *cut and paste* to move the text. First you select the text to be moved and then choose *Cut* from your editing menu. The text will be removed from or cut out of your paper and stored on a virtual clipboard. You then need only position the cursor at the place where the text should be inserted, choose *Paste* from the editing menu, and presto!—the text reappears at the cursor point.

Although these techniques are not difficult, you should practice before trying them out on your precious research paper. If you are feeling nervous or hurried, it is possible to lose text or accidentally reposition it in a completely irrelevant and unexpected place. If this happens, you could spend hours trying to find the missing material. Don't move too much text at one time or you may become confused, losing track of the logical progression of ideas you are trying to fine-tune. You also might consider copying your paper to a temporary file just before you do any dramatic surgery. That way, if anything disappears into the ether, you can recover the file without difficulty.

Editing for Style

The way in which you put words together is your writing style. Your main objective is to communicate clearly with your audience, so you want to express your ideas as smoothly and precisely as possible. Now that you have investigated the problem and have communicated the results of your investigation in your rough draft, check to be sure your reader can follow the process of your thoughts. Does your prose lead your readers from point to point? Have you provided enough information to be certain they understand each one before you move on to the next?

Using the Language of the Discipline. Every profession or academic discipline has a language of its own. As you read books and articles on your topic, you become familiar with the terminology used in that discipline. As you write your own paper, you should exhibit some knowledge of the discipline's language. However, this language can either clarify your ideas or make them more obscure. Therefore, make sure you understand the terms you use. The library reference collection contains specialized dictionaries to make these terms understandable.

Since research papers assigned in college composition classes are usually addressed to a lay audience, do not assume knowledge of technical terms; use them sparingly. In more advanced courses, like those in the sciences, you will be writing for a more specialized audience for whom technical terms are useful or even necessary to make your meaning clear. They serve as a kind of shorthand, allowing you to use one word where you might otherwise need a lengthy explanation.

Before loading your paper with technical jargon, however, be sure you are enhancing communication, not interfering with it. Explain terms your audience may not understand and, don't try to show off with an imperfect use of jargon.

You know from your own reading that some writers become addicted to jargon and use it in places where it is irrelevant and irritating to the reader. The federal government's bureaucratic jargon is the butt of many jokes, and it interferes with the ability of the government to communicate with its citizens. The military has also developed its own jargon which substitutes euphemistic phrases for the painful realities of war. Jargon of this type interferes with, rather than enhances, communication and should be avoided. If there is a clear, concise way of expressing a thought, use those words.

Using Abbreviations. In recent years our language has become peppered with terms like NRA, NOW, AMA, and a host of other abbreviations. Nearly every organization is becoming known by its initials. Although shorthand can be useful in avoiding tedious repetition, it can also be confusing.

The first time you refer to an organization by its initials, write out the words in full, followed by the abbreviation in parentheses. Thereafter, you may use the initials. If, however, you move on to another subject and then return a page or so later, your audience should not be forced to go back and look up the initials. Repeat the full name as often as necessary to avoid confusion.

Abbreviations can interfere with the flow of your writing and should be kept to a minimum. After you once write out the full name *American Association of Music Teachers*, references to the *Association* or the *Music Teachers* might be better choices than *AAMT* as long as your meaning is clear.

Choosing the Right Word. Make certain that every word you use means exactly what you intend it to mean. Many terms mean different things to different readers. For example, colloquial expressions vary from one region to another. Approximations of quantity, such as *many, few, several,* and *a lot,* mean something slightly different to each reader.

Pronouns can be confusing unless it is clear to whom or to what they refer. *This* and *that* are particularly troublesome. Instead of letting them stand alone, pair them with a noun, as in *this hat* or *that tree.* The reader should never have to search through paragraphs to determine the antecedent of a pronoun.

The best word in most cases is the shortest. In other words, use the simplest word that accurately conveys your meaning. The following are examples of unnecessarily long and pretentious words that can usually be replaced by simpler ones:

■ **If you mean this**   **Don't write this**

If you mean this	Don't write this
begin	commence
do	accomplish
extra	additional
go	proceed
happen	transpire
help	assist
later	subsequently
methods	methodology
much	considerable
show	demonstrate
suggest	hypothesize
use	utilize
use	application

Avoiding Clichés. *Clichés* are overused words or phrases that add little meaning. Our everyday speech is riddled with clichés and, for the most part, nobody objects unless we bore our listeners with the same ones over and over. We are especially tempted to add clichés in our conclusion when we are not sure what it was we accomplished and don't quite know how to end. Scholarly writing, however, requires that every word add meaning.

Avoiding Redundancy. Writers sometimes use a redundant phrase when they want to be emphatic, but too often the result is an excess of unneeded words. The word *tautology* means saying the same thing twice using two different words when one would have been sufficient. The following are examples of this sort of excess. In each case, one of the words can be eliminated without a change in meaning.

■ Too many words	Use instead
in actual fact	In fact
linked together	linked
postponed to a later date	postponed
related to each other	related
still in use today	still in use
tentative hypothesis	hypothesis

Tightening Your Prose. Eliminating redundancy is just one way of paring down your writing to make it say what you intend it to say in the fewest possible words. It is important to zero in on precisely what you mean, ruthlessly deleting all words, phrases and sentences that might distract your readers. This stripping down to the essentials serves another purpose as well. Saying things clearly and economically energizes your writing, propelling your reader rapidly along.

If you look carefully, you will probably discover sections that you wrote when you were bored or tired. Maybe it was late at night and you could not concentrate. You may have been too sleepy to pay attention to whether the words you typed actually meant what you intended. There seem to be times when one word follows another forming sentences and paragraphs that say little or nothing.

Avoiding Noun Strings. When you place more than one adjective before a noun, for instance, *hand painted, kiln fired pot,* you hear your own voice speaking the phrase. Your reader does not have that advantage and may have difficulty determining how the words relate to one another. Hyphenation can help clarify the relationship (*hand-painted, kiln-fired*), but the best approach may be to restructure the sentence so that you have no more than one or two adjectives before a noun.

Finding Synonyms. Because writers try not to repeat themselves, they struggle to find words with similar meanings. Reference books like *Roget's Thesaurus* and *Webster's Dictionary of Synonyms* are helpful for this purpose. In fact, many word processors also include an on-line thesaurus that is easier to use than the printed version. Take care, however, that you are using a word that really means the same. Rarely do two words mean precisely the same thing, and subtle differences between words may unintentionally change your meaning.

Revising for Syntax. The term *syntax* has to do with the way words are arranged in a sentence. Take a good look at your sentences to see if the syntax enhances your meaning rather than interferes with it.

- Are the elements of your sentences tightly linked together?
- Have you balanced the elements of your sentences? Are the clauses in a sentence parallel in structure?
- Have you placed closely related elements as close together as possible or is it sometimes unclear what modifies what?
- Do your sentences form complete, independent grammatical units?
- Are less important thoughts in subordinate positions in the sentence?
- Does your sentence structure help the reader focus on the important ideas?
- Did you use subordinate conjunctions to show that one clause or idea in the sentence was more important than another or did you connect ideas with coordinating conjunctions that made all ideas appear to have equal importance?

Even the best sentences, however, cannot stand alone. They must be woven into paragraphs, which in turn must be structured and organized into a tight, cohesive unit. The following are some tests of a good paragraph:

- Does the paragraph have a clear purpose?
- Is the paragraph necessary to the paper? Is its role obvious or does it just restate what has already been said?
- Does it clarify rather than cloud the issue?
- Is it sufficiently well developed to answer the reader's questions or does it just raise questions that are never answered?
- Are assertions backed up with supporting information and statistics if relevant?
- Is the length of the paragraph different from others nearby? Varying length adds interest.
- Is the structure of the paragraph too much like the others nearby?
- Is the paragraph unified? Does it contain one central idea?
- Are all the sentences in the paragraph concerned with this same point? Does the paragraph contain sentences that really belong in another paragraph?
- Is the paragraph well-structured? Are each of the sentences in the most appropriate position?
- Does the paragraph lead easily and logically to the one that follows?
- Are transitions made smoother through the careful use of transitional words and phrases?

Writing Correctly. Correct grammar, punctuation, and spelling all help to clarify meaning and avoid confusion. Punctuation, for instance, contributes to clear communication by showing the relationships between ideas. The reader cannot hear your voice, so punctuation must tell the reader where to pause and where to place emphasis. Overusing one type of punctuation is like always speaking in a monotone.

Punctuation adds meaning to written words, allowing your reader to interpret them as you meant them to be interpreted. It serves the same purpose as your tone of voice in a conversation.

A book of this size cannot cover the basic rules of grammar, punctuation, and spelling, so you might want to check out a recent grammar book from the library. A grammar book can also help you to decide which words to capitalize and which to leave in lower case. Be sure that you have begun every sentence with a capital letter and have capitalized the first letter of every proper noun.

Checking Verb Agreement and Tense. A verb is either singular or plural depending on its subject. In revising, every writer discovers at least a few singular verbs inadvertently paired with plural subjects or plural verbs paired with singular subjects. When we struggle with our sentences, changing the words around and making substitutions, we can easily lose track of what is supposed to agree with what.

Verbs must also agree in person with pronouns when the pronoun is the subject of the sentence. That is, a first-person pronoun like *I* must be paired with the first-person verb form *am*, the second-person *you* with *are*, and the third-person *she* with *is*.

Unnecessary changes in the tense of the verb also cause abruptness, giving your reader a sudden jolt. Present and past tense are normally used in a research paper, so if you need to depart from them for any reason, do so infrequently and come back as quickly as possible. The results of your investigation should be reported in the past tense, your conclusions in the present.

Using Quotations. Although the number of quotations in your paper should be kept to a minimum, most research papers contain at least a few. Remember that the quotation should be typed exactly as it appeared in the original source, even if it contained a misspelled word or grammatical error.

Incorporate quotations of less than forty words into your text and enclose them in double quotation marks. Quotations over forty words should be set off in a double-spaced block with no quotation marks. Indent one inch or ten spaces from the left margin and don't indent the first word as you would in a paragraph.

In certain situations, you will need to place one quotation inside another. You may be quoting the author of a book who is, in turn, quoting another authority. If it is a long quotation and set off in a block, enclose the inside or direct quotation in double quotation marks. If the entire quotation is under forty words, enclose the longer or indirect one in double quotation marks and the shorter one in single quotation marks.

Ellipses are a series of three periods with a space before and after each period. They are used to indicate that part of a quotation that has been omitted or left out. If the section omitted extends over two sentences, use four periods to indicate the omission. The fourth is the period that would normally end the first sentence, followed by the three spaced periods.

Occasionally, you will wish to insert some text of your own within a quotation. In order to make it clear that these are your words and not those of the author you are quoting, enclose your words in brackets.

Quoting Poetry. If you are quoting part or all of a single line of verse, treat it as you would any other text. Two or three lines may be quoted in this way if you use a slash (/) with a space before and after it to separate the lines.

Quotations of more than three lines should be placed in a block indented one inch or ten spaces from the left margin. Type each line exactly as it appears in the original. Use the same punctuation and capitalization and begin each line of the poem on a separate line of your page. Sometimes the spatial arrangement of the lines of a poem is unusual. Reproduce them just as they were printed. If a line is too long to fit within the right margin, continue it on the next line and indent an additional quarter inch or three spaces.

Getting Down to Details

Now that you are satisfied with the content, organization, and style of your paper, it's time to look at the myriad of mechanical details that must be dealt with before you can consider your paper finished. This part is what you might call the endgame. You're almost there, but you will need to keep yourself focused on your objective if you are to hone this fruit of your labors into a polished, professional research paper. All of these details can be seen in action in the sample papers on pages 193 and 218.

Choosing Paper

Always use heavy, white 8-1/2" x 11" paper for your final draft. Separate sheets like those used in a laser printer are preferable, but if you must use form-feed paper, be sure you separate the perforated sections as carefully as possible. Don't submit a final paper with ragged edges.

If you do not have access to a computer and must type your paper, do not use erasable paper because it becomes smudged. If you believe you're too poor a typist to manage without it, photocopy your final draft and submit the photocopy.

Spacing and Margins

Double-space your entire paper, including quotations, notes, and "Works Cited" or "References" list. If you are using a word processor, you should set the line spacing at two before you print. If you are handwriting the paper, skip every other ruled line.

Leave one inch for top and bottom as well as left and right margins. One-inch margins are the default settings on most word processors, so you probably won't need to make any adjustments. Some instructors prefer 1-1/4" margins since they are often required for theses and dissertations. Wider margins also provide space for the instructor to write comments. The first word of a paragraph should be indented one-half inch or five spaces from the left margin. Any quotations you set off from the text should be indented one inch or ten spaces from the left margin.

Numbering Pages

All pages should be numbered consecutively beginning with the title page (if you use a title page). Use Arabic numerals and position the page number in the upper right-hand corner, one inch from the right edge of the page and one-half inch from the top of the page If you must insert or remove a page, renumber all pages. Do not try a makeshift repair like 5A and 5B. If you are using a word processor, the software program will take care of the numbering, leaving you free to add or delete as much text as you like.

To prevent pages being misplaced, the MLA handbook recommends that you type your last name and the page number, for example, Smith 14. APA suggests typing the first two or three words of the title in the upper right-hand corner or five spaces to the left of the page number, for example, Genetic Testing 14.

If you are using a word processor, you may be able to create such headings using only page-numbering commands. If not, the program probably has a feature that allows you to include "headers" in the paper. Whatever you do, don't try to type either page numbers or headers manually into the computer. They will either end up in the middle of the page, or you will spend hours moving them.

Arranging Pages in Order

Undergraduate papers usually include little more than a title page, table of contents, text, and "Works Cited" or "References" section. However, you may occasionally wish to include additional material when it is appropriate to your topic. The following order is required for formal reports, theses, and dissertations:

Title page

Dedication

Preface and/or Acknowledgments

Abstract

Table of Contents

List of Figures

List of Illustrations

Text (begin with page 1)

Appendix

Glossary

"Works Cited" or "References"

Inserting Tables and Illustrations

If you are using graphs, charts, or other illustrative material, insert them as close as possible to the text to which they relate. Type a label (usually just "Table" or "Figure" followed by a number) and a caption at the top flush left and on separate lines. Type the source of the information and any notes needed to clarify the illustration below. In order to separate the table from the text you may wish to enclose it in a box or separate it with dotted lines.

Using Your Spell Checker

Although it doesn't hurt to run your spell checker over your text periodically, run it one last time before you print your finished paper. All sorts of errors seem to crop up at the last minute. A spell checker is not able to do the whole job, however. The computer will notice only the groups of letters not in its dictionary and has no way of knowing whether a word communicates the meaning you intended. For example, it will not know that you meant *two*, not *too*, or *their*, rather than *they're* or *there*.

Making One Final Check before You Print

Now is the time to ask yourself if you have forgotten anything. Is there some glaring omission that will be immediately obvious to your reader? The following checklist may not include every possible problem, but if you can respond positively to each question, you can safely move on.

- Does your paper have a fully developed introduction, body, and conclusion?
- Did you present your thesis in your introduction and keep focusing on it throughout your paper?
- Did you explain your argument fully? Does each point you made logically follow the one that preceded it?
- Did you support each argument fully with illustrations and supplementary material?
- Is each point or each part of your argument arranged logically?
- Does the writing flow smoothly?
- Is the language you used clear and precise?

- Did you use the same tense throughout, changing it only when there was a real need to do so?
- Does each paragraph have one central idea? Is it clear to the reader?
- Did you fully document all the ideas and opinions of others?
- Are you quite sure you understood the points raised by the experts you cited and that your notes were clear and accurate?
- Did you make clear distinctions between your own ideas and those of others?
- Is your "Works Cited" or "References" list complete? Are all the sources you used included? Are all citations correct?
- Have you proofread the entire paper, eliminating errors and rewriting as necessary?
- Did you run a spell-checking program on the document?

Viewing Your Paper in Page-Layout Format

If your word-processing program allows you to see your paper exactly as it will be printed, including page numbers, headers, footers, and margins, be sure to take advantage of this feature. The pages of the paper are displayed on your screen, one page at a time or with many pages displayed in small rectangles on your computer screen.

If several pages are displayed at once, you really cannot read the text but you can see how the blocks of black lettering will look on the printed page. Maybe the computer has arranged the text in a confusing or unattractive way, as for instance, when it positions a heading on the last line of one page and the text that follows at the top of the next page. What is known as widow and orphan protection can solve this problem. Check your word-processing manual for instructions. You will also want to be sure that the page number is suppressed on the title page but appears on the pages that follow.

Printing

If you are composing your paper on a computer, be sure that the printer can produce a crisp clear type. Although you need not use an expensive laser printer, avoid nine-pin dot matrix models. Be sure the printer has a new or nearly new ribbon or toner cartridge.

Despite the many interesting type fonts available for most PCs, be conservative and sacrifice art for readability. Choose a simple, widely used typeface like Times New Roman or Courier. Do not try to compensate for a too-short paper with extra large type or by increasing the space between letters.

If you have no access to a printer or typewriter, don't turn in a handwritten paper unless you have first checked with your instructor. If your instructor has no objections, write neatly and legibly with dark blue or black ink. Use only one side of the paper and be sure you make a photocopy for your own records.

When printing is complete, check to be sure that all pages printed and that they are in the correct order. Remove any blank sheets of paper that were accidentally fed through the print rollers. Check to be sure that every page printed correctly. Students occasionally wait until the last minute, grab pages as they emerge from the printer, and run to class without checking them. Even the best printers occasionally misbehave and it is not unusual to find yourself with a few e-mail messages or other oddities tucked between the pages of what you thought was your research paper.

Requesting Information from National Organizations

Natural Resources Organizations

Agriculture Council of America
1250 I Street, N.W., Suite 601
Washington, DC 20005
Telephone: (202) 682-9203

Alternative Sources of Energy
107 South Central Avenue
Milaca, MN 56353
Telephone: (612) 983-6892

American Forestry Association
Post Office Box 2000
Washington, DC 20013

American Wilderness Alliance
7500 East Arapahoe Road, Suite 355
Englewood, CO 80112
Telephone: (303) 694-9047

Center for Marine Conservation (oceans and habitats)
1725 DeSales Street, N.W., Suite 500
Washington, DC 20036
Telephone: (202) 429-5609

Greenpeace
1436 U Street, N.W.
Post Office Box 3720
Washington, DC 20007

Sierra Club
730 Polk Street
San Francisco, CA 94109
Telephone: (415) 776-2211

Arts Organizations

American Craft Council
40 West 53rd Street
New York, NY 10019
Telephone: (212) 956-3535

American Film Institute
John F. Kennedy Center for the Performing Arts
Washington, DC 20566
Telephone: (202) 828-4000

American Music Center
30 West 26th Street, Suite 1001
New York, NY 10010
Telephone: (212) 366-5260

American Symphony Orchestra League
777 Fourteenth Street, Suite 500
Washington, DC 20005
Telephone: (202) 628-0099
Facsimile: (202) 783-7228

Art Information Center (fine arts clearinghouse)
280 Broadway, Suite 412
New York, NY 10007
Telephone: (212) 227-0282

Dance/USA
777 Fourteenth Street, N.W., Suite 540
Washington, DC 20005
Telephone: (202) 628-0144

Jazz World Society
Post Office Box 777, Times Square Station
New York, NY 10108
Telephone: (212) 713-0830

National Theater of the Deaf
Hazel E. Stark Center
Chester, CT 06412
Telephone: (203) 526-4971

Poets and Writers, Inc.
72 Spring Street
New York, NY 10012
Telephone: (212) 226-3586

Education and Development Organizations

American Association of University Women
2401 Virginia Avenue, N.W.
Washington, DC 20037
Telephone: (202) 785-7700

American Council on Education
1 Dupont Circle, N.W., Suite 800
Washington, DC 20036
Telephone: (202) 939-9300
Facsimile: (202) 833-4760

Carnegie Council on Ethics and International Affairs
Merrill House
170 East 64th Street
New York, NY 10021
Telephone: (212) 838-4120

Council on Career Development for Minorities
1341 West Mockingbird Lane, Suite 412-E
Dallas, TX 75247
Telephone: (214) 631-3677

National Association for Sports and Physical Education
1900 Association Drive
Reston, VA 22091
Telephone: (703) 476-3410

National Education Association
1201 Sixteenth Street, N.W.
Washington, DC 20036
Telephone: (202) 833-4000

Health and Research Organizations

American Cancer Society
1599 Clifton Road, N.E.
Atlanta, GA 30329
Telephone: (404) 320-3333

American Foundation for AIDS Research (AMFAR)
1515 Broadway
New York, NY 10016
Telephone: (212) 719-0033

National AIDS Network
2033 M Street, N.W., Suite 800
Washington, DC 20036
Telephone: (202) 293-2437
James Holm, Executive Director

National Council of Community Mental Health Centers
12300 Twinbrook Parkway, Number 320
Rockville, MD 20852
Telephone: (301) 984-6200

Legal Organizations

American Bar Association
750 North Lake Shore Drive
Chicago, IL 60611

American Civil Liberties Union
132 West 43rd Street
New York, NY 10036
Telephone: (212) 944-9800

American Indian Law Center
Post Office Box 4456, Station A
Albuquerque, NM 87196
Telephone: (505) 277-5462

National Women's Law Center
1616 P Street, N.W.
Washington, DC 20036
Telephone: (202) 328-5160

NOW Legal Defense and Education Fund
99 Hudson Street, Twelfth Floor
New York, NY 10013
Telephone: (212) 925-6635
Facsimile: (212) 226-1066

Professional Associations

Association of Computer Professionals
230 Park Avenue, Suite 460
New York, NY 10169
Telephone: (212) 599-3019

American Psychological Association
1200 Seventeenth Street, N.W.
Washington, DC 20036
Telephone: (202) 955-7600

American Sociological Association
1722 N Street, N.W.
Washington, DC 20036
Telephone: (202) 833-3410
Facsimile: (202) 785-0146

Political Organizations and Watch Groups

Amnesty International of the U.S.A. (human rights)
322 Eighth Avenue
New York, NY 10001
Telephone: (212) 807-8400

Center for Holocaust Studies
1610 Avenue J
Brooklyn, NY 11230
Telephone: (718) 338-6494

Center for Media and Public Affairs (media research and policy)
2101 L Street, N.W., Suite 505
Washington, DC 20037
Telephone: (202) 223-2942

Coalition for Religious Freedom (First Amendment freedom)
515 Wythe Street, Suite 201
Alexandria, VA 22314
Telephone: (703) 684-9010

Consumers Union of the United States
256 Washington Street
Mount Vernon, NY 10553
Telephone: (914) 667-9400

Council for a Livable World (anti-nuclear weapons)
110 Maryland Avenue, N.E.
Washington, DC 20002
Telephone: (202) 543-4100
Facsimile: (202) 543-6297

Human Rights Watch
485 Fifth Avenue
New York, NY 10017
Telephone: (212) 972-8400
Aryeh Neier, Executive Director

Interfaith Center on Corporate Responsibility
475 Riverside Drive, Room 566
New York, NY 10115
Telephone: (212) 870-2293

League of Women Voters
1730 M Street, N.W.
Suite 1000
Washington, DC 20036
Telephone: (202) 429-1965

Martin Luther King, Jr. Center for Nonviolent Social Change
449 Auburn Avenue, N.E.
Atlanta, GA 30312
Telephone: (404) 524-1956

National Coalition Against Censorship (clearinghouse on book-burning
censorship in public schools)
2 West 64th Street
New York, NY 10023
Telephone: (212) 724-1500

National Council of Women of the United States (women's issues)
777 United Nations Plaza
New York, NY 10017
Telephone: (212) 697-1278

National Council on Crime and Delinquency
685 Market Street, Suite 620
San Francisco, CA 94105
Telephone: (415) 896-6223

National Organization for Women (NOW)
1000 Sixteenth Street, N.W., Suite 700
Washington, DC 20036
Telephone: (202) 331-0066

National Taxpayers Union
325 Pennsylvania Avenue, S.E.
Washington, DC 20003
Telephone: (202) 543-1300

Population Reference Bureau (research on population)
777 Fourteenth Street, N.W., Suite 800
Washington, DC 20005
Telephone: (202) 639-8040

Sports and Recreation Organizations

American Fitness Association
6700 East Pacific Coast Highway, Suite 299
Long Beach, CA 90803
Telephone: (213) 596-6036

American Ski Association
1888 Sherman, Suite 500
Denver, CO 80203
Telephone: (303) 861-7669

National Basketball Association
645 Fifth Avenue
New York, NY 10022
Telephone: (212) 826-7000

National Collegiate Athletic Association
Nall Avenue at 63rd Street
Mission, KS 66201
Telephone: (913) 384-3220

National Football League
410 Park Avenue
New York, NY 10022
Telephone: (212) 758-1500

National Rifle Association of America
1600 Rhode Island Avenue, N.W.
Washington, DC 20036
Telephone: (202) 828-6000

United States Olympic Committee
1750 East Boulder Street
Colorado Springs, CO 80909
Telephone: (719) 632-5551

Aerospace Organizations

Aerospace Education Foundation
1501 Lee Highway
Arlington, VA 22209
Telephone: (703) 247-5839
Facsimile: (703) 247-5855

American Institute of Aeronautics and Astronautics
370 L'Enfant Promenade, S.W.
Washington, DC 20024
Telephone: (202) 646-7400
Facsimile: (202) 646-7508

International Telecommunications Satellite Organization (INTELSAT)
3400 International Drive, N.W.
Washington, DC 20008
Telephone: (202) 944-7500

National Space Society
922 Pennsylvania Avenue, S.E.
Washington, DC 20003
Telephone: (202) 543-1900

Index